SPI
EGE
L&G
RAU

ALSO BY EMILY FOX GORDON

Mockingbird Years: A Life In and Out of Therapy

Are You Happy?: A Childhood Remembered

It Will Come to Me

BOOK OF DAYS

BOOK OF DAYS

personal essays

Emily Fox Gordon

SPIEGEL & GRAU

TRADE PAPERBACKS

New York

2010

A Spiegel & Grau Trade Paperback Original

Copyright © 2010 by Emily Fox Gordon

All rights reserved.

Published in the United States by Spiegel & Grau,
an imprint of The Random House Publishing Group,
a division of Random House, Inc., New York.

SPIEGEL & GRAU and Design is a registered trademark
of Random House, Inc.

Some of the essays were originally published in
The American Scholar, Boulevard, and *Salmagundi.*

LIBRARY OF CONGRESS CATALOGING-IN-PUBLICATION DATA
Gordon, Emily Fox
Book of days: essays / Emily Fox Gordon.
p. cm.
"A Spiegel & Grau Trade Paperback Original."
ISBN 978-0-385-52589-3
eBook ISBN 978-0-679-60401-3
I. Title.
PS3607.O5936B66 2010
813'.6—dc22   2010005889

Printed in the United States of America on acid-free paper

www.spiegelandgrau.com

2 4 6 8 9 7 5 3 1

FIRST EDITION

Book design by Barbara M. Bachman

For
Anne Farber

contents

—

EMILY FOX GORDON:
THE REAL THING

Phillip Lopate

—

True personal essayists are extremely rare. At first it might seem an easy thing to do: you need merely chatter away about yourself, your experiences and opinions. But then the complications set in. How to know where to begin the monologue, and how much or how little historical background information to include; how to choose each time a topic of appropriate scale, one that will not be so trivial as to peter out after three pages, nor too complex to allow for sufficient depth in less than forty; how to merge seamlessly anecdote with reflection, scene with summary; how to inject enough tension into the rumination's spine so that the reader will pursue a mind tracking itself on the page with the same engrossment as he would a mystery story. The requirements for the job are stiff: they include a quirky, cultivated, unconventional mind, the detachment to be able to laugh at oneself (or at least not take one's wounds too solemnly and self-righteously), a quick wit, for condensation's sake, a talent for elaboration, and a sparkling, textured prose style that can sustain attention when all else fails. To keep refining a voice that is at once charmingly likable and shockingly frank, alive to its owner's flaws and its own contradictions, and to do this in essay after essay, over decades—this is a game few can play.

Emily Fox Gordon *can* play it. She does do all of the above and more, and this is why she is, to me, the most consistently interesting and satisfying personal essayist to have newly appeared in the last ten or fifteen years. I relish her comic genius for self-mockery: for turning the "I"/Emily character into an alarming social danger to herself and others, one forever longing to be accepted into a club she secretly (or not so secretly) disdains. I love her sharp satiric eye for the pretenses of bourgeois academia, the insecurities of bohemia, and the ideological fashions of the politically correct: see, for instance, her hilarious portrayal of the Kangas in "Faculty Wife." I cherish her ability to engage Kafka and other weighty literary or philosophical texts, without losing sight of the human-all-too-human, subjective investigator who is rummaging through them. And withal, I find deeply admirable her ability to sift through her feelings about serious, sober subjects, such as long-term marriage, illness, and the need for extended family, with a tenderness and maturity that always have the final word. She is an evolved human being; she has done her psychological homework; and in that respect she gives us what we who love the personal essay are seeking underneath all its wit and style: wisdom.

There is one more impediment, or temptation, that gets in the way of someone who would like to swear devotion to the personal essay: the greater popularity of the memoir. A writer has no sooner to effectuate a few graceful, sure-footed personal essays than the editors or literary agents she solicits will be telling her she should recast her book proposal in the form of a memoir—preferably one revolving around addiction, abuse, poverty, or some other nasty problem whose overcoming will yield the desired triumph-of-the-human-spirit results. In her essay "Book of Days," Gordon tells ruefully the tale of how she was seduced, not once but twice, to write and publish memoirs, instead of being allowed to bring out a collection of personal essays. She also has some intriguing things to say about the differences between the two forms: the almost formulaic narrative, with its redemptive, triumphalist imperative, found in memoirs being published today, and the circling, skeptical, less imperiously conclusive mentality of personal essays, which, to her, reflects more faithfully the truth of daily life. As it happens, I do not share her reservations about her own prior efforts: both *Mockingbird Years* and *Are You Happy?* strike me as priceless accomplishments, happy examples of the best in contemporary memoir. But I applaud her for continuing to brood intelligently and scrupulously about the consequences of memoirizing her life; and I am glad that she has finally gotten her wish, in the form of the present book. For this superb, delightful, thought-provoking collection of personal essays gives us the *sublime* Emily Fox Gordon (how she, who so dislikes receiving flattery, will hate me for saying that!) in top-notch form, and in the genre of prose writing with which she most identifies.

BOOK OF DAYS

FACULTY BRAT

—

The photograph is small, printed on shiny black stock, black and white and curled at the edges. It represents me, at age two, sitting in the lap of what we called Library Hill, my arm loosely slung around the neck of our German Shepherd. His big head is cast upward as he tolerates my embrace, and his tongue lolls rakishly. We sit in a dent in the long grass. The wind has unsettled my tam o'shanter; the shoulder button of my overalls has come undone. My dog and I look happy, and a little idiotic.

Photographs like this are marked by the pathos and authority of a different time. In another, my mother poses with me and my infant brother, standing in front of our boxy Plymouth station wagon, grayish white in the picture but in historical fact a pale aquamarine. The year is 1949. She is wearing a mouton coat and heavy shoes with ankle straps. Her hair looks frizzy—she had probably just home-permed it—and her face is tired and pretty and young. My brother is a faceless bundle in the crook of her arm. Enough time has passed, enough of destiny has been realized for all three people in this picture so that looking at it gives me a little shock. It's as if I'd been waiting for a chronically turbulent pool of water to clear and, as a reward for my patience, had seen at the bottom a small brightly colored stone. We lived in two houses, one after the other, both rented from the college for, if I recall correctly, $125 a month. The houses sat next door to each other in a gentle declivity on a small meandering street next to the library and across from a freshman dormitory and the small white clapboard building which housed my father's department. In both houses we children felt the influence of the undergraduates, their beer parties and the shouts of their impromptu lacrosse games, from one direction, and the emanations of the alumni at the Williams Inn from the other, their chuckles and hoots over martinis in the lounge. Williams is a very old school; its campus is uncloistered, mixed with the town. At least it was then. Now both of my childhood houses are coeducational dorms.

The first house was low-slung and rambling and painted gray. After my family moved next door it housed the chairman of the Williams drama department and his dramatically bohemian wife. Wild parties spilled out onto the lawn and were gossiped about. Thornton Wilder, there for the Williams Theatre's production of *Our Town,* woke us up one early morning when he stumbled about on our lawn drunkenly, calling "Here, kitty, kitty, kitty." Still later, when scouts went looking for a quintessentially academic setting for the movie *Who's Afraid of Virginia Woolf?* that house, I'm told, was nearly chosen.

The other house was larger, a white Victorian wedding cake with tent-shaped attic rooms and a butler's pantry. A great chestnut tree grew in our yard, and every fall my brother and I gathered fallen pods, slit open the moist spiky green jackets and popped out the glossy inner nuts. We kept them in sacks and dragged them along to football rallies, threw the nuts into the bonfire for the pleasure of hearing them hiss and explode.

My memories of the first house are internal, centered on the furniture, the corners, the dark-yellow hopsacking curtains that turned morning sunlight butterscotch as it entered the room, the odd wallpaper in the dining room, diamond-shaped broken-line enclosures containing red-combed roosters. I remember moving my three-year-old hands along that cool wall, mumbling "A rooster, a rooster, a rooster," until I ran out of roosters. When my own daughter was the same age it occurred to me that another child might have counted the roosters. For me it was enough to repeat the name, over and over.

The second house I remember more for the views out of its windows. One of those stretches diaphanously across my mind's eye while I process grocery lists and weekly plans, like the faint background wash of flowery fields running under "Pay to the order of————" on the more expensive variety of personal checks. It's not a particularly interesting scene, just an uncropped view of the slanted roof outside my bedroom window, and the portico and green awning of the Williams Inn (a "Treadway Inn"). I also remember, but not so persistently and eidetically, a view from a later period, when I was allowed to move into one of the attic rooms. From there, high up, I could see College Place snaking along around the library. I could read the inscriptions carved in a marble scroll that ran below its roof—Ovid, Horace, Euclid, Plato. I could see the elms, which even then were moribund and leafless, sketchy goblets filled with air. The wind that shook the healthy, foliated trees left them unmoved.

In my early childhood my mother was a significant blur to me. I have trouble remembering her face when it was youthful, and I've had to piece together the person she was. Multitalented—indifferent to music but a competent pianist, a prolific seamstress, a watercolorist and cartoonist, a brilliant cook, a wit, a teacher with advanced pedogogical notions, an unrealized writer with perfect literary pitch and a deep love of the language, a sort of aesthetic heroine, a Renaissance woman. It seemed to me that my mother could do anything. Now it seems to me that my mother was trapped in an odd paralysis because she was so good at so many things. As she perfected her skills they became smoother and smaller; they became miniature.

There were other types of faculty wife, of course. A few were seriously but ineffectually intellectual, taking multiple advanced degrees, doing translations. More were musical. Others were odd, with a predilection for solitary pond-wading and insect collecting. What united them was a pride in accomplishment for its own sake, unremunerated and often unrecognized. My mother, I felt, was the queen of faculty wives.

Faculty wives still exist. I have turned out to be one, if only by default. These women staff the charity thrift shops, sell potted mums for the school benefit, hold season tickets for the symphony. At every potluck supper I attend, I can find them in the kitchen dressing salads and finding room in the oven for all the casseroles to warm. They are mostly middle-aged, but occasionally some shy young pregnant wife, who knows that her husband's professional future is so uncertain that when the baby comes she may be living in Salt Lake City, will find a harbor with them. These women seem grayer, chattier, more self-effacing every time I see them. They cluster together and make their own society, while out in the living room the female academics circulate freely among their male counterparts. There is a tension between these two varieties of women, and extended conversations between them are rare. Sometimes it happens that a female academic will arrive at one of these parties with a new baby, and she will bring it, as if in a ritual of obeisance, into the kitchen where the faculty wives will surround it, to coo and praise.

Once my mother had a bad dream which kept her quiet and low all day: our German Shepherd, whom she loved like a fourth child, had shrunk to the size of a bird, and been caged. She was subject to depression. I remember her in her sewing room, a length of periwinkle-blue corduroy draped across her lap, her mouth full of pins and her eyes full of tears. She had unexplained, and to me inexplicable, idle days, when she sat at the desk in the hall musing and doodling, drawing women's fingernails, perfectly oval, with delicately shaded quarter-moon cuticles.

My father was a big, fresh-faced man, balding from his early thirties. He grew up in Philadelphia, where his parents ran a corset shop. He and his younger brother lived in a household where several nephews were boarded; one of my cousins told me that the place had the feeling of a boys' dormitory. My grandparents lost all in the depression, recouped, lost money again because my grandfather—a savant who could do inventory in his head—had a weakness for the horses. Consequently, my father was tense about money all his life.

My father had the mark of brilliance on him and he shot up through the academic ranks of an emerging meritocracy fast; Phi Beta Kappa, editor of the newspaper at Swarthmore, Rhodes Scholar in economics. He had, I've been told, the "coup d'oeil," an ability to see the whole panorama of an abstract landscape at once. His studies at Oxford were interrupted by the war, and he returned to be drafted and serve behind a desk in Washington, D.C., where my older sister was born. Then he was recruited by Williams, and later on the Ford Foundation, and almost immediately after that the Kennedy administration. Things happened so fast to my father that he never got around to completing his Ph.D., and he was so busy thinking—he would often sit at the dinner table in a kind of cataleptic trance, his eyes wide and blank, his jaw hanging—that he never produced a book. Today, with these deficiencies, my father would never be able to get tenure at any university. Forty years ago, the academic world was roomier, yet to be regulated. But even then, I believe, my father felt himself to be out of place in academic life. He had an itch for action, an impatience with circumlocution, a blunt and colorful sense of humor.

H. L. Mencken was his favorite writer, and his own style, in the few articles he wrote, was a model of balance and economy. He was admired by his students, who stood up to applaud him at the end of every semester, and he made many friends among the economists and their kinsmen, the political scientists. Many of these people sat over the remnants of my mother's very good dinners, talking for hours about things I found mystifying. I paid attention to tone, though, like an intelligent dog, and I always pricked up my ears for gossip and judgments. "Unsound," my father would say of somebody unknown to me, "bright but unsound," or "abysmal, just abysmal."

My father, who has now been dead for fifteen years, was a disastrous parent, worse than he deserved to be. He was deficient in self-knowledge and easily angered. When he turned to his children he seemed unable to modulate the hearty cynicism with which he looked at the world. "Who is Jack Frost?" I asked at the breakfast table. "Friend of your mother's," he answered, and smirked into his coffee cup. He could also be cruel: when I fell down the stairs at age five he stood over me for what seemed like a full minute, his expression disgusted. "I don't know whether to laugh or cry at you, Emily," he said finally, and walked away. He was mostly preoccupied, but he had some crudely behaviorist notions about child-rearing, which I got the worst of because I was so clumsy and absentminded. When I left the soap on the edge of the sink instead of in the soap dish, he would stand over me and make me replace it properly, remove and replace it again fifty times. And the same corrective was applied to all my other lapses: leaving the top off the toothpaste tube, forgetting to turn off lights, scratching the paint on the car when I parked my bike in the garage. "Careless" was his word for me. His provisions for reward were equally crude; after a good day he would usher me into his study and give me a quarter. My brother and sister were shrewd and strategic about my father; they anticipated his reactions and dodged his wrath. I continued all through my childhood to do all the things that infuriated him, and he continued using negative reinforcement in an effort to train me. Stupidly, bullheadedly, my father and I kept at it until at ten or eleven I conceded and retreated. I got back at him later, when adolescence gave me a new head of steam. At seventeen, when I had come home late and drunk from a party and he met me scowling at the door, I ran up all five flights of our Washington townhouse shrieking with laughter, flicking off lights as I went, leaving him—he already had a heart condition—in the dark. And in the late sixties, when my sister's Machiavellian boyfriend and I arranged a Christmas Eve insurrection, a drama of confrontation at my mother's festive dinner table, I let him have it. The boyfriend and I blamed him for everything—my mother's alcoholism, which by then was full-blown; the Vietnam War, which he abetted by supporting; the general unhappiness of our family. We left him in tears, and hugged each other in triumph while my mother and brother and sister looked on in dismay.

Sometimes, rarely, my father was kind. When a bad hot dog at a picnic made me sick, he put his hands on my heaving shoulders. He called me pet names—Um and

Umbly—always full of implicit insult, but affectionate. I shuddered, and still shudder, with ambivalence about those names.

But I feel a solidarity with my father, perhaps because I look like him, bigger and heavier than the others in my family, with his long face and heavy eyebrows. Only my incongruously retroussé nose tells of my mother. And like him I'm chronically angry and love food more than I should, and insight has come hard and late for me.

My mother was magical. She floated birthday candles anchored in halved walnut shells in the tub when my brother and I were bathed. She turned off the light, lit the candles, and stood smoking a cigarette in a shadowy corner of the bathroom as we sat in the midst of a small shining armada.

MY FATHER'S BACKGROUND was Jewish, my mother's Presbyterian. Both of them were agnostic rationalists, and I grew up hearing almost nothing of belief or doctrine. My mother preserved the aesthetic parts of her Christian heritage. We spent two weeks before Christmas, my mother, sister, brother, and I, at the kitchen table mixing food coloring into vanilla icing in small glass dishes—pale green, pink, a shade I called chocolate blue. We used toothpicks to paint striped frosting trousers on the rudimentary legs of gingerbread men, buttoned up their blurred pastel waistcoats with silvery sugar balls. We also collected pine cones and sprayed them, over newspaper, with silver and gold (the wonderful toxic reek of those spray cans, which were also preternaturally cold to the touch!); we saved the tops and bottoms of tin cans and used metal shears to cut them into stars and spirals for the Christmas tree. We made Santas, gluing triangles of cotton on the chins of walnuts and red felt hats on their foreheads. When we were very small, my mother let us have Advent calendars. We hung them in our bedroom windows against the white winter light and opened a door for each day, finding a translucent symbolic favor revealed, a pear, a sprig of holly, a mournful doll. The final door opened to show the manger scene, of course, but I can't picture it. Because of some tangle of neural strands, or the operations of an internal censor, I remember instead a miniature view of the Williams College skating rink.

We children learned nothing of Judaism, except a vague understanding that the pickles and corned beef sandwiches my father loved, and the demonstrative relatives from New York and Philadelphia we occasionally visited, were things from the Jewish side of the universe, as were abstractions like justice and the gross national product. We understood as Jewish the sometimes jarring jokes and epigrams my father loved to repeat. A dog goes into a bar, they typically began. Maybe I should have said DiMaggio, they ended. We children looked quickly toward our mother when my father told these stories, to catch the quiver of distaste which flickered over her lip.

Much later I understood that my father was one of the first of the Jews who beat down the pre-war quota barrier erected to keep them out of academia. He and his friend the laconic, brilliant Emile Despres were among the few

Jews to come to Williams in the late forties. Williams president Phineas Baxter, one-lunged but a blowhard nonetheless, who called the undergraduates "a bunch of fornicating earthworms," regularly referred to my father and his friend as "those two Jews."

I am the only one of my siblings to marry a Jew, and from her birth my daughter has always been Jewish to me. My brother and sister consider themselves and their children to be unaffiliated, but they celebrate Christmas and Easter. I'm not sure what I can call myself, but now, having a child, I find I cannot celebrate the Christian holidays, even though the memory of some carols—"It Came Upon the Midnight Clear," and "Lo, How a Rose e'er Blooming"—brings tears to my eyes when I find myself humming them in December. I know more about Judaism now, and I have a great abstract respect for it, but my mother's holiday Christianity, its sweetness, the memories of food and music and the surfaces of familiar things embellished and glittering, is like a beloved country from which I have exiled myself.

My parents made strange bedfellows. When they faced the world, they did so in perfect alliance. They both came from barely middle-class parents, not far removed from great-aunts and great-uncles who died in steerage. My parents were united by upward mobility. Their politics were smoothly merged; they lived in a time when it was still possible to believe in human progress and they both did—blithely and rather arrogantly, it seems to me now. My mother, as president of the local League of Women Voters, worked for the cause of fluoridation, which many local people feared as a Communist plot. My father ran Adlai Stevenson's campaign in Williamstown, and spun strategies in the back rooms of New England Democrats. My parents and their friends, a lively, hard-drinking group of young faculty liberals, shared an attitude of amused contempt toward McCarthyism and the forces of religion and reaction. Dim-witted prejudice, superstition, fearfulness: these impediments were soon to be burned away by the light of reason. One of my father's favorite anecdotes, which he recalled many years later at Washington parties, told of me, at age four, traipsing into the lounge of the Williams Inn with our German Shepherd and showing off the tricks my father had taught him to the alums. "What do politicians do to babies?" I asked him, and he promptly licked my face. "Would you rather be dead or Republican?" I demanded, and he lay down, putting his paws over his ears and whimpering. At that point, my father loved to recall, I always lost my audience.

Together my parents made an unstoppable aesthetic/political flying wedge, she with her graces and accomplishments and the elegant dinner parties she managed on my father's meager salary—the homemade pâtés; the salad served, in the French style, after the entree; the pots de crème in terra-cotta ramekins—he with his intellect and the intimidating force of his presence. Without realizing it, we children lived in the broad, invisible end of the wedge, where it widened into the past, into separate and irreconcilable histories and traditions. And so, with us children, and especially with a difficult and naughty child like me, the differences were enacted. My mother, with her half-acknowledged background of aestheticized Christianity, believed that knowing the beautiful meant knowing the right. To correct was clumsy and ill-advised. Surely, children brought up with good food and good literature and sane, moderate principles and the example of beauty all around us would flourish and turn out well. My father—and here I perversely credit him with some parental feeling—saw that this was not happening, at least in my case. Half the time he was too busy to be bothered; he took out his tensions and frustrations on me, but I believe that he also acted from an obscure desire to help me, to teach. Only his methods were brutal. My mother protested to the degree her sense of fittingness allowed, and when her gentle intervention got her nowhere she withdrew from both of us and, with a perfectionist's shame at failure, eventually from my brother and sister as well. I blundered into the widening space that separated my parents, to fall between them for years.

AS MY MOTHER RECEDED—cocktail parties and much praised dinners at our house twice a month, evenings at other houses twice a week, more days spent withdrawn and sometimes weeping—my brother and I made the town our parent. My pretty, popular older sister, who was a stranger to me, went off to boarding school and her oddly marginal role in the family was written out entirely. I took her sending away as a just punishment for her alternately exemplary and petulantly moody behavior.

I think my brother, Andy, and I understood that our mother had passed her authority to the town, acknowledged its surrogacy. And what a gentle, fostering place it was! Ringed with wild ponds, fields, and granite outcroppings, ringed further by the rounded risings and fallings of the ancient Berkshire mountains, in summer it felt to us like another mother, in winter like a kind cold father. Sometimes together and sometimes apart, we spent every afternoon, weekend, summer day wandering under the elms and through high grass, down past the Haystack Monument and married-student housing, around the tennis courts to the frog pond or beyond, to the train tracks where we left pennies to be flattened and pried off the track the next day, then struggled soggy-footed through crackling uncut fields back to the Williams Inn garden, where we induced hysteria in the chickens by knocking on the henhouse window. One spring we watched as a rabbit, her eyes filmed with shock and fear of us, gave birth in the dark soil of a tulip patch.

I had an odd collection of friends, Williams freshmen and a few of the elderly people who lived in the Williams Inn annex. I waited every afternoon for two old gentlemen, Mr. Allen and Mr. Cartwright, whose daily constitutional took them past our house. One was tall and courtly, with tortoiseshell spectacles, the other deformed, a near dwarf with a built-up shoe and a face that sagged to the right. I intercepted them, and we had a little formal talk, Mr. Allen inquiring about my dog and my parents (never, bless him, a word about school!) and Mr. Cartwright managing with his tortured lips a remark about the weather. They stood over me, leaning in to hear my replies, and I wonder now at the gratitude I felt toward them, the importance to me of these daily, stereotyped encounters.

I also visited an elderly lady, a southerner named Mrs. Thorn, in her rooms at the annex. I have very little memory of these occasions, only the feel of the shiny mahogany banister as I went up the stairs, the painted boards of the ceiling above me receding away, teaching me my first lesson in perspective. I remember the wicker loveseat in which I sat and a cloissonné jar of peonies somewhere at the end of the long peaceful room. Mrs. Thorn, a widow, had a widowed sister named Mrs. Rose. Mrs. Thorn always received me cordially. She kept a stock of shell-shaped chocolates and crystallized ginger. Once she gave me a string of real pearls, the value of which I understood only later. Subtly but unmistakably, I felt like a pest when I visited Mrs. Thorn.

When I dropped in on my friends in Lehman Hall, the freshman dorm across the street, I was never left in any doubt about my reception. I gained access to their rooms by climbing the fire escape and knocking on their windows. Sometimes they waved me away. Beat it! they would call through the glass. Your mother's calling you! Come back when you're sixteen! In another mood, they would usher me in and feed me salami, let me sip the foam off their beer, teach me dirty words or play catch with me in the stairwell. My brother, obedient and steadily quieter, never accompanied me on these visits. He grew into a gentle, self-effacing man, a devoted father, a gardener and carpenter and musician with none of my father's ambition, a near ascetic about food and drink.

As time went on I made the college radio station one of my regular stops. I waited politely outside the door of the broadcasting booth until the "On the Air" sign went from red to black, and eased into the room so quietly that it was often a few moments before the announcer— I remember him; big and prematurely balding, wearing the Williams uniform of chinos and blue oxford-cloth shirt, penny loafers and no socks—realized that I was standing behind him. By this time the sign had gone back on. Out! Out! he would mouth at me, making sweeping motions in the direction of the door, or he would turn to his microphone, intoning in his loud round "On the Air" voice, Why it's Miss Bennington again! A few words for the audience, Miss Bennington? What about that hemorrhoid operation Mr. Dulles just underwent at Bethesda Naval Hospital? Any thoughts on that, Miss Bennington? Handed the microphone I would splutter, breathe, giggle lamely. Not a lot to say, Miss Bennington? I thought you Bennington girls had an opinion on every subject.

LATENCY TRANSFORMED ME for the worse, and I was a pariah at school. Fat, grubby, a shame-faced mumbler with a bowl haircut and a double row of teeth, I came back to myself only when the bell rang and I escaped into the woods. I failed academically, making passing grades in English only. I forgot homework, lost my books, spent hours in the detention they called Study Hall until it occurred to me that I could simply climb through an open window, hop a brook, and clamber over a barbed-wire fence, tearing the crotch of my tights and the hem of my handmade red corduroy jumper in the process, and be gone. I understood that there was no hope for this situation, that my job was to endure and avoid. School was irrelevant and my life was elsewhere.

Today the child I was would be diagnosed as learning disabled, recognized as suffering from poor self-esteem, offered remediation and counseling. I would be hugged by professionals, assured that I was all right, given inspirational stickers to paste on my lunch box. Well-meaning adults would hover over me, surrounding me on every side, leaving me no escape. Perhaps this was exactly what I needed, but even as an adult the prospect leaves me feeling trapped. I was, I want to protest, a happy child! My happiness was in being of no account, being forgotten by preoccupied adults, having for practical purposes no gender. My happiness was freedom.

My mother took me to a doctor—not my usual one, an avuncular refugee who called me "chatterbox" and congratulated my mother on my blooming cheeks and girth, but an Englishman who spent the consultation railing against socialized medicine. As an afterthought he weighed me and prescribed pills that made my stomach feel as though it had been plugged with foam rubber. She took me to a psychologist at North Adams State Teachers College, a man with a yellow tie who played checkers with me and asked me to draw a picture of the members of my family. My father took me on a tour of local dentists, two of them in faraway Pittsfield. In the end he found one who said I didn't need orthodontia.

All this, too, was irrelevant. I had found some comrades, two brothers, David and Timmy, the sons of a Williams professor, a political historian who was soon to be famous. David and Timmy were pariahs like me, faculty brats like me. Their father was tall, a benign, shabbily aristocratic kind of academic. Summer afternoons we sat around him on the sagging porch of their brown-shingled house while he told us time-machine stories. He assigned us star roles in these fictionalized history lessons. I was Marie Antoinette; David was Savonarola, Timmy Attila the Hun.

David was a fat Buddha-like boy, afflicted with asthma and addicted to ChapStick. He was self-possessed and sensible, and probably the brightest student in our school. Timmy was another kind of character, tense and guarded, with a martial feeling about him. I don't know what he became as an adult, but I can picture him as a political adviser or a shadowy second-in-command, discreet and tight-lipped. The last I heard, and this was twenty years ago, David was living in Scotland, an acolyte of R. D. Laing.

We had a fourth compatriot, Roger, who was not a faculty child. His father worked at Cornish Wire in North Adams, and his family lived in a small blue house in one of the first suburban developments in Williamstown. With my unconscious snobbery, I looked down on Roger and his family. He was an introspective boy with a Dostoyevskian gloom about him, and he was already an autodidact, roaming the stacks of the college library. In the sixties, Roger became a revolutionary and distributed Marxist pamphlets at Cornish Wire after his father had retired.

The four of us plunged into a shared imaginative world. We roamed the town, going farther afield than I ever had in my solitary wanderings. We zoned it, renamed it. Indian Country was the area of brush and swamp that stretched between David and Timmy's house and the back road to Bennington. New Inverness was a sweep of rising meadow beyond it. We penetrated every college building, and set up elaborate initiation rituals which were enacted at night and required sneaking out of our houses. I found it easy to escape during my parents' parties. When the drone of anecdote and explosions of raucous laughter reached a certain pitch, I knew I could ease my way down the stairs and out the first-floor study window, which my father kept open. I was gone sometimes half the night and got caught only once, returning from a cave-exploring expedition to find that all the guests were out on Library Hill, searching for me with flashlights. It was after midnight, and some of them were giggling. I hid behind a hedge and watched for a while, but our dog caught my scent, howled, and flushed me out.

During the football season we fanned out under the bleachers and picked up dropped change. After alumni weekends we knew where to look for church-key openers, and collected bags full. Once we found an obscene Polaroid snapshot, a headless naked woman sitting on a linoleum floor, perhaps one of the dorm bathrooms, her legs spread to disclose pubic hair and vulva. We were unsure what to do with this prize, eventually decided that I should keep it for the group. The theory was that a girl was less likely to get in serious trouble than a boy if such a thing were intercepted by a parent. I kept the picture under the blotter on my desk, taking it out to show my brother, who held it gingerly by the edges and looked at it for a long moment without comment. Eventually it disappeared, and I knew my mother had found it.

Toward the end of my family's Williamstown days, David and Timmy's father decided to run for Congress against a Pittsfield Republican named Silvio Conte. We were caught up in the exhilaration of that campaign and for one summer it united my family. We hung streamers, distributed leaflets, baked sheet cakes and decorated them with red, white, and blue icing. On Labor Day we rented a donkey; it traveled from Albany in a special covered truck and clumped down the plank to David's driveway with its mouth full of hay and its eyes demurely lowered. We were allowed to ride the donkey.

My mother composed campaign songs. Andy, Timmy, David, Roger, and I performed them proudly in front of the Williams Inn. "He's for me, He's for you, He's a candidate true blue!" we bellowed, to the tune of "As the Caissons Go Rolling Along," before a small puzzled group of guests who had wandered out to listen.

Silvio Conte's campaign was not such a ragtag affair. I'm not sure whether or not his supporters rented an elephant, but they probably could have afforded to. That David and Timmy's father lost the election came as a surprise to us children, but to none of the adults. I was shocked that this vulgar Republican with too many vowels in his name had so conclusively trounced the forces of enlightenment. This defeat was my first inkling that my parents' order was not always going to prevail. And in fact, Silvio Conte's tenure as congressman from that district remained unbroken until his recent death. I can't think of a more striking example of historical continuity in my time.

WHEN I RETURN to Williamstown, I see that the town has changed very little. There's more peripheral sprawl, a little fast food around the outskirts, but the core of the town, where I lived as a child, has the feel of historic preservation about it. College Place is blocked off now, and no cars move along it. Our two houses are dorms, tenanted museums. I've considered walking in to them, explaining to some polite and uncomprehending young face that this was my home, but that seems quixotic. I stand at the head of Library Hill and wonder that what once was so fluid now seems so still.

The truth is that sometimes we were happy, a happy family. Periodically, some spell would lift from us, and it would be as if we had always been happy. The great glass jugs that the milkman left on our cold back porch would spontaneously pop their corks, and all of us at the breakfast table would laugh. Or my father would sing, basso profundo, his chin tripling on his shirtfront: "Rocked in the cradle . . . of the . . . deeeeep." Or my mother and I would take a short evening walk to the end of College Place to admire a crescent moon, and we would sing as we ambled:

> *Au claire de la lune,*
> *Mon ami Pierrot.*
> *Prête-moi ta plume,*
> *Pour écrire un mot.*

Happiness challenges everything. It upsets causality, undermines explanation. Because we were sometimes happy, I can never make sense of my childhood.

We emptied the wedding-cake house and returned it to the college, packed the aquamarine Plymouth, and moved to New York. As we drove by the pastures of Housatonic, where cows looked up from their grazing to gaze at us, my mother turned to Andy and me and said, "Children, this is the end of an era." I remember thinking my first consciously critical thought about my mother then; her pronouncement seemed embarrassingly stagy and portentous.

After a year in New York, my father was called to join the new president's Council of Economic Advisers. We packed up again and moved to Washington. We all attended his swearing-in ceremony, and a reception at the White House where we shook hands with President Kennedy and the first lady, the vice president ("How do you do, my little cotton-tailed bunny rabbit?"), Earl Warren, and Adlai Stevenson. My mother made her own dress for the inaugural ball, a long beige sheath and a matching brocade coat with silk frog fasteners. I wore a black-and-white-checked shirtwaist with oversized pink rosette buttons that my mother ordered from the "chubbette" section of the Sears catalogue. We ate petits fours at the White House, and my brother was forced to dance with me as the Marine Band played "The Syncopated Clock."

I was sent back to Williamstown to a boarding school. I learned that I could shake my pariah status by being mean and funny. After two years I was expelled, and returned to my parents in Washington.

I was sent to a progressive school where I spent most of my time smoking in a butt-strewn courtyard. While still hefty, I had lengthened, and at fifteen, on my best days I managed to stay on the right side of the line which divides the attractive from the unfortunate. I grew my hair long, washed and ironed it every morning, and by noon my scalp had generated enough oil to turn my bangs into long vision-impairing spikes. I was proud of my hair; it was thick and shiny, the pelt of my nubility. I began to hang out at Dupont Circle, where an emergent hippie scene was gathering. I became obsessed with a boy, and my days were filled with sweaty lyricism.

On the day Kennedy was shot, I sat cross-legged in a far corner of the school courtyard with this boy, trying to read a poem he had abruptly decided to show me. One quick furtive skim showed me it had nothing to do with me, or love, or anything immediately gratifying, but the distinction of being asked to read it was enough to send me into physiological overdrive. My heart was banging, perspiration trickled down my inner arms under my heavy black turtleneck. I was trying to summon a response to this poem, which I found obscure, when another student rushed out, radio in hand, with the news.

Mild shock, a sense of dislocation, annoyance that I was to be sent home early on such a promising day; these were my reactions. On the bus I rehearsed my attitude; I was not to be surprised by this upending of the world. My friends and I were on the side of anarchy and convulsion now. There was nothing in the assassination of a president to threaten me.

I found my father, who in those days I rarely saw at all, standing in the driveway, clutching my brother to his chest. His mouth was contorted, tears coursed down his face. Andy, who kept his tender heart intact, was weeping too. I realized my father was waiting for me, and when he freed one arm to gesture me toward him I had to resist an impulse to turn and run in the opposite direction. My father pulled me to him, got my head into a kind of half nelson, pressed painfully against his hard unfamiliar chest as it vibrated. This was an embrace to which I could not respond, and I let my arms hang limply while I breathed through my mouth to avoid my father's scent, which was like the resinous deposit on the bowls of his pipes. I let my thoughts go back to the courtyard and the poem.

Where was my mother? Looking with one eye over my father's shoulder I saw her—exactly the age, then, that I am now—as she stood hesitating at the window.

MOCKINGBIRD YEARS

—

I.

When I was eighteen my parents were faced with a problem: what to do with a sullen, disorganized daughter who had failed to graduate from high school and who had returned home to Washington, D.C., wrists bandaged, from an extended stay with her boyfriend's mother in Indianapolis. They took me in tow to the psychiatrist I'd been seeing off and on through my high school years, who recommended that I spend some time in a "therapeutic environment." He suggested Austen Riggs, a hospital in Stockbridge, Massachusetts, where patients—none of them too sick, he reassured us—were free to come and go, and where I might spend some months away from the immediate source of my confusion, the boyfriend and his mother.

I stayed at Riggs for three years, one as an inpatient, two as an outpatient, living in apartments with various roommates. These were years I should have been in college, and they were so empty and aimless that when I remember Riggs now my mind pans around the corridors of the big comfortable patient residence, the Inn, as we called it, and in my imagination it is absolutely uninhabited. I drift through the central hall and into the dining room, where the fruit bowl and the iced-tea urn rested on a polished sideboard, replenished by the staff at regular intervals. I cross the hall to the living room with its twelve couches, grand piano, and tall windows hung with flowered chintz curtains. Then I withdraw to the wide central hall and approach the reception desk below the great curving central staircase, and wander in memory through the back door to the grounds, where deck chairs were arrayed in pairs under the trees. I skim by the volleyball and tennis courts and across the parking lot behind the medical building, where patients met with therapists, past the patient-run, staff-supervised nursery school and the greenhouse.

Riggs was an anachronistic institution even then. (I often wonder what it's like there now; the patients are a lot sicker, I'm told, and they stay for shorter periods of time.) The population was very young, very bored. There were a few middle-aged people there, but we younger ones tended to avoid them. They looked baggy and defeated, truly sad in a way we sensed had more to do with life than with diagnostic categories. Years later, when I actually went to college, I read *The Magic Mountain* in a seminar, and I felt I had a certain advantage over the other students. How well my Riggs experience prepared me to understand the convalescent languors of the tuberculosis patients, reclining on their deck chairs, blankets draped over their knees, eyes fixed on the middle distance. Now, whenever I see one of those chairs, the white-painted wooden Adirondack type which seem to show up in soft-focus lithographs on the walls of so many doctors' offices, I feel a familiar jelly-limbed ennui.

My suicidal gesture had been feeble, a few swipes with a pair of nail scissors. I knew when I arrived at Riggs that I was quite sane and only mildly sick; I had no business being there. But I had no business anywhere else either— no diploma, no prospects, and no ambitions.

I arrived excited; going to Riggs was the fulfillment of an adolescent fantasy. The status of mental patient would invest me with significance. The frantic little act that landed me there had been my entree to a process; life would work on me in this particularly colorful way, and who knew what might happen? Riggs had a special interest for me because by coincidence I had spent some time hanging around there at age fifteen, when I visited the home of my friend Caroline, whose father was the financial manager of the institution. We had recently seen the movie *David and Lisa,* and we were smitten with the romance of madness. I think we believed that if we cultivated dissociation we would become as beautiful as Lisa: our complexions would turn luminous, our faces grow expressive hollows, our hair lie flat and glossy. We spent our days edging cautiously around the grounds, taking drags on shared cigarettes and muttering "A touch can kill," hoping to be noticed by the patients, drawn into their glamorous orbit by the magic of proximity. The patients frustrated us by staying indoors, their windows open to the July breezes, playing "Mockingbird" on their stereos. We heard this song constantly, from multiple windows under which we passed, and for us its refrain became the perverse anthem of mental illness:

Mock, yeah!
Ing, yeah!
Bird, yeah!
Yeah, yeah!
Mock-ing-bird!

When the psychiatrist in Washington recommended that I be sent to Riggs, I quivered inwardly, afraid to blow it all by showing my pleasure, and the moment I got home and free of my parents I called Caroline long distance. "Guess what?" I whispered. "Guess where I'm going?" Caroline was going to college, but I was going to Riggs, and I knew by the envy in her voice that I had double-trumped her.

AT COMMUNITY MEETINGS patients sat cross-legged on couches, or lay sprawled on the carpet, and were encouraged to ventilate their feelings by the nurses and a small, round-eyed man, a nondoctor whose function I couldn't understand at first, a kind of professional gadfly and controversialist. Years later I found a category for him: he was a proto-facilitator, perhaps the first of his kind to emerge from the fledgling family-systems school of psychiatry.

These meetings, meals, and therapy sessions were the only real structure of our days. We were assigned tasks, called "work-jobs," in the mornings, but most patients slept through the hour reserved for them. It felt a little gratuitous to spend an hour sponging down baseboards when that hour was being charged to one's account. The issues of work-jobs and D.N.R., or day-night reversal (this was the late sixties, and already we were using acronyms: Riggs was both anachronistic and ahead of its time), were the staples of discussion at community meetings—not so much discussion, really, as nagging and resistance. The nurses and the proto-facilitator kept after us. Why couldn't we take pride in our environment? Could we get to the bottom of this, please? The patients sank deeper into silence and into the contorted positions young bodies assume in shamed repose.

The essential passivity of life at Riggs, a life lived to be examined in therapy, worked against the staff's attempts to get us to clean up after ourselves and keep sensible hours. The domestic staff in the Inn, the nurses, and Richard operated at cross-purposes with the therapists, those austere beings in the big white building across the way who received us singly in their offices and were seen in the Inn only when a patient was having what the nurses called an "upset," with the accent on the first syllable of the word, late at night. The therapists viewed our sloth as symptomatic, and we all tacitly understood that any attempt to expunge what was symptomatic in our behavior was antitherapeutic. The therapists were the radicals, the staff the exponents of realpolitik. The conflict between these factions was never open, and perhaps it was never a real one, but rather a deliberately engineered tension, a therapeutic master plan, a good-cop, neutral-cop ploy. But even if that were true, I know that like most master plans it was often lost sight of, even by its designers.

Not all of us were essentially normal late adolescents. Some were seriously depressed, not just sluggish. Some were harmlessly odd, like L., a lapsed seminarian who carried on a constant internal debate about the supremacy of the papacy. He would emerge from his room to keep a running score on the blackboard above the mailboxes— L. 24, Pope 17. Some of the elderly outpatients seemed beyond hope. The parameters of their worlds shrank as they aged; their compulsiveness stiffened. Never quite accepted by the townspeople, they shuffled up and down Main Street, stopping for the lunch special at the drugstore, ducking into the library for a nap.

A few patients were mad. I can think of two in the early days of my stay there; one somehow got her hands on an antique cannon, fiddled with it to make it operational, and fired it out of her bedroom window. She also pulled a gun on her therapist, made him plead for his life. The other, a young man who could have doubled for Charles Manson, stuffed hard boiled eggs into his rectum and laid them publicly, dropping his pants and squatting in the hallway.

Still, making allowance for the effects of idleness and boredom, most Riggs patients were much like people in the outside world. Graduate students, for example, don't seem much saner as a group, or even much happier. The striking difference between Riggs patients and comparable young people living outside was that Riggs patients were richer. I believe I came from the least wealthy family of any patient while I was there.

MY MOTHER DELIVERED me to Riggs. She spent the first night with me in the local guest house. We were shown into our room, with its flounced twin beds and space heater, its view of Stockbridge's famous main street, the one painted by Norman Rockwell. She closed the door and took her flask from her purse. "I guess the sun's over the yardarm," she said.

The next morning was frosty and bright; we said good-bye in the parking lot of the therapy building, and she alarmed me by bursting into tears, very uncharacteristic behavior. "Goodbye, my dear," she said, and clutched me. The sun bounced off the lenses of her dark glasses and blazed in the car windshields. I remember staring over her shoulder blankly, eager to see her go, eager to get started.

I was led from office to office in the warren of small rooms in the basement of the therapy building, tested and interviewed by five or six of the psychiatrists on staff. I was given the standard Wechsler Intelligence Scale test for adults. (What is the Koran? What does the following quotation mean: "A single swallow does not a summer make?" Assemble these blocks so that the result exactly reproduces the pattern in this booklet. Tell me a story that explains this picture—a boy stands at the head of the stairs, a broken violin in his hand. A man stands over him.) I was given a Rorschach, a Personality Inventory. When I hesitated, the examiner leaned back in his chair, drummed the desk with his thumbs, took a furtive look at his stopwatch. "Take your time," he said.

After my diagnostic workup was complete, I was the subject of a full-dress staff conference in which my prognosis was discussed and my treatment plan drawn up. I think I may have been the last patient at Riggs to be brought into her own conference. The custom was dropped, probably because it had an unenlightened, nineteenth-century feel to it.

I remember entering that room, led in by a nurse, shown to a chair at the head of a polished oval table that seemed to me the size of a fishing boat. The nurse withdrew. Seated there, looking down the rows of faces which looked back inquiringly into mine, I was visited with an impulse to say "Perhaps you gentlemen were wondering why I called you all together today." That made me smirk inappropriately. "Emily," said one of the doctors, "I'm interested in this detached feeling you described in your interview—that floating, disengaged sensation. Are you feeling that way right now?"

"I guess I am," I said, and I lifted my lowered eyes to hazard a smile at the assembled doctors. They smiled back encouragingly, and at that moment I felt a desolate certainty that now there would be no backing out. Now I had left home for good.

I WAS A HOG for attention and welcomed nearly any kind, but the doctors' questions, the nurses' charting of my moods and actions, all this had the feel of the speculum about it.

Within a few months, though, the staff's vigilance had dissipated, and I took my place among the other patients, lounging on the leather sofas in the entrance hall, ashtray balanced on my knee, running my eyes over back issues of *Horizon*. I learned to scorn the activities Riggs offered, ceramics and woodworking in the shop, repotting plants in the greenhouse. I learned to pretend that I hated the food, which was actually the best institutional food I had ever eaten, or ever have since. My adjustment was quick and unproblematic.

I was assigned to a therapist, a research psychologist. I learned later that I was only his second clinical patient. He was a man in his middle thirties, amiable, earnest, eager. He had a spade-shaped, high-cheekboned, luminous face—a beautiful face, really—which sat at an odd angle to his neck, a disc facing up rather than out, and he stood rocked forward on his toes, his shoulders so hunched they were nearly level with his ears. My adolescent sensors instantly registered something alien and slightly goony in his aspect, and I never fully accepted him. Now I understand him better; experience has provided me with a context into which I can place him. He came from the Bronx, a *yeshiva bucher* from a Yiddish-speaking household. When I think of him now, I put a yarmulke on his balding head and append Hasidic curls to his temples, and I see his face as a throwback to visionary and ecstatic ancestors.

—

I WAS RETESTED a year after I arrived, and my IQ had declined significantly—how much, my therapist wouldn't tell me. He would only say the test results were "disappointing." My diagnosis was altered. Now my anxiety neurosis had become a "schizoid personality disorder with borderline trends." This is a bad diagnosis, and an insulting one, I've been told since, but at the time I rather liked the sound of "borderline trends." It made me think of a stylish flourish, an extra, like piping on a jacket or white-wall tires on a car.

Apathy wasted us. I had been a failure as a student, but I had always read voraciously. At Riggs I stopped. We lost our normal adolescent interest in sex—for the most part, at least. We hung out in groups, but we tended not to form real friendships; we saw one another as fundamentally inaccessible, three quarters submerged. We wore kimonos and hair curlers, jeans and slippers as we padded around the Inn—half dressed, half there. News of the Vietnam War protests reached us; we crowded into the patient library, where the record player was kept, to listen to *Blonde on Blonde, Music from Big Pink,* and *Abbey Road,* but still we felt wistfully peripheral. The great counter-cultural storm was rising, but far away from us. Actually, to the degree that a therapeutic view of life has been a legacy of the sixties, we seem in retrospect to have been an advance guard. But at the time we viewed ourselves as the last of the stragglers.

Many of us got worse rather than better, and for some,

getting worse was dangerous. By the time some patients ran out of money, and this was bound to happen eventually, even to the multimillion-dollar trust-funders, their parents and doctors had come to view them as too debilitated to go back into the world. Instead they moved on to state institutions, where sometimes they stayed for life.

MY THERAPIST BECAME inappropriately attached to me. Our meetings were charged with feeling; every session seemed to end in an epiphany. But it was Dr. Schiffer's eyes that beaded with tears, not mine. My parents, we acknowledged in therapy, had rejected and abandoned me. I had known this for years, but pretended it was a revelation because I found his emotion too gratifying not to play on. At the same time I felt itchy and uncomfortable, instantly sated with his love, made queasy by it. I'm not sure whether this was because I felt myself to be in bad faith or whether I was unaccustomed to this kind of moony empathy, this cherishing pity. I was not the kind of young girl a lot of men fell in love with. And I always felt that the object of Dr. Schiffer's love was not me, but some phantasmal waif who only half inhabited the chair in which I sat.

"Thank you," I would say as we paused at the door of his office at the end of an hour. "No, thank *you,*" Dr. Schiffer said. I had opened up the world of feeling for him, he told me. The years of charts and statistics and rat mazes were over for him now. We began to take walks on autumn days. Dr. Schiffer taught me to drive and accompanied me when I took my driving test. I taught him to smoke cigarettes.

Around the time when Dr. Schiffer's wife was due to deliver a baby, I became an outpatient. Dr. Schiffer began to appear at my door. One evening we drank a lot of wine, he and my roommate and I, and we all took a tipsy walk after dinner. Dr. Schiffer put his arm around my waist. This was the first physical contact between us, and the only, but it changed things unalterably. I woke the next morning charged with a theatrical anger and teased by doubts about its legitimacy.

In therapy I remained mostly silent after this incident, and glared. Dr. Schiffer became frantic. He told me one day that he had spent the morning weeping in his parked car on a farm road in Lenox, one of the routes we often took on our drives. Hearing this confession puffed me up with scorn like a blowfish. I was thrilled and enraged. Inwardly, I felt some alarm at this reaction; it seemed partly out of my control. My disgust at Dr. Schiffer had something to do with the way his clammy feelings for me entwined with professional ambition—at my second staff conference, he presented our work together as a new way of doing therapy in which the therapist makes himself vulnerable, fully embraces his own transference, drops his therapeutic distance. A triumph, except for my unfortunate deterioration, documented in testing. But that was easily finessed with the familiar psychoanalytic rationalization that explains an increase in symptoms as a necessary precursor to a breakthrough. As for my baleful new diagnosis, that was drawn from the testing. Having forsworn objectivity in his dealings with me, Dr. Schiffer took no part in it.

I was witnessing the final collapse of adult authority, and my anger was a cover for fear. But it also served to conceal a kind of sexual frustration. I think my semiconscious thought process went something like this: if I'm going to do something so extreme and destructive as to have an affair with my married therapist, I want him to be so powerful, so seductive, that my culpability is washed away. I want his passion to overcome me and leave me blameless. But Dr. Schiffer's feeling for me was more emotional than sexual, more tender than passionate. I could feel a smug slackness in the arm that encircled my waist, tentativeness in his dangling fingers as they brushed against my hip, and it made me mad. I never fully acknowledged this to myself at the time. But let me give my former self the highly qualified credit she deserves: my self-suspicion was like a thready, persistent extra pulse.

I began an unsystematic search for a new therapist, approaching doctors who looked sympathetic and explaining guardedly that I felt I would do better with somebody more experienced than Dr. Schiffer. The answer was always the same: this is an issue to be worked out in therapy.

II.

The new director arrived, startling us all with his appearance. He was tall and bony, with a comic villain's brilliantined black hair and a waist that seemed to begin six inches below his lantern jaw. He wore cowboy boots and string ties, and he brought with him a bevy of beautiful psychotic young girls from the hospital he had directed in Washington, D.C. He was a swashbuckler, a florid, impulsive personality. Going crazy is an occupational risk for therapists who work with psychotics, and the new director was famous for his hands-on treatment: if the patient crawled under a bed, the story went, he crawled under too, and conducted the session right there.

But those girls! They were like a team of NBA all-stars trooping in to watch a junior college practice. They quickly showed us their tricks; one inserted needles in the pupils of her eyes; another plastered her face with chalky makeup and walked around the Inn with her eyes closed and arms extended, a kabuki somnambulist. A third became a member of my therapy group (Subgroup C), and she enlivened the proceedings by screaming at unpredictable intervals, full-throated operatic screams that lasted for fifteen seconds. The arrival of these girls precipitated an avalanche of competitive upsets among the patients, and the nurses had their hands full for a few months. Then these patients, too, "settled in," being human as well as mad.

DR. LESLIE FARBER had come to Riggs with the new administration. He was an old friend of the director, who lured him with promises of time to spend on his writing. I first saw him when he visited our community meeting, which began with the usual nagging by the nurses and

Richard about the work-jobs left undone, the unwhole-some hour at which most of the inpatients had gone to bed, followed by the usual silence, and then the dribble of patient complaints. Sue M., the lanky Floridian, wanted to know why scrambled eggs could not be substituted for the food offered at every meal, not just breakfast. Howard Z., a new patient housed in the east wing of the Inn, com-plained that trucks making early morning deliveries to the kitchen were waking him.

Diana D. spoke next, from her cross-legged position on the floor, leaning forward from the waist, arching her neck and gesturing extravagantly. Diana's speaking style was expressive and tormented. She would make a stab at saying something, fail, erase the air with flailing palms, cover her face with her hands and rock back and forth on her haunches, then try again. Today she said: "I . . . I don't feel very good about this, but I'm just so uncomfort-able. I don't think this is something I can say."

"We're listening, Diana," said Richard. "We want to hear what you have to say."

"It's the outpatients," Diana finally blurted. "The out-patients are making me depressed. Especially John Haviland. I wish he didn't have to come into the Inn. I wish he didn't have to eat with us. He's so depressing, the way he eats." John Haviland, wearing a soiled wind-breaker, looked up from the piano bench by the window. He was a little man with a built-up shoe. He was often the object of imitations by the late-night crew in the patient kitchen; stuffing a roll of toilet paper down the front of one's pants and locking one knee helped to evoke his off-center lumpiness and his fractured gait. "When they're around, the older ones, I feel like that's how I'm going to end up, and I don't want to have to look at that. I don't really think I should have to."

I had been stealing looks at Dr. Farber, who sat quietly in the wing chair by the fireplace. I had noted that he was slightly plump, balding, and middle-aged, with an elfin-Semitic face and an air of masculine elegance that none of his constituent physical parts accounted for. (Later I learned from him how he felt about his embodiment: "a fat little Jewish dentist," he said, quoting a former patient.) In the silence after Diana's remarks I slid my eyes in his direction again and saw on his face an unmistakable expression of shocked contempt. His eyebrows were arched, his lip curled, his nostrils distended.

This look jolted me. I knew instantly that Dr. Farber was a different kind of being from the other therapists. His was not the neutral watchfulness I had become so used to; he judged, and revealed his judgment. This was striking enough, but it was really just the first layer of my reaction. I think I also sensed, if obscurely, that he was a person whose way of looking at the world—unlike that of any therapist I had encountered—was integrated with, and undetachable from, his self.

I learned later that Dr. Farber was well known not only in psychoanalytic circles, but in the wider intellectual world as well. He was a maverick, humane and culti-vated, who challenged his colleagues to confront what the science of psychology had refused to acknowledge—the inextinguishable presence of will in human behavior.

In one of his essays Dr. Farber wrote of the therapist who is like a man who has spent decades building a splendid mansion, a great complex multistoried edifice with wings flung out in every direction. But when the man has finally completed his dream house he settles contentedly into a shack next door. So in his view the house of psychoanalysis was impressive but unfit for human habitation.

Dr. Farber's face, its expression that afternoon, was a life lesson for me, the first I had received since I willingly immured myself at Riggs, a very dense, impacted lesson which I would spend years absorbing and have yet to learn completely.

I MADE AN APPOINTMENT with Dr. Farber immediately, and once seated in his office I wasted no time in blurting out the story of Dr. Schiffer and the driving lessons and the baby Mrs. Schiffer had just given birth to and the arm around my waist and his tears. I felt some terror as I spoke; Dr. Farber's dour expression was not encouraging. He heard me out without interruption, though, and when I was finished he agreed it would be impossible for me to continue in therapy with Dr. Schiffer. Which doctors on the staff would I consider compatible? I didn't really know, I said. They seemed kind of indistinguishable from one another. Would he, Dr. Farber, take me on as a patient? No, he said; his docket was already full. We sat in silence for a few minutes.

Next Dr. Farber startled me by asking what I thought of Washington, D.C. He had just come from there, he said, and he had noticed a Washington address in my file. I stalled, floundered. What could this question mean? Finally I said that I liked Washington, although it was kind of a weird city. He nodded gravely. It is kind of weird, and I like it too, he said. He added that he was having some trouble adjusting to Stockbridge. Did anybody actually work around here, or were the townspeople all models for Norman Rockwell? I laughed explosively. A joke!

We went on to talk about other subjects. Poetry: did I like John Crowe Ransom, a special enthusiasm of his? Yes, I did, I replied, although I had never read or heard of John Crowe Ransom. Dr. Farber stubbed out his Camel and propelled himself headlong out of his chair so abruptly that for a moment I feared he was having a seizure. He rummaged in one of the cardboard boxes that surrounded his desk—he was still unpacking his library— and drew out a book. He tossed it to me, and I caught it two-handed. Take it, he said. You can return it when you come back to talk to me next week. He moved to the door and opened it. What about therapy? I asked, rising from my seat. Do without therapy for a while, he said, ushering me out. Just come back next week and we'll talk.

MY FATHER WAS understandably outraged when he learned that I had gone without therapy for three weeks. Just talking, he shouted over the phone, at eighty dollars a day? Just chatting? He handed the receiver to my mother.

I read the Ransom anxiously, preparing myself to be quizzed, but when I awkwardly got out of my chair to give back the book—even the simplest physical transactions between patient and therapist made me self-conscious—Dr. Farber took it, opened it, and leafed through it, reading passages aloud in his fine deep voice, smiling, shaking his head in confounded admiration. "The curse of hell upon the sleek upstart," he read,

> That got the Captain finally on his back
> And took the red red vitals of his heart
> And made the kites to whet their beaks clack clack.

(I copy these lines from the same Vintage paperback Dr. Farber threw at me twenty-six years ago, one of many books he loaned me which I never returned.) Involuntarily, in a burst of delight, I clapped my hands and repeated "clack clack." I blushed. Dr. Farber smiled his odd, wounded smile and we lapsed into a long, for me unnerving, appreciative silence.

I was desperately eager to please Dr. Farber, but the open-endedness of our arrangement made me so anxious that my conversational timing was thrown off. I sensed that he was wavering in his refusal to accept me as a patient, that I was being auditioned, and the more urgently I wished to pass this obscure test, the more clumsy and aggressive my efforts to win him became. Too shy and fearful of rejection to plead, I sometimes veered off into truculence, imposed my own attention-demanding silences. I wanted to talk about Dr. Schiffer, my parents, myself. So we talked about these things, but in a novel kind of way. I told him the particulars of the mess that had precipitated my suicidal gesture—the boyfriend and his mother, the train ride from Indianapolis to Washington when I lay in a roomette and wept myself sick. And instead of inviting me to continue with a receptively neutral psychoanalytic silence, he forthrightly responded with an anecdote from his own life. He told me about the breakup of his first marriage, the car trip he took from San Francisco to New York, driving for eighteen hours a day and collapsing in roadside motels for six. I hung on these stories, these amazing offerings, but when they ended I lapsed into panic. What now? How was I to respond? And could any response be adequate? I wanted to lift Dr. Farber's confidences out of the hour, out of their contextual bedding, and take them home with me to gnaw on in private, extract all the nourishment to be had from them.

Did I like Joanne Woodward? This one came from way out in left field. Did I? I asked myself, and rummaged frantically in the underused opinion-forming sector of my mind. Finding no ready-made response, I asked myself what movies I had seen in which Joanne Woodward appeared. I knew I'd seen some, but my memory was clouded and roiled with anxiety. I called up an image of Joanne Woodward's face. "Yes," I said, "it's her face I like. It's plain and handsome at the same time. It's very direct." Yes, said Dr. Farber, with gratifying emphasis. That's the thing about her, all right. And we went on to talk about Joanne Woodward movies, a few of which, now that I had relaxed, bobbed up naturally onto the surface of my recollection.

> Thus does the despairer appear before us to ask that most extraordinary and truly diabolical question—especially when addressed to a psychotherapist—"Is there any good in talking?" After this, we may recover our composure and succeed in engaging him imaginatively, so that real talk does, after all, begin to come about. Despite his absolute certainty of a few moments before that even momentary relief from the torment of despair was no longer possible, his despairing self-absorption may yield to forthright interest in the subject at hand, a yielding which goes beyond mere distraction. Relief has, in spite of everything, actually been granted him; his despairing certainty has been exposed to the real world of discourse and proved false. We might even say that a minor miracle has occurred. What are we to answer then, when, as the hour nears its end, our patient or friend, preparing to take his leave, turns to us and asks, "But haven't you something *useful* to say to me—something I can use after I leave here?" If there is an answer to this question, it has not occurred to me.

This passage comes from Dr. Farber's essay "Despair and the Life of Suicide," and it describes exactly the experience of therapy—or friendship; for him the two were inseparable—with Dr. Farber. "The real world of discourse": this is where we are all free to live when we live outside of systems, but I had lived inside one for a long time. Years of psychotherapy (I started at age eleven) had made me smoothly practiced at collapsing into my components, exposing them for convenient inspection on cue. I had learned to "assume the position" so automatically that Dr. Farber's requirement that I come to our talks as pulled together as possible—ready to exercise judgment, to make distinctions, to listen and respond, to view myself first as a moral and then a psychological being; most important, to tell the truth; the high value he placed on tact, empathy, intellectual substance, wit—all this bewildered me at first. It bewildered me later too. In fact, it bewilders me now all over again, having lived for nearly fifteen years after Dr. Farber's death in a culture that has become saturated with therapy, in a world that has become a hospital.

The patient or friend in this passage is in despair, for Dr. Farber a very specific state, which he vividly describes and carefully documents as a drastic spiritual condition that presents its sufferer with an opportunity for redemption (not recovery) at the same time that it provides "fertile soil" for the "intrigues of suicide." What bothers me when I read this passage is a nagging sense that I never was the patient or friend of whom Dr. Farber speaks here. "Despair seems to afflict only those whose relation to life is a serious and potentially responsible one," he remarks later in his essay. While I hope I was "potentially responsible," I don't believe I was "serious" in the way that Dr. Farber's hypothetical friend was serious. Despair was not my condition; neediness was. In fact, from my perspective now, in middle age, the story of my attachment to Dr. Farber would seem more likely drawn from the annals of primatology than from philosophy or theology (the latter, really, was Dr. Farber's stomping ground). It seems plain to me now that while I felt the purest and most ardent admiration for him that I had ever felt for anybody, I was also an unprotected young female trying to find refuge in the care of a "silverback," a dominant male.

DR. FARBER WAS extremely sedentary; his idea of exercise was to fumble energetically for his lighter when it fell between the cushions of his red leather chair. Now that they had moved to the country, his wife persuaded him to buy a bike and ride it to Riggs in the morning. He fell off the bicycle almost immediately, cracked a rib, and broke an arm.

He sat uncomfortably upright, twisted to shield his injured right side from collisions with the arm of his chair, lighting his innumerable cigarettes one-handedly. He looked miserable. After a few minutes of halting monologue I reverted to the politeness I had been taught in early childhood and suggested he go home. He thanked me, and we broke the session off.

The next week he greeted me with warmth. His arm was still in a sling, but he looked much better. At the end of the hour he announced almost casually that a space had opened up and he would, after all, be able to take me on as a patient.

Dr. Farber insisted that I have a final, civil talk with Dr. Schiffer. I protested that I was too angry at Dr. Schiffer to speak to him. Dr. Farber suggested that I consider the connection between guilt and anger. I countered with genuine indignation that Dr. Schiffer was far more guilty than I. Dr. Farber allowed that, and observed that the greater guilt did not completely mitigate the lesser. I made the appointment and spent an hour with Dr. Schiffer, the details of which I can't remember. I think he cried, and I do remember walking into his office with the sullen air of a child forced by adults to apologize. Now I want to say to my former self: you didn't need to apologize, you dolt! You needed to ask to see the baby pictures, and to say goodbye.

I HAD COME to view guilt as a noxious psychic byproduct, something to be gotten rid of in the interests of health. It took me a while to grasp that Dr. Farber's idea was different: for him, guilt was a state that must be acknowledged and, only if possible, expiated. Farber believed that people have real moral claims on one another, and that a full honoring of each of these claims is always impossible. Guilt—some of it a permanent burden—is thus inevitable. For Dr. Farber, guilt was a moral, not a psychological, category.

Dr. Farber's attitude toward me was never the "unconditional positive regard" with which therapists are charged to view their patients. His regard was highly qualified and partial, and it was as real as rock.

III.

I studied for and passed my GED certification. I took a few night classes at the local community college. I began to read again, mostly books loaned to me by Dr. Farber—Goncharov's *Oblomov* (appropriate for me), Martin Buber's *I and Thou,* which I still fail to appreciate, poems by Randall Jarrell and Philip Larkin. I got a summer job in the kitchen of a summer camp. "Girl, we've got to teach you to *work,*" said the cook, and I quit after a few weeks.

I also began to get myself in trouble with alcohol and bad companions. When night fell we could be found at the Stockbridge Inn, known to regulars as Simmy's, drinking beer and waiting to be picked up. Simmy's was full of local characters, pool players laid off from their jobs at G.E., reprobates thrown out of their houses by their wives, glumly stewing at the bar, low-life free riders on the sexual revolution, buying us drinks and dragging a carpe diem line.

I became promiscuous, and I confessed my promiscuity to Dr. Farber. I think I told him about every encounter. His response was surprisingly muted. Again? he would say. Once he called me a "female jerk." He got truly angry only when the man in question was married.

Why did I behave like this? I can think of psychoanalytic explanations: perhaps I was "acting out" the unconscious feelings that Dr. Schiffer's seductiveness had aroused in me, or, more likely, punishing myself for having rejected him and having won Dr. Farber as a protector. I can think of obvious explanations: I was bored, and getting picked up was fun.

I tried out my hypotheses on Dr. Farber. His response was to cut me off. "I'm not interested in that," he would say. His approach, as always, seemed to steer a slalom course around the causal markers I had put in place. Instead he turned the discussion to my drinking, and drinking in general. We talked about the coarsening of feeling, the blurring of distinctions and the deadening of thought that habitual drunkenness brings about. He also talked about the joy of another kind of nonhabituated drinking. Stop the bad kind of drinking, he advised me, so that you can regain the good kind. You were meant, he told me during one of those talks, for the conscious life.

I carry that around with me still, and also the "female jerk" remark. One negative, one positive, they were both his gifts of confirmation.

THEN I GOT PREGNANT, not by one of my Simmy's pick-ups, but as a result of a brief re-encounter with another patient who had been my boyfriend for a summer.

I had skipped a period, felt sick in the mornings, but I refused to acknowledge my condition until one of the nurses, a local woman with a pungent sense of humor, whacked me on the rear as I stood serving myself in the Riggs dining room and made some remark about eating for two. Then I panicked.

A Pittsfield gynecologist confirmed my condition. There are certain circumstances in which bringing a pregnancy to term may not be advisable, he told me. Do what you can do on your own, and call me in two weeks if you haven't had any luck. Perhaps they can help you at Riggs. I wonder now why I didn't take this as a veiled and provisional assurance that he would give me an abortion (then illegal). That was surely what he meant. Instead, I put emphasis on his instruction to "do what I could."

When Dr. Farber asked me if I wanted my parents told I said *no*. I did tell two of my inpatient friends about the pregnancy, though, and soon everybody knew. The director barged into Dr. Farber's office and demanded that my parents be called immediately. The institution would be liable, he insisted, for anything that happened to me. He picked up the phone receiver. Dr. Farber grabbed it away from the director, he later told me, and a physical struggle ensued. The image of a wrestling match between that aging Mutt and Jeff pair seems hilarious to me now, and Dr. Farber's part in it heroic.

Dr. Farber reported to me that the director had suggested a therapeutic abortion. This would require Dr. Farber's assent, and his signature on a document attesting to my unfitness to bear and raise a child. Dr. Farber explained his refusal carefully; he could not arrange the abortion because he could not agree with such a statement. I nodded, barely listening. He had raised my hopes and dashed them, but I felt no resentment, no reaction except an acceleration of panic.

I spent a week on the phone, following leads, being scolded long distance by abortion activists for my past failure to get involved in the issue. Finally I was instructed to dial a New York number, to wait until the phone was picked up and to give my number and area code to the silent person at the end of the line, then to wait for a call. I followed these instructions; the phone rang and a deep, emphysematous male voice told me to be at the Port Authority bus terminal, standing by the third phone booth at the Forty-second Street entrance, carrying six hundred dollars in cash at a certain time and date the following week.

I got the money from the ex-boyfriend, and the two friends in whom I had confided drove me to New York. I waited at the designated place until I was approached by a little man in a green suede feathered cap, who beckoned me out of the terminal and into the back of a limousine, where I was soon joined by an engaged couple from Teaneck. We were all blindfolded and driven to some place in the Bronx (my friends, I learned later, were following in their car). I waited in the parked limousine while the couple were ushered into a building. They emerged a half hour later, the girl walking a little unsteadily, the boy shielding her solicitously with his arm.

Then it was my turn to follow the little man up the back stairs, to shake hands solemnly with "Dr. Adams," to lie down on my back on the linoleum table in a kitchen furnished as sparely as a stage set while five or six radios blared, all tuned to different stations, a crude wall of sound. It was over soon, and I was given pads and an envelope full of antibiotics, and allowed to go.

I was delighted to see my friends waiting for me at the end of the block, waving and jumping. They had spent the time eating a late lunch at a nearby Chinese restaurant, and they had saved me an eggroll.

LATER THAT EVENING, I stood dialing Dr. Farber's Stockbridge number, up to my wobbly ankles in sawdust in the back of a West Village bar and steakhouse, full of Brandy Alexanders and Demerol. Dr. Farber's wife answered and handed the phone immediately to Dr. Farber. "You're all right?" he said. I heard his wife whisper "Thank God!" in the background. Years later, when I got to know her well, she told me that Dr. Farber had spent hours that day in acute anxiety, pacing back and forth in his study.

I launched into a description of my experience, but he cut me off. "Tell me later. You really feel all right?" I feel *fine,* I said, and I did. I was celebrating my passage through a rite; my friends were treating me with respect and solicitude; the adventure had ended safely and I was high as a kite. At the end of the conversation I said something like "You're really a great guy!" or perhaps "I love you!" I don't remember.

MANY OF THE THINGS Dr. Farber said have acted on me much later with a time-release effect. Only a few years ago, some time after Dr. Farber's death, I realized what Dr. Farber meant by his refusal to endorse a therapeutic abortion for me. At the time I had dismissed it, if I thought about it at all, as adult boilerplate, the kind of carefully worded refusal every adolescent recognizes. Now I realized, *he really meant it.* Let me put it another way: he did not refuse to sign this statement because of a legalistic moral scrupulousness (i.e., he could not say that I would *not* turn out to be a fit parent). He refused to sign it because he believed I was able, even then, to bear and raise a child.

Living in the world has been hard enough for me without the complication of what then was called an illegitimate child. I'm retrospectively relieved that I had an abortion. I cannot imagine myself in one of my many chaotic apartments, feeding and rocking and changing a baby. Apparently Dr. Farber could, though, and perhaps he was right. But whether or not he was right doesn't matter; what does is his faith in me, which took me some twenty years to appreciate, or perhaps to accept.

Was Dr. Farber acting out of an anti-abortion agenda? He was, after all, a religious man, a private and nonobservant but passionate believer. Was his refusal to endorse a therapeutic abortion an attempt to influence me? No. He was an anti-ideologue, and no manipulator. He took the crisis of my pregnancy far more seriously than I did; he understood it as a true dilemma, and he showed a respect for me which I perhaps did not deserve by allowing it to be mine.

Have I found myself, now that I am older and the mother of a living child, capable of guilt about that abortion? Not really. I find I can't advance very far along the path of speculation about alternative fates for that dead fetus who would now be twenty-five without backing up in confusion. The voice of the conceptus is too faint, too garbled and muted by the distance of time and the cross-cutting static of possibility for me to hear it clearly. He is no more apparent to me than Dr. Farber's God.

I am just as needy now as then. But perhaps by now I've also become the serious friend—the despairer—of whom Dr. Farber wrote. This is the question that continues to haunt me: What would Dr. Farber make of me now? How would he judge the person I've become?

MY THIRD STAFF conference came and went. "They made you sound like a little machine," Dr. Farber reported, "a little machine that could barely make it to the bathroom."

Things were jumping at the Inn under the new regime: plenty of upsets, angry contention in the community meetings. Dr. Farber waved it all away with a gesture of disgust. For the most part, it didn't interest him. He was an enthusiastic gossip, though, and sometimes he would find some piece of exhibitionistic lunacy diverting. He loved the story about the patient (the same one who laid eggs in the hallway) who shaved his head bald except for one sideburn and then felt so delighted with himself that he jumped up and down on his bed until it collapsed.

Dr. Farber began to complain about Stockbridge. I hate this place, he said. I hate this goddamned maple sugar Norman Rockwell tourist-infested place where you can't find a decent corned beef sandwich. He announced that he was moving to New York, where he would set up a private practice and continue his writing. "If you don't believe I'm going," he said, quoting some old blues lyric, "just count the days I'm gone."

You're welcome to come along, he told me. Or perhaps that was my idea. At any rate, all three of us who were his patients at Riggs packed up and followed him to New York, as if on a dare. He beckoned, and we were sprung.

THE MOST RESPONSIBLE GIRL

—

I. The Rose Court

She was the most responsible girl, the leader of our dormitory floor, and twice monthly we all trooped into the room she shared with two high-status roommates. I remember her, sitting in her Lanz nightgown at the end of her neatly made bed, with its colorful afghan, hand-embroidered throw pillows, and pyramid of stuffed animals. Her hair was rolled up on giant-sized orange juice cans—these produced the full, sleek effect we were all after in the early sixties—and she managed to paint her toenails, chin balanced on one knee, while listening judiciously to both sides of disputes about runaway rumors or food left on the radiator to attract ants. The girls arranged themselves on the floor around her bed in a fan formation, the most favored in the rank nearest to her.

I was the least responsible, or close to it, and least favored. I stood by the door. Sometimes another outsider would join me, and we would lean together smirking and giggling subversively. These companions came and went; nobody was as steadily incorrigible as I. Often I would arrive at a meeting to find my latest co-conspirator reabsorbed by the group, sitting somewhere in the outer ranks, casting guilty glances at me over her shoulder.

My behavior was beneath the notice of the responsible girl and her auditors, but I caught scathing looks from the dorm adviser. This was our drama teacher, Virginia, a failed actress and singer in her early forties. She kept a baleful black-and-white neutered tomcat named Booey and she was full of campy mannerisms—double takes, facetious gasps of horror, derisive snorts. She wore her hennaed hair in a beehive and plucked and redrew her eyebrows into tufted peaks. She was one of those odd adults who rattles around for years before settling down to discover the pleasures of engineering and enforcing adolescent hierarchies. She acted as a kind of palace guard, and her allegiance to some particular girl signaled that girl's ascendancy as unmistakably as white smoke hanging over the Vatican. I hated her, and she hated me back with a shocking directness. It was Virginia who got me thrown out. She caught my roommates and me drinking Chianti and ginger ale on the roof, identified me as the ringleader, and persuaded the directors of the school that I was too immature to benefit from the experience that the school had to offer.

WHAT DID IT TAKE to be most responsible girl? This is a question I've pondered for years. Not looks or wit or academic superiority. Any marked distinction that might help a girl's chances in the world of men, or in the mixed world of men and women, actually tended to work against her candidacy. While never ugly or unattractive, the most responsible girl was often rather plain and solid, but with good bone structure. She was a high-average student, quiet and even-tempered. More frequently than would seem likely, she had a small physical defect—a slight limp or a noticeable but nondisfiguring birth-mark—or some mild chronic illness like asthma.

The most responsible girl often rose up out of a dis-carded carapace of shyness: she had been, for example, the wardrobe mistress for the school play rather than the lead, the recording secretary or treasurer of the student govern-ment rather than the president. But her developmental pace was as regular as a healthy pulse; by the time she reached her junior year she had begun to show new poise and a quiet confidence. She was the tortoise, confounding all the upstart hares; the wattage of her glow grew steadily. Around this time, she often acquired her first boyfriend, a big, earnest masculine one, a muscular-Christianity type, not quite handsome but nearer to the male ideal than the most responsible girl was to the female. He and the mrg walked together hand in hand, giving off a powerful musk of responsible ardor. I remember sensing this as I watched the two of them, hit in the solar plexus with my first apprehension of what married sex might be like, in all its hairy maturity.

The mrg was surrounded by a kind of rose court of the pretty and the witty. This most inner circle was the place allotted to girls with natural gifts. When the mrg had a fight with her boyfriend, they clustered around her as she sprawled on her bed weeping, and their celebration of her grief gave it a special gravity.

Now we had to credit Virginia with an eye for spotting dramatic potential; suddenly the mrg was transformed, a new creature with a vastly expanded emotional range. Her hollow-eyed pallor became her: now we could feel the depth of her female authority. She was Medea-like in the haggish glory of her rage and sorrow. A hush hung over the second floor; the mrg's attendants scurried up and down the back stairs, carrying trays of tea and chocolate pudding up from the kitchen, ordinarily out of bounds between meals but opened up on this occasion by special arrangement with Virginia.

I felt a faint dismay, a sense of disillusionment. Was all love imperfect, even the love between these two paragons? And I was deeply shocked when I learned, some months after the fact, that the most serious of these fights—I can still remember the sobs of the mrg and the shouts of Virginia—was the consequence of the betrayal of a member of the inner circle; she was caught by Virginia in the alley of pines behind the dormitory necking with the mrg's boyfriend. They were both stripped to the waist when she discovered them, according to the report I heard. Virginia marched them back to the school, prodding the reprobates in the smalls of their backs with a stick.

For the mrg, female society was bedrock. However perfidious men might turn out to be, women could always be trusted, at least once the traitors had been weeded out of the garden. She and the girls surrounding her took refuge in a pre-feminist female solidarity. The group provided a soft place for retreat from the pre-feminist gender wars, and it offered an alternative view—somewhat more broad-based and democratic than the erotic wishes of the boys—of ideal and desirable female traits. The ordinary-looking girl who knew what to do with her hair, or how to dress, who had a sense of style and groomed herself immaculately, was closer to this ideal than was, for example, one particular friend of mine, a good-looking slob with an air of fey distraction and a need for solitude. A great emphasis was placed on communitarian virtues— reliability, organization, maturity, a willingness to subordinate one's desires to the interests of the group.

Sometimes I speculate about the mrg from a Darwinian perspective; perhaps she and her court represented a check, a refining influence, on the indiscriminate operations of natural selection at work behind simple male lust, the hard-wired tropism of males toward females with clear skin and large breasts and a ratio of .7 between the measurements of their hips and their waists—all very rough indicators of health and superior genetic endowment. Too rough, too dismissive of the moral and the social; so the girls got together and created an mrg, an intelligent young woman built to the specifications of responsible motherhood and civic participation, and offered her to the male camp as a sensible alternative to the sweet-smelling decoy-flower females for whom they clamored.

The mrg was more the locus of the group's feelings and values than its leader, more emblematic than active. But she was also more than raw material for the construction of a cult object; she had real authority, grounded in a finely tuned sense of psychic proprioception. She knew at all times exactly where she was in the complex terrain of social interaction, just how the various parts of her social being were positioned, and how far into the imaginative worlds of other people they extended. This is an aptitude that blossoms with developmental maturity. I've shown so little of it myself that I have to wonder whether I lack it the way some people lack a spleen or whether I lack it because I never fully grew up. Even now, the world makes sense to me mostly as something to look out on; once entered into it, I'm vulnerable to a panicky sense of dislocation, floundering without coordinates as faces move past me and horizons loom and disappear. It's this deficit, I suppose, that explains my style of friendship, which is nearly always predicated on a shared sense of exclusion, and on shared conspiratorial sniping. "Come my dear, let us abuse the company!": this invitation, offered to Becky Sharp by her outrageous aunt in *Vanity Fair,* has always delighted me.

I was certainly a slow and uneven developer. I arrived at boarding school—a progressive coeducational one in the Berkshires—dazed with anxiety and homesickness. At thirteen I was really still a little girl; I needed reminding to bathe and pick up after myself. This my roommates did, bluntly and effectively. They wadded up the dirty clothes I'd left strewn around the room and threw them over the balcony into the empty swimming pool. They locked me in the bathroom with a box of tampons until I could learn to use them. It's hard for me to say, from the distance of thirty-five years, whether this treatment was damaging or just the right rough remedy for my backwardness.

I SOON DISCOVERED that I had one social card to play, a quick wit and a willingness to put it to whatever unkind use might win me friends. I became the Dorothy Parker of the smoking porch, or so I saw myself, blowing rings and drawling witticisms. I gravitated toward the boys, who always gave me plenty of commissions for limericks and imitations. Among the boys I found some solid, if necessarily partial, friendships. Early on I became a kind of mascot figure, a tagalong treated with alternating affection and contempt.

At the end of my freshman year I was taken aside by one of the graduating seniors, a charismatic boy named Dutch with floppy blond hair and an elegant aquiline nose. I had been in love with him for some weeks, and when he beckoned me to follow him into the woods I did so with knees shaking.

We walked some distance, following a trail of muddy tire tracks through a forest of maple saplings just coming into yellow-green leaf, arriving finally at the door of a little abandoned shack, half hidden in underbrush. I recognized this as the legendary place the older boys called "the house," passed each spring from one senior boy to his chosen successor, a hideout where rumor had it six-packs of beer were consumed and sex acts performed. I felt a little frightened, though even then I was in touch enough with reality to think it unlikely that Dutch had designs on my pudgy, barely pubescent person. He gestured me into the shack, which was cold, dusty, and tidy, neatly fitted out with surplus classroom chairs and a military-style cot.

I also recognized a small mosaic coffee table on which Virginia had displayed ceramic ballerinas, a photographic portrait of Booey, and a montage of snapshots of herself mugging with a series of most responsible girls. It had stood against a wall in the short hallway outside her suite of rooms. She inspected the dorm the morning it was discovered missing; flanked by two henchwomen from the inner circle, she swept through the rooms and closets of likely suspects.

The shrine had been neatly reassembled in a corner of the shack, all the objects placed in their original positions, though by now of course the ballerina statuettes were headless, the photographs of Virginia and the mrgs were vandalized with devils' horns, supernumerary breasts, and crudely drawn pubic bushes, and the silver frame from which the smoldering eyes of Booey looked out had been pitted with BB shot.

"Yours," Dutch said, waving to indicate the shack and all its contents. "I bequeath it to you." I was the first girl, and the first nonsenior, to receive this honor, and while I was sensible of it, I was also obscurely disappointed.

BY THE FOLLOWING FALL I had matured a bit, and while my chances for acceptance by the mrg and her court remained as remote as ever, I found my roommates more inclined to tolerate me. They, in turn, had rounded another developmental bend far ahead of me and become cautiously disinhibited, though still far less naughty than I was. I remember this school year, when I turned fifteen, as my happiest in adolescence. It was the year I began to do well in my classes, the year my roommates taught me to take care of my hair and clothes, the year I found a confidant in my kind, elderly French teacher, a man who treated me with a delicate respect when we met for our weekly talks.

It was also the year I began to get myself into male-pattern trouble. My ostensibly docile roommates were often just as guilty of misdeeds as I, but they lacked my flair for getting caught. At our last meeting, after I had been expelled, my French teacher rose from his chair, bent over from the waist, and kissed me on the forehead, a light, dry kiss like a blessing.

That year I contracted passionate crushes on a series of boys, mostly the older ones. Around these boys I spun intense, near hallucinatory fantasies; in the earliest ones, I was often a nurse, flying to my beloved as he lay wounded on the golf course, crouching to attend him as bullets whizzed over my head. (Wounded how? By some shadowy "opposition group," whatever that meant. Why the golf course? Because I saw one in the distance every time I looked out my window.) The elements of the fantasy were makeshift and arbitrary. What mattered was the flow at the center of my imagination, the oceanic pull of feeling as I lowered my cheek to his chest, the lingering of the sensation as I tore myself away from him, his cries of gratitude to me, the failed rescuer, ringing in my ears.

Later, my fantasies took the form of imagined dialogues in which I confronted and challenged the beloved. I took as my text Jane Eyre's address to Rochester at the foot of the great chestnut tree:

Do you think, because I am poor, obscure, plain and little. I am soulless and heartless? You think wrong!—I have as much soul as you,—and full as much heart.

I was, of course, not able even in imagination to chivvy the object of my fantasy with an eloquence like Jane's, but I did my best to imitate her brave, tremulous dignity. And I ended with an attempt at the same transcendent claim to essential equality, my own paraphrase, after which the beloved rewarded me by taking me into his arms, just as Rochester gathered up Jane:

I am not talking to you now through the medium of custom, conventionalities, or even of mortal flesh:—it is my spirit that addresses your spirit: just as if both had passed through the grave, and we stood at God's feet, equal,—as we are!

How this thrilled me! I have to admit that it still does. It remains my paradigm for relations between men and women. The dyad! How much I prefer it to the group. In my heart I believe that the presence of more than two introduces a tragic warp into the world. From a developmental point of view, no opinion could be more retrograde, but I can defend it by pointing out that, on one account at least, God agrees with me.

I WAS SENT TO a new school after my expulsion. There, I began to develop the rudiments of a sexual style. A certain kind of male, I could now see, responded to a boldly frontal approach, a challenging, slightly teasing manner. I learned that it was possible to walk up to certain boys and simply engage with them. Never, of course, with a directly sexual intent; my innocence protected me from even conceiving the notion. My longings were unfocused and the erotic was hidden behind a hundred lyrical veils.

Often, this technique misfired, but sometimes, to my delight and surprise, it worked! I had found a way to run out, briefly, from under the cover of androgyny, to feel, just for a few moments, quite dangerously feminine. How satisfying it was to walk through the halls of my new school, deep in conversation with some boy, and to catch in the periphery of my vision the stupefied stares of girls who had been trying to snag him for months. It was not so much the envy of the very pretty girls that gave me this visceral and vindictive pleasure; I knew myself to be out of their league entirely, and felt a little ashamed at my apparent presumption. (When I look at pictures of my seventeen-year-old self I'm chagrined to realize that I was more adequate than I thought. I was almost pretty, or would have been if only I had known myself better.) What really gratified me were the looks I got from the girls I had identified as mrg types, the mature girls, the *womanly* girls. I had confounded them by innocently and fearlessly crossing the zone that divided me from men, the territory that Virginia and the mrg would have you believe was strewn with hazards, and only to be attempted if you could be sure that the company of women stood waiting to succor you when you staggered back across the border into home territory.

II. Anna

Five years ago I embarked on a promising new friendship. I had just moved, with my husband and daughter, to a new city. After my daughter started school, I began to make tentative moves toward establishing a life in this new place. I audited a course at the university where my husband had taken a teaching position and met a few people, one of whom introduced me to this interesting woman—I'll call her Anna—who, like me, was married to a faculty member, had literary leanings, and felt alienated by the academic establishment. My husband and I were both charmed by her; she had a touchy rectitude, a bluestocking intensity, and an endearing vulnerability. She seemed available to friendship—still open, still thinking, still, like me, on the outside of things, peering in. I find it's not easy to make friends in middle age; so many of my contemporaries seem closed and completed.

Anna served as my guide to the people in the academic and writing communities to which she belonged and I aspired. What's So-and-So like, I'd ask, and, after some protestations and shows of evasive tact, Anna would blurt out her opinion of that person, whom she almost invariably viewed as arrogant, rude, self-involved, and treacherous, or as the innocent dupe of others with these qualities. And there was always an illustrative anecdote.

An example: Anna belonged to a university women's group, ostensibly leaderless but actually run by a politically powerful group of women in the English department. To her, Anna, they had delegated all the clerical work, all the typing, copying, and note-taking, because, as she noted bitterly, they assumed that her time was less valuable than theirs. I laughed sympathetically and made some observation about the cultural contradictions of feminism—or any ism, I was quick to add. I also said something about the ironies of groups with utopian agendas and dystopian dynamics. Anna's reaction—I barely registered this at the time—was rather veiled. She went opaque for a moment, but I interpreted this as a welling up of her incompletely discharged anger.

I too knew about the maddening condescension of the credentialed toward those they took to be their inferiors. I felt indignant on Anna's behalf. I also assumed—wrongly, as it turned out, and perhaps this was a symptom of my continuing failure of psychic proprioception—that I was free in this new friendship to express my opinions, even those that ran against the conventional grain.

For example: as Anna and her husband sat with my husband and me in our living room one evening, finishing our coffee, the conversation turned to the Senate hearings on the confirmation of Clarence Thomas which were then in progress. I was in a convivial mood, feeling comfortable with these new friends, feeling the wine I'd drunk at dinner. We seemed on the brink of a real intimacy, and so I gathered the nerve to express my real feelings about this contretemps, something I would have known better than to try in the company of most academics. I remarked—laughingly—that while I considered Clarence Thomas an inadequate nominee for the Supreme Court, I thought Anita Hill's (an mrg, by the way, if ever I saw one) protestations of horror at Long Dong Silver and the other indignities were ludicrous and transparently trumped-up, and I went on to say further that this new strand in feminism, this new sanctimony, this soppy protectiveness of female innocence—well, I said, it was pernicious indeed. In response to Anna's husband's polite inquiry about how I would feel if the Coke can with the pubic hair on it were brandished in my face, I said, Just fine! Wouldn't bother me a bit. I've had worse waved at me. I went so far as to invoke the name of Camille Paglia before I began to realize that my guests had gone cold on me, and that it was time to change the subject.

As we all stood at the doorway, some minutes later, saying goodnight, I pressed into Anna's hands the manuscript of a novel I had just completed. Anna had offered to read it and I gave it to her with the hope that we could recover from the small chill I had felt on our friendship that night.

Three long weeks later—days pass with a gluey slowness when you're waiting for reaction to a manuscript—I broke down and called Anna. She answered the phone after six rings, out of breath and apologetic. She and her husband, she explained, had been putting in some plants. Her voice was cheerful. We talked for a few moments about the gardening she'd been doing. As she spoke I went blank—gardening is terra incognita for me—but I pictured Anna, standing in the shade of the screen porch, her hair pulled back under a bandana, wiping the sweat of Indian summer from her forehead with the back of her wrist as she talked on the cellular phone. Her husband was barely visible to the eye of my imagination, viewed in diminished perspective at the bottom of their property, his gray head lit by late afternoon sun, bending over a wheelbarrow like a figure in a Diego Rivera painting.

"So," I said, "did you get a chance to read the novel?" I was prepared to hear that she hadn't yet; Anna taught at a local community college and the preciousness of her leisure time was a persistent theme in her conversation. "I did," said Anna, with a bell-like forthrightness. A silence followed.

"I thought there was a lot of good technique," she began. I made some registering noise. "A lot of good writing. Of course, as a whole it's a deeply misogynistic novel."

"What?" I said.

"I said it's deeply misogynistic."

My novel, originally titled *The Mall Walker,* concerns an academic couple with a small child. The wife of the couple, Miranda Blau, is a passive and detached personality. Now that her daughter is in day care, she finds herself at loose ends; she makes a few gestures toward finding a part-time job and drifts into a kind of half-life, watching reruns of *Marcus Welby, M.D.* on television and wandering through shopping malls like an anomic ghost. She is surrounded by charged-up, goal-directed female exemplars—it's a comic novel and I'll grant that they are portrayed parodically—but the prospect of imitating them leaves Miranda more languid than ever. I had intended her as a sort of female Oblomov; I wanted her stillness to serve as a surface on which reflections of the comic and chaotic world around her might play. Her ruminations, her internal dialogue, represented the best of whatever wisdom I had managed to acquire. For Miranda, I hardly need to mention, read me. "Misogynistic?" I said.

I've had years now to replay that conversation, to erase the spluttering and the lame rejoinders, to fill my incredulous silences with wit and sense. But now I can't separate what was said from what I wish had been said. I do remember clearly how the conversation ended. I put myself in the wrong by shouting an obscenity and slamming down the phone.

That was the end of my friendship with Anna, and my anger and remorse caused me acute pain for three months. I tortured my husband with my moodiness; he was patient, willing to engage in marathon sessions of ventilation and consolation, quite ready to agree with me that Anna's stand on artistic solidarity with other women was rigid and unreasonable, especially in light of her complaints about the group of university feminists who had misused her. But why did she send such conflicting signals? He had no idea, he said.

I was continually prying the incident apart, as if by disassembling it I could disarm its power to hurt me. I should have seen it coming, I said, and my husband concurred. I went on to anatomize all the hints and foreshadowings that should have warned me. Soon I was talking to myself, and my tired husband was nodding dully. At the end of these talks, when it seemed that his sympathy had only exacerbated my agitation, he repeated his observation that, in spite of her charm, Anna carried a large chip on her shoulder and was not very rational. What more was there to say? He shrugged and left the room.

What more? I was irritated at my husband for pitching the whole mess into the miscellaneous bin. I wanted to push on the incident until it yielded some insight. What I couldn't convey to my husband was the peculiar quality of the shock Anna had given me. She was like a grimly cheerful physician producing, with a flourish, the giant wriggling tapeworm that had been causing a multitude of obscure and apparently unrelated symptoms: here's the culprit! As long as I protested the injustice of Anna's accusation, I was sparing myself a confrontation with the real source of my pain. This was the rearing up, after years of semi-dormancy, of the loneliness, the sense of anomaly in myself, that I felt when I walked into a dorm meeting to see some erstwhile friend's back, now one in a circlet of female backs ringing the bed of the mrg. My hard-won middle-aged equanimity, my years of steadying wife-and-motherhood, my place in the world of adults: all this dropped away. At some point in the phone conversation with Anna, I had been hit by a wave of recognition and the shock of sudden exposure. I heard her calling me something worse than misogynist; I received her words as confirmation of my fear that I was an unnatural woman.

III. A Male-Identified Mutant

At this juncture, I'll admit that my identification with men runs deep. While I recognize and acknowledge the historical fact of the oppression of women, I don't have much firsthand feel for the rancor against patriarchy that informs the movement.

And in fact, some expressions of that rancor make me rancorous in return. I bridle, for example, at the casual offering of antimale slurs as conversational gambits by women I have only just met. I take umbrage at the notion that women cannot or should not find guidance in male mentors. Indignation leaps into my throat when I hear it said that women cannot be expected to identify with male protagonists in literature, or worse, when I read, as I did a few years ago, that all men are to be considered potential rapists, and that sexual intercourse between married partners (the dyad! the dyad!) is always, in its essence, rape. I've come to feel that same visceral, reactive response in defense of men that many women feel when they spring to the defense of other women.

How is it that my experience has been so different from that of other women—particularly those many feminists who have documented their transformation from dupes of the patriarchy to participants in a group rebellion against it? I can get closer to the source of my contrarian impulse by acknowledging that my childhood was non-standard. I grew up encouraged by my talented and unhappy mother to express a masculine side she suppressed in herself.

I was butch to my older sister's femme; she wore pinafores and braids while my mother cut my hair in a bowl and dressed me in overalls. I was never encouraged to put any stock in my appearance or to dream of marriage and children: instead I was urged to roam and play freely, and to read. My mother was advanced in many ways; quiche appeared on our table fifteen years ahead of the world-historical schedule, and I was raised in a scrupulously nonsexist manner.

I grew up pained by the absence of just those influences which so many feminist accounts recall as noxious and stifling. I wondered what was wrong with me, that my mother pressed the bauble of femininity into my sister's hand, but kept it hidden from me. Never mind about that, she seemed to be saying, hastily concealing the glittering thing behind her back. You wouldn't be interested. You were meant for better things.

But I couldn't help noticing that she cultivated her own femininity, that she enjoyed clothes, that she flirted, that she became semianorexic in her determination to stay slender. And the nonsexual side of her femininity was perhaps even more important to her; how hard she worked to make her cooking and housekeeping seem effortless and offhand! How important to her, much as she dismissed it as the mere performance of an animal function, was the fact of her motherhood.

What I assumed was fundamental and unquestioned in the lives of other girls was problematic in mine. It was only quite late, after I had provided myself with a secure substructure of marriage and motherhood, that I was able to turn my energies to writing, the vocation my mother had foreseen for me.

Over the years I've assembled an adequate stock of conventionally feminine experiences. Those boys, for example, who responded to my frontal approach usually did so only temporarily, and soon enough I was complaining, just like other women, about the common male syndrome of emotional withdrawal after the fact of intimacy. I've given birth, and suffered the ordinary maternal pangs of love and worry. I'm a veteran of a long, struggling, and ultimately successful marriage. Still, even now, in the presence of women whose womanliness runs deep, I often feel like an overgrown child, a shy, sad monster—dim, clumsy, incompetent, but somehow, in some transcendent but useless way, superior.

I grew up with a blustery contempt for all things feminine and a secret longing for them. My exclusion from the mrg's rose court was defensively self-imposed, but no less painful for that.

My mother sent me out as a proto-feminist scout into a future which she trusted to catch up with her enlightened notion. I wandered for years in what seemed to me a wilderness. Feminism, when it came along, should have rescued and vindicated me, but instead it has left me more isolated, I think, than I would have been without it. Here at last was the cavalry, rumbling at full gallop—but in the wrong direction! Here I remain years later, still apart, still watching as they thunder by.

IV. Shama's World

As I observed earlier, I'm a slow developer. A few years ago it began to dawn on me that fear of anomaly in the self is as common as the condition itself is rare.

When I first read V. S. Naipaul's novel *A House for Mr. Biswas,* I encountered a passage in which the protagonist, Mohun Biswas, ruminates about his pregnant wife, Shama, and the matriarchal family structure which surrounds her. What Shama wants is

> to be taken through every stage, to fulfill every function, to have her share of the established emotions: joy at a birth or marriage, distress during illness and hardship, grief at a death. Life, to be full, had to be this established pattern of sensation. Grief and joy, both equally awaited, were one. For Shama and her sisters and women like them, ambition, if the word could be used, was a series of negatives: not to be unmarried, not to be childless, not to be an undutiful daughter, sister, wife, mother, widow.

This passage hit me with the force of revelation. For me, it was a kind of Rosetta stone, a means by which I could translate my language into the language of others.

Instantly, I knew it to be true, not only of Shama and

her sisters, but also of me. Given a feminist quarter-turn, updated and purged of language that assumes any connection with men, it applies to nearly every woman I know. We understand this fear, this negative imperative—"not to be . . . not to be." It predates feminism, but the matriarchal movement that feminism has become exploits it, threatening to unwoman anyone who dares to lay claim to any but the prescribed narrative of the rejection of patriarchy followed by identification with the group, any but "this established pattern of sensation."

The mrg wept, surrounded by her sisterly court. I was left feeling sick and spiteful, full of an insupportable envy because I knew that just as I would never feel the fullness of the mrg's satisfaction, so I would never feel the fullness of her misery. Her groans were everywoman's, echoed by a chorus. They had a roundedness, a primal dignity. To wail while cradled and celebrated; this was surely a good kind of pain. Like the agony of childbirth, it laid a claim on universality. My hurts, on the other hand, were private. I felt them as stinging reminders of my own anomalousness, and I hid them.

Naipaul draws a comic and horrific portrait of a matriarchal extended family. The daughters of Mrs. Tulsi, the widowed matriarch-in-chief, all live together in a compound, bringing up one another's children in true "villager" style. They support and protect one another, and they also make each other quite miserable. Shama, for example, feels compelled to beat her children brutally in order to save face before her sisters, and her marriage to the hapless Mohun Biswas is continually undermined by their mockery. The group makes a cult object of the eldest sister in a way that instantly reminded me of the mrg: all compete to wait on her and to attend to her numerous ailments. The sisters hold one another hostage through shame. It is the fear of exclusion from the mainstream of feminine experience that motivates them. Above all else, they fear the charge of unwomanliness.

Naipaul reminds us that female solidarity is often found in enclaves of poverty and backwardness like the West Indian Hindu colony where Mohun Biswas and his family live, societies where women live in subjugation, where their choices are few and their power indirect. This is the natural milieu of matriarchy. The system of values matriarchy enshrines—the celebration of competitive self-sacrifice, of a militant relatedness to others, of a gestural "macha" defiance in the face of male domination—all this develops where and when patriarchy is most oppressive. It occurs to me that this kind of "strong" woman is not always, or even usually, a free woman.

V. Two by Two

What went on in their minds, those girls in the third and second and even the first ranks, as they sat listening to the mrg? And the mrg, for that matter: what was her subjective state? Is it possible that some or all of them were feeling, or at least suppressing, something like what I was feeling, some degree of that sense of anomalous isolation?

Their backs told a story of creaturely fealty; seen from that angle they were as charming as a school of dolphins swimming in formation. But what did they look like from the mrg's vantage point? She was the only one with a privileged view of all their faces, individual and vulnerable, tipped up into her gaze like bowls awaiting the distribution of oatmeal.

How could I have failed to perceive that the mrg's anguish, even when the others pressed around her like a poultice, came from a lack of exactly what the group could never give her—that is, intimacy and mutuality? How wearisome the group must have seemed to her then, what a burden. She must have felt herself to be a singular creature indeed, like the great turtle on whose back some mythologies have placed the world. Where, she must have asked herself, is a mate fit for me?

GROUPS HAVE NO MIND; only in dyadic relationships can I, or anyone, be known, or know another. Only in friendship—and particularly in the long, combative friendship that has been my marriage—have I been able to free myself of the feeling of anomalousness that I've harped on so obsessively here.

Which is not to say that my marriage has been unproblematic. Over the course of the first fifteen of its twenty-five years, through a protracted, sometimes agonized process of (here I pause to consider a sequence of possible words—confrontation? negotiation? encounter?—only to reject them all as euphemistic) fighting, my husband and I each formed full, separate selves.

All my life I had been itching for a good fair fight, and

my husband was the man to give it to me. He has been a formidable adversary, lucid and dogged, with an extraordinary capacity for sustained feistiness. For me, these purely personal wars have been the only ones to end in peace. Better a battle with a single antagonist, even a resourceful scrapper like my husband, than a hopeless struggle to preserve myself in the face of the grossly numerical superiority of the group, an entity that can only subsume.

Here at last, inside my marriage, I've been able to express, and eventually to temper and control, the aggressive, masculine side of my nature. Here I was able to be—and to become—my unwomanly self without shame. How many other women have had some variant of this experience?

MEANWHILE, AS WE FOUGHT, I sensed the presence of an invisible panel of feminist judges suspended in the air of the kitchen or the bedroom that was the scene of the engagement. (Every woman carries them in her head. Surely it was this same manifestation that hovered translucently before Anna as she spoke into the cellular phone on that warm autumn afternoon, renouncing and denouncing me and all my works.) Any impulse I felt toward compromise or capitulation set these white-wigged apparitions to frowning and shaking their heads in concert. They exhorted me to bravery; they reminded me of my duty to myself, and I obeyed. But always, at exactly the moment when the battle grew most heated, they took sudden alarm. "Leave him!" they shrieked, and fled. Now? I wanted to ask. Just when we were starting to get somewhere?

It seemed the terms of engagement had changed, and that to remain in any relation to my husband at all, even a belligerent one, was to admit defeat. This demand to sever bonds was a call to honor, and one it hurt me to refuse. I accused myself of weakness.

The cognitive dissonance I endured! I was angry at my husband, who was quite capable of being pigheaded without being cast in the role of a pig. I was angry at the spectral judges, because I had never invited them to preside in my consciousness, and I was angry at myself, for allowing an ideology I viewed with such ambivalence to colonize me against my will. I was angry most of all at the complexity of the situation, because I had to grant that sometimes women *do* need some sense of solidarity, some backup, in order to negotiate their part of the great collective bargain being transacted between the sexes. I have to acknowledge that I need it too, but only a little bolstering—something a friend might offer—not the great unbalancing blast of wind that has blown marriages apart in such great numbers.

PATRIARCHY DIED WHEN MARRIAGE broke its connection with the extended family. Deprived of an intergenerational conduit, it could no longer perpetuate itself. I believe that much of the social history of the last fifty years can best be understood as a competitive scramble to reconfigure society after this profound alteration. Has anyone noticed that marriage has changed? The hierarchial role-bound form which found its origins in the division of labor has now been replaced by the companionate egalitarian dyad.

Surely we are witnessing the continuation of Tocqueville's "irresistible revolution, advancing century by century over every obstacle and even now going forward amid the ruins it has itself created." The Tocquevillean juggernaut has plowed through our society, leveling inequalities and leaving flattened in its wake all the complicated foliage of social organization, the shadowy places of refuge. Only marriage seems to have adapted and survived, transformed by the equalizing process that destroyed so much else.

The insides of marriages have always been obscure, but in earlier days one could presuppose a certain uniformity in their furnishings. A good marriage was tranquil and fecund, supportive of the male partner. The extended family had its means of penetration and inspection; at least one front parlor had to be kept neat and dusted.

Marriages like my mother's were semiprivate accommodations, but marriages like my own are radically private. While intact, they are scaled against the outside world; any penetration tends to destroy them. When prompted to view my marriage from the outside—from the perspective of the feminist judges—I find that I can't see into it at all. Or, rather, I can, but only through a sort of pinhole which gives me a distorted, leering view, like the reflection of a kitchen seen in the shiny surface of a toaster. Only when restored to my place inside it can I remember the realms of solace that my marriage contains, the real proportions of our shared space.

BY NOW IT HAS BEEN amply demonstrated that children can be raised outside of marriage—some even say successfully—and that families need not rest on a marital foundation. Marriage can no longer claim the begetting and raising of children as its primary reason for being. But if not that, then what is marriage for? Why does marriage remain?

It remains to provide the simplest and most essential of psychic shelters, a sort of human lean-to inside which truth can be told and selfhood can unfurl. In the desert of mass society, it provides the patches of shade necessary for the cultivation of shared private worlds.

Marriage is a mutuality reservation: as such it is absolutely necessary, but from another point of view it seems dangerously inutile. When marriages have broken free of extended families, what becomes of the lonely children who hang unsupported from these mysteriously self-contained unions? And when the breach between married couples and the families that engendered them cuts off the transmission of cultural norms, how are children to be socialized? And for that matter, aren't marriages themselves impoverished by an absence of the limitations and expectations once imposed on them by extended families? How dearly bought are freedom and equality!

—

SOCIALLY PROBLEMATIC OR NOT, the new kind of marriage exactly suits the new kind of woman that my mother raised me to be. Sometimes I feel a faint nostalgia, not particularly for the extended family—I hardly knew such a thing—but for the lively community of faculty wives that surrounded my mother, for the slow-growing friendships of affinity and shared interest that flourished among them and that no longer seem possible in an age of ideology. But I find I can't sustain this prelapsarian mooniness for long. I know I could never accept the terms of my mother's marriage, relatively enlightened though it was. Here at last is my feminism. For just this moment I seem to be sitting with the others, not standing by the door grousing. But as I've said, it's the next step I can't seem to take, the baptismal immersion in the group, the terrifying loss of self.

Marriage has been a kind of salvation for me, and for many others, I feel sure, including some of those feminists who regard it with official suspicion. But it can't be salvific in any more general way. Unlike individuals and families, dyads cannot be added up to make a society. If anything, the insular privacy of marriage works against social cohesiveness. More and more, marriage becomes a purely human good.

The gap between the human and the social continues to widen. I've taken a contrarian pride in staying on my side of the divide, watching from a distance as the others file in and arrange themselves in rows. Marriage has confirmed me in that old habit of withdrawal.

But even now I sometimes imagine what it might be like to walk across the space that separates me from the others, to sit down and take my place among them. Would I feel a sense of homecoming, a gratifying internal collapse?

My husband and I look out at the world together from within the protection of our marriage. Year by year we feel further removed, so much so that recently we've begun to imagine ourselves as colonists reconnoitering the landscape of a blighted planet, parched by the unmediated heat of an ideological sun. Our module is self-contained and highly maneuverable; it can skim the blasted surface or withdraw to a perspective of high, hovering detachment. Our removal sometimes leaves us feeling a little cramped, but also dizzyingly free. We carry our own atmosphere. Our craft is ingeniously designed and stocked with nearly everything we need.

FACULTY WIFE

—

They're nearly gone now, victims of attrition and destruction of habitat. The sociology of academic life may never record their dwindling and extinction.

I speak of the faculty wives of my mother's generation. Rare as they have become, I still spot them occasionally. That near-elderly woman I see on my walks, for example, out in the swampy fields gathering grasses: there is a diffuse benevolence of her aspect that marks her. And the museum docent leading a group of grade school children through the Gainsboroughs; surely she's one too. "Children," she whispers, leaning down to address them intimately, draping her arms around the necks of two representatives, "look at the lady's shoulders. Aren't they just like two scoops of vanilla ice cream?"

1. The Kangas

Once, at age ten, on my way home from school, I stood watching as two dogs mated in Mrs. B's yard. Neither of these belonged to anybody I knew—they were members of a pack of yellow, dingo-like dogs that roamed our small

New England college town in those unregulated days. As I stood, ashamed and riveted, the strap of my bookbag cutting into my shoulder, watching the conjoined vibrating of these curs, Mrs. B emerged from the door of her house and padded out to join me. Mrs. B was a small woman who wore her glasses on a velveteen rope around her neck, walked on the balls of her feet, and hummed airs from Mozart. "Isn't it fascinating!" she stage-whispered as she joined me, taking my arm while the glazed-eyed dogs shuddered to stillness and decoupled, the female, once released, twisting to snarl and snap at the male.

Mrs. B was insufferable, but she was happy and virtuous. She belonged to the subspecies of faculty wife that I've privately named the Kangas, after the intrusively maternal kangaroo in *Winnie-the-Pooh*. They were the super-competent elite. Their gardens spewed healthy produce; their homemade bread rose high and evenly pocked; their children were born gifted and raised according to psychoanalytically sound principles which the Kangas felt no compunctions about applying to the children of others whenever possible. That was what Mrs. B was doing on that fall afternoon when she mortified me so; she was demonstrating that I need feel no shame about my curiosity. She was commending to me an attitude of appreciative detachment toward all the processes of nature. Instead, of course, she opened up to me the true depth of my shame, acquainted me with the reek of my own horrified arousal. I will always associate that experience with the sulfurous smell of the egg salad sandwich remnant lying smashed in the bottom of my bookbag.

Did she consider me capable of the detachment she modeled for me? Or was she deliberately shaming me? I remember her profile as we watched the dogs hump, the enlightened elevation of her chin, her lower lip slightly pursed. She lacked only a pair of opera glasses.

The Kanga households were a grid of interlocking fiefdoms circling the college campus. Their shaggy back-yard gardens abutted one another brandishing sunflowers and booby-trapped with monstrous zucchinis in August, still bearing frost-blighted brussels sprouts in October. My brother and I tromped a zigzag path through those gardens like bear cubs, foraging for tomatoes and beans.

On my way to school I heard snatches of violin and flute, also the whirr and thump of the kiln in Mrs. R's mudroom. I saw the sparks of Mrs. L's blowtorch as she worked in the garage she had converted into a sculptor's studio. And silent work was going on all around me; in the long spaces of school day afternoons sestinas and novellas were being composed.

This was the era of the Feminine Mystique, of women languishing in suburban isolation, manifesting their unhappiness somatically with ulcers and rashes. But Kangas (a demographically insignificant group, I'm sure, a tiny powerless elite) seemed immune to the general malaise. They were a vigorous bunch, highly educated and accomplished. Their musical consorts, book discussion groups, charitable and political activities all served to confirm these women in their conviction that their lives were beautiful and useful, even if their work was unpaid.

The Kangas consciously resisted the domestic cleanliness obsession that gripped American women in the fifties. The big Victorian houses they rented from the college were cluttered with evidence of their enthusiasms. Unwieldy arrangements of dried flowers spilled out of giant hand-thrown pots; surfaces were littered with children's collections of seashells and butterflies. Sometimes a harp or a loom occupied a corner of the living room. With Kangas, the rule was accretion; where they nested, culture thickened and deepened. Unpressed by the mold of employment, they grew into all the eccentric spaces of their differently cultivated leisure.

At the top of Kanga society was a select group of the older wives, the permanent staff of the Women's Exchange, a consignment shop that supported the local Visiting Nurses' Association. These were Kangas of an earlier generation, less educated than the postwar faculty wives and even more tightly bonded as a group. I spent many hours at the Exchange while my mother worked there as a volunteer; I remember lying on my back in a litter of snowsuits in the back room, inhaling dry-cleaning fumes and staring up at a buzzing, blinking fluorescent light. I listened, on and off, to the conversation between the women working there. Sometimes they would exclaim over the quality of a new consignment—a clutch of the Rudolph girls' cashmere sweaters, perhaps, in six pastel shades, never worn—and their voices would lower and hover together deploringly as they allowed themselves the pleasure of touching the soft wool. Or they would speak more softly yet—this was always my cue to listen hard—about failed marriages, illnesses, birth defects. The older wives were amateur eugenicists, shrewd judges of the health and viability of newborns. Often I heard them speak about "good" and "bad" faces, and when a local doctor's daughter dropped dead at age nineteen of an undiagnosed heart ailment they all swore that they had privately predicted it.

The most benign of the Kangas was my parents' friend M. She was a big, soft woman with a heap of disordered hair worn in an outsize twist. Her voice was more than musical; she was the only person I've ever known who consistently sang her speech.

M's house was full of dhurries, woven baskets, brass bowls, batik hangings—things commonplace enough nowadays, but exotic then. Here I'm reminded of an interesting generalization I can make about the faculty wives of my youth: their tastes and interests were culturally prophetic. As I've grown up and then older I've watched various customs and items of cuisine and decoration favored by my mother and her friends which were odd and singular at the time become trendy and widely disseminated. The Kangas grew their own herbs, ground their own coffee, cut up their own chickens and cooked them in olive oil, drank wine with meals, made sure that their children's diets included fiber, or "roughage" as they called it, inquired about the availability of endive at the A&P. They favored earth colors and matte surfaces. Now that I find these provisions and proclivities all around me, it's as if my mother had been writ large and faint upon the culture.

M was a Californian exiled in a cold New England

town where her expansiveness of spirit could never quite find room. The other Kangas viewed her enthusiasms— during a Polynesian phase she hosted a cocktail party in a grass skirt and a lei—with affectionate irony. I was grateful to her because she was kind to me in a way I could have found acceptable only in somebody whose air of breezy dissociation made her incapable of intrusiveness. Once when she was giving me a ride somewhere in her big rattling station wagon, she began to muse about me and my prospects. "How wonderful," she sang, "to get taller and stronger and just grow out of all the misunderstandings and fears. How wonderful to have all that time and to know that things will get better and better." She gestured extravagantly, but she kept her shining eyes turned forward toward the road and toward a vague and glorious vision of me and the transforming future. I felt a slight mortification at being reminded that for me there was nowhere to go but up. Even so, as she spoke I began to feel buoyed, like a grounded ship slowly lifted by the tide. She had good will by the gallon, and the impersonal banality of what she said served to dilute it enough so that I could absorb it.

In those days I was busy with a complicated internal project; at the same time I was trying to assimilate my mother's aesthetic (which contained her ethic) and casting about for alternatives to it. I had to do both simultaneously, because the more I attempted to apprentice myself to my mother, and the more I learned about her through this effort, the more I saw that her worldview would ultimately exclude me. So M and her big loose enthusiasms became significant to me; she lodged in the back of my mind and stayed. When I think of the future she imagined for me—and suffer the attendant shock of realizing that for me any such future is past—the picture that accompanies my thoughts is a Polynesian landscape, a stylized palm tree against a mauve and black sky.

II. The Princeton Party

A faculty wife remnant seems to have survived into my own generation as well, but this group hardly recognizes itself as such. I would not have acknowledged myself as one of their number if my husband and daughter and I had not spent his sabbatical year seven years ago at the Institute for Advanced Study in Princeton.

There the "members" lived with their families in a housing complex on the grounds of the institution. The wives—or spouses, as the administration took pains always to call us—were mostly a self-selected group, or at least the Americans among us were. These were women who had chosen to accompany their husbands on leave. Absent were the professionals, the lawyers, businesswomen, doctors, tenure-track academics. Present were the potters, the painters, the jewelry makers, the academic "part-timers," the writers. Also present were some particularly enterprising and devoted mothers of small children. Kangas, in other words, were everywhere. My daughter, then five, tore around the grounds with her cohort of faculty brats, safe and free and watched over as she would never be again. For a year, she lived my childhood.

The institute, where Einstein and von Neumann once worked, was a weird place, full of cultural contradictions. The receptions we attended in the vine-covered administration building were high-toned, chilly affairs. White-coated waiters circulated with flutes of champagne and nest-baskets of deviled quail eggs. Life in the housing units was another, humbler story: too poor to use the communal laundromat, the peasant mothers of young Chinese physicists stumped out of the units every morning to string hand-washed towels and sheets from tree to tree across the grounds.

The institute was a reservation for faculty wives. We gathered daily at the school bus stop, a multicultural group wearing our coats over our pajamas, herding our children and breathing steam, shuffling in place to keep warm. We loaded the children onto the bus and then dispersed into our days of solitary unpaid busyness, our grocery shopping, house cleaning, reading, translating, flute playing, novel writing. We gathered again at three when the bus returned.

I had found myself so isolated in my daughter's early years that at first the daily bus stop ritual seemed a reassuring emblem of community. I felt the novelty of knowing that I was among my own kind. But soon I began to understand that it would be difficult to make friends among the wives. I looked at them more carefully and I saw all the stigmata of shyness. This generation of Kangas had been affected by some curious attenuation. Except for a few loud, hale, natural-leader types—and only a month or two were required to reveal these as even more deeply insecure than the rest of us—we were a self-doubting, introspective group, abashed and reproachful, accustomed to solitude. We wore our graying hair in long ponytails; we favored wraparound skirts with commodious pockets and Birkenstocks with knee socks. Our noses were raw from the continuous colds our children brought home from school. Many of us had suspended the connections to the world we had established back home—the part-time job in the library, the graduate program, the circle of supportive friends—and we resented the loss. I did some internal thrashing around that year, anxious that I was being left out of something and yet baffled about what that could be, eager both to identify myself with this group and to distance myself from it. I also began, haltingly, to work on a novel, the first really serious and sustained literary project I had ever attempted. I think I picked up something confirming in the air, just enough to get me started.

Early in the fall semester, some of the institute fellows and their spouses were invited to a Sunday brunch at the home of a Princeton professor, a gathering of academics, mostly philosophers with an interest in politics and the social sciences. In spite of the well-meaning efforts of our hosts, themselves both philosophers, to put everyone at ease, this was an intimidating occasion. Guests arranged themselves through the book-lined spaces of that house in the mysteriously nonrandom and meaningful way that guests always do. The pattern here was established early, and it was striking. One room reserved itself for the wives, who huddled together in a semicircle, softly discussing vaccination reactions and orthodontia. Two of them were nursing babies.

In an adjoining room there was loud lively talk, punctuated by the laugh of sudden, delighted insight that philosophers seem particularly prone to. Perhaps a third of these disputatious intellectuals were female, but they seemed a different species from the wives in the other room: they were upright, mobile, angular, assertive, expressive. They were, I was thinking from my place among the Female Women in the other room, the Female Men.

To move from one of these rooms to the other was to feel a change in emotional weather so extreme that a kind of physical barrier seemed to erect itself. I noticed a few of the male academics hovering at the doorway, sending two-fingered waves and guilty smiles to their wives. But somehow they seemed to balk at the prospect of actually entering the room. This scene was too primitively female for comfort, and I suspect the sight of breast-feeding made these men shy.

The only person who traveled freely between the two zones was our hostess, a woman far too gracious not to make an effort. She stood over us and offered anecdotes about her daughter's infancy, but these stories soon began to sputter in the face of our assembled passivity. (I think we were exaggerating the bovine act out of hostility.) She had been careful to acquaint herself with our interests, and several times she leaned into the Female Women's room in an effort to coax one or another of us out. "Julia," she would call, "didn't you write your dissertation on the social contract in a Nepalese village? Why don't you come out here and tell us about it?" But I was the only one to take the bait and follow her. "Emily," said my hostess, drawing me into the ambit of a famous intellectual whose books I had read and admired, "wrote a doctoral dissertation on Kafka."

"Master's thesis," I corrected. "Ah," said the famous intellectual, giving me a faint, bilious smile and turning back to his eager interlocutors. I had no choice but to return to the welcoming circle of round-shouldered women, remarking to myself on the wild irony of this situation. Of all places and times, I thought, to be relegated to the prison of gender, the home of two distinguished married academics in Princeton, New Jersey, in 1989 seemed the least likely.

In one room, a scene of vigorous free intellectual exchange, apparently genderless. In the other, like atavistic phantoms, a group of females, babies, and small children who might as well have been huddled on an earthen floor in a thatched hut, poking at a fire with sticks. (Two or three of the small children being monitored by the Female Women at the Princeton party actually belonged, I should add, to Female Men.) But, of course, strictly speaking, the dividing line here was not gender, because women stood on either side of it. Nor was it education or aptitude. Most of the Female Women had advanced degrees; all were highly intelligent. Instead, it was something more like temperament. For whatever reasons, and if only temporarily, the Female Women lacked the assertiveness and ambition of the Female Men. Or perhaps, to put it more positively, they felt the nurturing imperative more strongly. And of course, the Female Women lacked one thing essential in order to be taken seriously these days at a faculty party—a university affiliation.

Maybe the odd nature of this gathering was a product of the artificial situation from which it sprang—guests were chosen from the roster of the institute's members, academics spending a year among strangers and forming bonds on the basis of shared intellectual interests and accomplishments. So perhaps the wives, along for the year's ride, were unduly thrown back on one another and on the common denominator of baby and child talk. But this is not an adequate explanation; I've seen the same dilemma many times since, plausibly diluted, at various faculty functions.

Our hosts' dismay and embarrassment were obvious; it couldn't have been comfortable for them to preside over this apartheid-riven afternoon. What was happening? Why were the wives so sullenly resistant to the efforts of our hostess to integrate us into this gathering? I think we were unconsciously reaching back into our sixties arsenal of passive-resistance ploys, playing that trump card of postmodern ideology, the claim to authenticity. We had lost the respect we felt was our due; we had been marginalized, and so we arranged ourselves in a tableau which we knew would instantly evoke a shock of guilty recognition. We were far too liberated to plant ourselves at our husbands' sides to smile artificially until the ordeal of the party ended. We would revert instead to a more primitive, more compelling set of images. We would act the part of Woman—the burdened, the earthbound, the oppressed.

Which was ridiculous, of course. Whatever room we occupied, we were all of us members of a class of people who take for granted unprecedented comfort and liberty. We had freely chosen our roles. Even so, the Female Women had reason to feel defensive and depressed. We had lost access to the protective environmental niche that an earlier generation of faculty wives had enjoyed. Gone was the set of understandings and expectations which established the idea that a wife and mother could enrich and decorate her family life by bringing to it the benefits of her education, festooning it with her art and learning. She lived outside the real-world economy, but inside a private economy that rewarded her efforts with validation and approval. Some of this reward came from her husband and children, but perhaps even more of it issued from the sisterhood of faculty wives. Without this reward, the latter-day Faculty Wife's efforts come to seem pointless to her, cranky and anachronistic.

III. Bad Wives

I recall no such separation at my parents' parties, which were frequent. There was an absolute gender divide along professional lines, of course, no females at all among the faculty members. The men talked shop and the wives talked babies, but only at the beginning. As the evening progressed and the guests became more lubricated, the room integrated itself; groups of fours and fives, only a few of them single-sex, began to form, dissolve, re-form. When viewed directly from above, high up on the stair landing (children were expected to perform one turn with the hors d'oeuvres tray and then vanish), these human constellations looked like blossoms or starfish drawn in rough outline.

With experience I was able to recognize the stages of the party: after an awkward half hour, the manic yammer began to build, the conversational groups slowly contracting, then flaring outward in reaction to the punchline of the joke or the point of the anecdote. At this moment the party would feel to me like something single and organic, a breathing beast.

The noise would begin to modulate and steady until it had attained a raga-like drone. Then began a gradual migration toward the periphery of the room and a slow trickling into other parts of the house. The convivial roar was replaced by intelligible words and phrases, spoken softly and with a new earnestness. Now that the guests were seated I could see that they had arranged themselves in pairs and threesomes, and that many women were talking to men who were not their husbands and many men were talking to women who were not their wives. The hectic flirtation, the explosion of Dionysian energy and noise in the earlier stages of the party: all that had been in the service of this scattering and rearranging, and finally, this coming to rest. Conversations during this latter phase of the party had a relaxed intimacy, a quality I would later come to recognize as postcoital. During this magic interval—the hour of the coffee cups—men and women got to know one another as equals. Real talk went on, or so it seemed to me from my post on the landing.

The element of flirtation is utterly absent at the academic gatherings of today. (Let me disarm the reader's suspicion that I draw this conclusion only because nobody is flirting with me. Believe me, nobody is flirting with anybody at these functions.) Children are often present; alcohol is far less central than it was in my parents' day. These parties—mostly potluck suppers and Sunday open houses—usually begin with the establishment of zones: wives and small children gather on the couch, recapitulating in less dramatic form the pattern of the Female Women at the Princeton party. The older wives cluster in the kitchen, overseeing the food, while young faculty and graduate students congregate near the beer cooler; senior members of the department find nooks in which to lean together talking serious shop. Thus the party continues until it reaches its sober, sensibly early end. It is all very cozy and wholesome, but to my mind it is as much like a party as a shopping mall is like a town square.

Some devil gets into me on these occasions and makes me behave badly, or want to. I'm irritated by the sight of these men and women with their innocent eyes, their gentle and slightly fuddled manners, helping themselves moderately to drink and grazing among the raw vegetables. Where is their aggression? I ask myself. Where is their lust? I feel cheated of my childhood expectation that adult life would be charged with violent emotion, and all the more aggrieved because it happens to be true that I would be content to enjoy violent emotion vicariously, if only somebody would provide me that gratification.

They seem capable, these academics, of peevishness

and spite, but none of the forthright, elemental energy that people on the outside have in abundance. Especially as we all grow older, they begin to seem marsupial to me. They have lived too long in an unevolved paradise; no wonder they were unprepared when conditions changed and a horde of young theory mongers, red in tooth and claw, dropped from the trees and ate or colonized them.

I don't mean to imply that what went on at my parents' parties was seamy, that it was anything like the suburban adultery clusters one encounters in Updike's early fiction. My parents' parties served to acknowledge and release sexual tension in a socially sanctioned way, and for the most part they were harmless. Only a few guests seemed unable to resist the temptation to ride the beast of the party out the door.

Among these the most memorable was J, the wife of a distinguished sociologist, the mother of a large brood of children and overseer of a big messy ambitious Kanga household full of musical instruments, books, baskets of rotting apples and unfolded laundry. She was a plump, busty woman with a slightly overblown Celtic prettiness. I disliked her, partly because my mother did, but also because I dreaded her temper. She had a terrifying way of moving from a fugue-like state of dreamy preoccupation to sudden quivering rage with no intermediate steps. I have a vivid memory of her small feet in scuffed flats, planted on dusty floorboards. As I tilt the memory upward I can see her face, broad and rosy with anger as she berates me for dropping her son's violin.

J took pains to preserve appearances; she volunteered

at the Women's Exchange and played the cello in a local quartet, but she was very promiscuous. I remember watching her from my top-of-the-stairs vantage point at a party. She stood on tiptoe as she talked animatedly with a much taller man, one hand flattened with spread fingers against her breastbone in the classic flirting position, the other flung across her half-open mouth and flaming cheek in feigned amazement. Her high color—it frightened me to look into the oven of her face—her insinuating smirks and roguish smiles: how all this amazed and repelled me. Rumors circulated about her affairs, at least one of which was certainly true: she served as the mistress of a disreputable townie, a figure of fear to faculty children, a big rough man with picket teeth and a perpetual five o'clock shadow who once clambered drunkenly onto a float at a football rally to imitate a woman wriggling into her girdle. Eventually J's marriage broke up. Later she married a wealthy widower within a month of his wife's death; the two could often be seen downtown, J clutching her frail husband's arm tightly and steering him from store to store. My mother and her friends clenched their teeth and rolled their eyes at the mention of her name.

J was one of the cautionary tales of my childhood, but she was also a kind of inspiration. I didn't like to think about, nor did I know enough to imagine, the couplings of J and the disreputable townie. (Today I can picture them spilling out of a parked car on a rural road late at night. I can hear her coy shriek and his laughing growl as he pursues her through the long grass of a field and brings her down with a thump.) But she gave me a sense for the parameters of adult passion; even as I recoiled at her gaminess I marveled at the power of what burned in her. "She thinks with her glands," I overheard my mother say, and I wondered how she had mastered that trick and whether one day I might be able to do it too.

I believe that what J did in her life would be impossible for a similarly situated woman today. She lived out a specifically female destiny, one fated to end in low comedy or in tragedy, or in some mixture of the two. Such a destiny is no longer available to a woman of J's socioeconomic class. While a woman might be just as compulsively unfaithful as J, society is no longer configured so as to register her actions, to mirror her back to herself as anything but unhappy. And nobody has time or energy to go in for promiscuity as a calling. My own daughter has no such bad examples to watch and wonder at. It would be hard to imagine the mothers of her friends in the role of courtesan or harlot. They are lean and healthy and tense; they wear beepers on their belts and carry daily planners in their bags. My daughter gets her notions more efficiently than I got mine: she watches MTV, where Salt-n-Pepa do squats and point at their vulvas.

One often hears the African folk saying that it takes a village to raise a child. True enough, but it also takes a village to produce a first-class adulteress.

IV. Femina Ludens

At least for a while, our small-town college society provided J just the combination of reluctant tolerance and steady, mild disapprobation that she required.

It was not so kind to R, a painter who looked like a dancer past her prime. She dressed in leotards and calf-length skirts. Her face was as pale as Anaïs Nin's, her hair a bleached, broom-shaped helmet. She drank heavily even by the standard of that place and those days, when two stiff drinks before dinner and wine with it were a daily ritual. I can summon up a clear image of R drinking publicly—in front of people and at somebody's house—straight out of a bottle of gin. But that picture may come from the vault of apocrypha that occupies half my memory.

R was married to a historian, a tall man whose wry insouciance was undercut by weariness. She seemed constantly in a rage—I remember making way for her on the sidewalk as she swept by, black cloak flaring, pulling her two pale daughters behind her, her mouth written into an angry slash with red lipstick. Eventually her marriage broke up and she moved to Cambridge with the two girls.

I knew that my mother and her friends disapproved of R even more intensely than they did of J, and so, as usual, I followed suit. When, on a school trip, I saw R walking across Harvard Square, thinner now and more raddled, I felt a frisson of horror. How unseemly that R should continue to exist, I thought, when by now it should surely all be over for her (she was forty or so). For her, continued animation could be only a hideous reflex, like the galvanic twitching of a dead frog's legs.

The wives never sanctioned R's high bohemian style. They looked askance at her railroad flat with good light in the back room, which she furnished minimally with low-slung couches and Japanese paper-moon lamps. Casual to the point of negligence about their own children's hygiene, they clucked at the wax visible in the ears of R's lovely, solemn, conscientious daughters.

When R persuaded the art department to let her display her paintings in the college gallery—and that must have taken some doing—her husband played a practical joke on her. He sneaked in after hours and tacked up his own primitive crayon drawing of a horse and barn, priced at $14.95, between two of her big abstract canvases. I'm not sure whether this was the proximate cause of her removal to Cambridge, but I know that it delighted the Kangas, particularly my mother, who told the story at dinner tables for decades.

R had offended faculty-wife society with her pretension, her incivility, and her flagrantly excessive drinking. But what the Kangas really held against her was her ambition to be professional. This brought out all the latent clannish nastiness that enlightened training had taught them rigorously to suppress. There was something dangerous about the violation of this taboo, as if the placing of a real price tag on a painting put the private Kanga economy itself at risk. I believe that it was the Kangas who exiled R, who ran her out of paradise.

And they were prescient: it was the linked forces of professionalization and feminism that were to bring about the extinction of the role of faculty wife. As a result of these developments, a great undifferentiated space was opened up for women—a kind of savannah, a wide open plain on which one could wander and hunt. What was lost was shade, cover, protection, a place to hide. But this is nothing new; more and more of these niches have disappeared as institutionalized hiding places like the clergy and the military have lost their protective status for men, and the solid walls of bourgeois marriage, behind which women found privacy, have become transparent.

Some fit, keen-eyed people are well equipped for the savannah. Others, weaker and slower, are soon picked off by predators. Still others, deprived not only of habitat but of fixed points of reference, wander into the place where the savannah becomes desert and perish slowly of thirst and exposure. The savannah is no place for reverie or distraction. Passive people, dreamy and contemplative people, don't do well there.

I'm a faculty wife by default, because I'm married to an academic, whose salary supports me. We live in the great diaspora that academic life has become. I'm no potter, no gardener, no musician, and I've never been a particularly resourceful or inventive mother. What I am is a writer, and during the twenty years when I was producing nothing, covering my existential nudity with an inadequate garment composed of patches of housewife/graduate student/mother, I was serving the writer's apprenticeship, letting the world trickle through me to leave behind sedimented layers of impression. All through my protracted apprenticeship I felt anomalous and apologetic, subject to fits of self-loathing and panicky self-consciousness, inclined to take refuge in the comfort of grandiose fantasies. The fact is that for years I was a social parasite, the same years when dependency has been a condition of shame for a woman of my class and station. In my case, the absence of shade has meant the absence of a secure and secluded vantage point, a place from which I could observe without being observed. How can I hide where there is no shade?

My apprenticeship might have been shortened if I had been a faculty wife of my mother's generation. I might have been happier surrounded by other amateurs, other experimenters, in an atmosphere that encouraged artistic endeavor for its own sake. But what would have happened when my apprenticeship was complete, when I was ready for metamorphosis? Would the wives have turned on me as they turned on R?

Faculty-wife culture was healthiest in the late fifties, just at the time when bohemia was flowering. I think the two social phenomena are interestingly similar. Kangas and beatniks: both lived out, demonstrated in their lives, the vital link between art and the gratuitous, between art and play. Postwar affluence floated these groups for a while. Then, like the tadpole societies that spring up briefly in puddles after storms, they disappeared.

Would I then wish myself back forty years, in my mother's place? Like all arcadians, all unreconstructed lovers of the past who ask themselves that question, I have to reluctantly admit that the answer is no. I would not wish myself back. Faculty wives were free spirits only to a very limited degree. In spite of their educated backgrounds, their enlightened views, they were also those anachronistic things called ladies, which few of us today could imagine ourselves to be. We wear looser, rougher clothing now; our language is fouler, our patience shorter as we slouch toward the millennium. I would be unable, of course, to accept the circumscription of their lives. Like R I would trespass, and like R I would be expelled.

But how I envy their playfulness! In high summer, when the inevitable zucchini glut overtook their gardens, they drew faces on the outsized squashes, wrapped them in christening robes, put them in bassinets, and left them on one another's doorsteps like foundlings.

How I envy their sense of community, the long deep friendships they maintained through days and years of steady, uneventful proximity, and continue to enjoy in their dotage.

How I envy them their safety, that lost prerequisite for so much else. But here perhaps I'm falling into confusion; perhaps I'm confounding their safety with the safety I felt as a child, protected and fostered by those many mothers. Perhaps I'm remembering them wrongly, with a deceiving, simplifying clarity. Perhaps I'm projecting my wish for protection onto the past, as people are often said to do. Can the wives have been so tightly banded, so consciously what they seem to me to have been? Can the trees have been as deeply leaved, the shade as thickly dappled as I remember?

KAFKA AND ME

—

Some years ago, when my daughter was a toddler, I read all of Kafka's works except *Amerika,* which I could never finish, all his journals and letters, all the existing biographies, and much of the critical literature. Out of this reading I produced a master's thesis, which I called "'TO HELL WITH PSYCHOLOGY!': Kafka's Life in Kafka's Art." I keep a copy of this long paper in a bound volume in the lower drawer of my desk. Like nearly all theses and dissertations, it's a useless document. As I look through it now, it strikes me as fairly readable but badly argued and written in a coded academic language which could only conceal from my readers—all five of them— the story I really wished to tell. This was the tale of my friendship with Franz Kafka, and I will tell it now.

I.

AT THE TIME I embarked on the course of study that led me to Kafka, I was living in a small New England city with my husband, who taught in the philosophy depart- ment of the state university. Our eighteen-month-old daughter had recently begun to attend a drop-in day care center for three mornings each week. I had stumbled on the place through dumb luck just as it opened, and it soon emerged as the most enlightened day care establishment in town.

Here was where the affluent and educated brought their only children to be introduced to the idea of separation—a rather blurred notion for children and mothers alike, since so many mothers contrived to hang around as volunteers. At naptime these women sat cross-legged on mats, each cradling her own child and crooning lullabies, while the paid attendants paced the darkened hallway, doing the jiggling, rocking day care dance, carrying one baby in each arm and a third in a frontpack.

Another group of mothers subscribed to the official cold turkey policy of the institution. These were the women in narrow skirts and pantyhose who squatted in the doorway making earnest eye contact with their wailing, barely ambulatory infants, gripping their frail shoulders and reciting the formula all of us had by heart: I'M GOING AWAY NOW BUT I WILL BE BACK WHEN IT'S TIME FOR LUNCH. I belonged to neither of these camps, or both, persuading myself of the merits of one side and then the other, undermining my judgments with insidious counterarguments and scolding myself for my indecisiveness. The staff grew exasperated with my inability to make a clean getaway from my howling, begging child, and I made matters worse by impulsively returning half an hour later to a scene of passionate reunion and yet another, still more painful, separation.

But one morning my daughter pushed herself away from my chest and matter-of-factly climbed down to join the action at the water table. I walked out of the building into a transformed inner landscape. The path that the midwives and doctors and visiting nurses had laid out at my feet three years earlier had been growing fainter and more equivocal for months, and now it had run itself out in the weeds.

The term of earliest motherhood had just expired, and I was unceremoniously delivered back to myself. Now the question was, what to do? At thirty-six, for the first time in my passive and dreamy life I was asking myself this question with some urgency. And the only answer, I concluded after a few weeks of self-torture, was to finish the degree I had abandoned in my seventh month of pregnancy, when one day I left Spenser's *Faerie Queene* sprawled facedown on the desk of my library carrel, waddled home to put my feet up, and stayed.

I felt very little enthusiasm for this project. I harbored an attitude of angry contempt for all but a few of my professors, and I knew that the degree—a "terminal MA," as they called it—would be nearly useless to me in practical terms. But somehow it seems to be my fate to pursue an extended education indefinitely.

AS I BEGAN to study for my comprehensive exams I found the mornings spent in the library calming; another trudge around the stacks, a few more index cards filled out, and it would be time to get a bean burrito and a pink lemonade from the food truck and eat my lunch sitting on a marble bench in an open courtyard, an entourage of squabbling pigeons at my feet, and then, finally, with a sensation of trembling relief, to head for my car to pick up my daughter at her day care.

I passed my comps with shaming ease, and then—with more difficulty—the foreign-language requirement. The next step was to plan my thesis. Here I got stuck for six months, wedged between the horns of the English graduate student's dilemma: much as I loved and admired the work of George Eliot, I found I had very little to say about it that was not, on the one hand, broadly and simple-mindedly appreciative, or would not, on the other hand, require so much dull slogging through bibliographies and chronologies that I would give up before I finished. (Fifteen years ago, studying in a backward and provincial English department, I had no access to the randomly additive strategy available to today's graduate students—the stringing together of conveniently prefabricated jargon-chains.)

But then I happened, by chance and in a mood of idle desperation, upon Kafka's short pieces and parables, and also the collection of his letters, journals, and autobiographical pieces compiled by Nahum Glatzer, called *I Am a Memory Come Alive*. I had read "The Metamorphosis" and *The Trial* with spooked incomprehension in high school, but the rest of Kafka's oeuvre was new to me. I found the stories deeply charming, and some passages struck me as funny, drastically funny in a way that startled me into laughing aloud and also brought tears to my eyes. Here, for example, is the long-winded canine narrator of "Investigations of a Dog."

> The hardest bones, containing the richest marrow, can be conquered only by a united crunching of all the teeth of all dogs. . . . If I remain faithful to this metaphor, then the goal of my aims, my questions, my inquiries, appears monstrous, it is true. For I want to compel all dogs thus to assemble together. I want the bones to crack open under the pressure of their collective preparedness, and then I want to dismiss them to the ordinary life that they love, while all by myself, quite alone, I lap up the marrow.

I also happened upon *The Terror of Art,* a book-length study of Kafka by the British critic Martin Greenberg. I spent half an hour on my feet in the stacks looking through this book and found it incisive and elegantly written. I was immediately impressed by the clarity and suppleness of Greenberg's thinking, the subtlety of his distinctions. Here is an observation from the first chapter—one which corrected and guided my reading of Kafka:

> His stories exercise a magical effect, but his magic is not the magic of illusion but of revelation. His gift is only superficially a gift for the fantastic and unreal. In fact his art is devoted to reality. We see this in his style, which is sober to the point of plainness, and in his humble realistic detail.

Unlike Joyce or Mann or any of the other great modernist "wordmen" who used language to construct alternative realities, Greenberg's Kafka was an anti-literary writer who saw truth and words as fundamentally opposed. He was a "poet-seer" rather than a "poet-maker," oriented more toward truth than art. Greenberg describes Kafka's writing as "literature trying to be revelation."

Greenberg goes on to explain Kafka's complex relationship to the Freudian thinking that, as a Prague intellectual, he absorbed by osmosis: "Kafka's subjective world of apparent irrationality hiding a heart of meaning is Freudian through and through." The real utility of Freud for Kafka, Greenberg observes, was that Freud's influence "helped to give him the courage to understand his quarrel with his father as a worthy contest rather than a puerile one, which he could 'discuss' in his stories rather than turn away from." This passage is typical of Greenberg's clear-eyed sympathy for Kafka. That wonderfully tactful "discuss" says it all.

But, Greenberg goes on, Kafka was eventually to reject psychoanalytic thought:

> [H]e is also concerned, as he moves from his early to his middle and last years, with defending the human against being itself reduced psychoanalytically to "nothing but" this or that illness or "neurosis," and here he becomes positively anti-Freudian— "From now on, to hell with Psychology!"

Greenberg quotes Kafka in a letter to Milena Jesenská: "I consider the therapeutic part of psychoanalysis a hopeless error. All these so-called illnesses, sad as they may appear, are matters of faith."

To a veteran of psychotherapy like me, living at the century's end in a therapy-marinated culture, this pronouncement seemed prophetically shrewd. My half-addicted dependence on psychotherapy and my struggle to get free of it: this was exactly what I had been longing for the courage to "discuss," if only in my own mind. And now Kafka, with Greenberg acting as a kind of channeler, had extended that courage to me across the century. Was it possible to think in a way that transcended the therapeutic? I had been granted occasional glimpses of this vision, but like Georg in "The Judgment," I was continually forgetting. ("At this moment he recalled this long-forgotten resolve and forgot it again, like a man drawing a short thread through the eye of a needle.")

To hell with psychology! This expostulation thrilled me, and I decided on the spot to write my thesis on Kafka. The English department balked at my proposal, insisting that this was a comparative literature project, and that since there was no such department at the university, it would not be feasible. With uncharacteristic resourcefulness, I looked through the bound theses in the library and found three on translated works. The English department relented, and I approached two of the three members of the department with whom I was still on friendly terms and asked them to serve on my committee. I recruited my thesis adviser, the only member of the faculty with any Kafka expertise, from the German department.

II.

I remember this time with pleasure because my daughter had recently become so engaging, verbal enough to register and comment on the meals and naps and walks and stories, the daily round of errands which I found as comforting and steadying as she did—the trip to the local cider mill, where the proprietor always made a great show of polishing an apple on a clean corner of his pulp-smeared apron before presenting it to her, the perambulation through the frozen food aisle in the grocery store where she would shiver ritualistically and I would rub her hands and put up the hood of her sweatshirt. I felt honored to be the protector of her small, simple, radiantly meaningful world, composed of basic shapes and primary colors and the continual reassurance of routine.

But it was also a time filled with agitation and anger and bad fights with my husband, who had recently become deeply preoccupied with a scholarly project. I developed an obsessive self-consciousness around the other mothers at the day care; whichever side of the staying or leaving debate they took, they all seemed so calmly confident and fluent in their mother talk that I was sure my own clumsiness and uncertainty were obvious by contrast. Fumbling frantically with the recalcitrant zipper of my daughter's snowsuit, I muttered audible curses at myself, then glanced up to see if I had been overheard. Even after she learned to let me go, I found myself swamped with panic whenever I entered the day care, stung by the sense that I had been identified as incompetent or even unfit, whispered about and excluded from the society of mothers.

I could feel myself beginning to disappear into the obscurity and isolation of faculty-wifehood, and I dreaded the prospect of becoming as worn and sweet and invisible as some of my fellow wives (just now beginning to be called "spouses"). These women were earnest and eternal students with multiple degrees, quick to recognize one another but too shy and demoralized to make common cause. Wearing odd collections of ethnic clothing, they bent over desks in the back of the classroom taking voluminous notes, hovered in the halls during office hours, carrying sacks full of library books and checklists of questions. They came closer to being my natural kind than anyone else, but I rejected their tentative overtures, turned away from their wan smiles. I shared neither their intellectual purity nor their gentle defeatism, because in my arrogant heart I nurtured the conviction that I was a writer—a writer who had failed to be recognized only because I had not yet written anything worthy of recognition. And in fact this was the time, I can see in retrospect, when the writer in me was beginning to stir, to differentiate and define itself, to grow elbows and knees and jointed fingers.

Somehow in my preoccupation with my daughter I had managed to shed all my friends. The only people I saw regularly, apart from immediate family and people at the day care, were my periodontist, who was planing and scraping every few months to slow the progression of the gum disease which pregnancy had accelerated, my daughter's pediatrician, whose reassurance I sought so often that I was sure he considered me a pest, the woman who cut my hair, the produce man and the checkers and baggers in the supermarket, and my newly acquired therapist, Dr. B.

And also my husband's parents, who had jumped eagerly into the breach left open by the absence of my own family, from whom I had been semi-estranged for years. Every six weeks they came to us from suburban New Jersey in their giant black Lincoln, carting along everything they needed to maintain their kosher arrangements during the four- or five-day visit—pots and pans and plates and silverware and canned goods.

They were already in their seventies during those years, but amazingly energetic, full of philoprogenitive zeal and anxious fussiness. The moment they arrived they fell on their knees to embrace their granddaughter, to present her with one extravagant and carefully chosen gift, and all through the days of their visits they doted without ceasing. They spent the nights at the nearby Sheraton, ostensibly because they wished not to burden us, but actually because the standard of hygiene in my house was too casual for their comfort. They ate their meals with us; my mother-in-law put on her apron and moved into my kitchen, using her own crockery and utensils, or—in a pinch—mine, covered with aluminum foil.

We ate potatoes, baked chicken, canned vegetables. My father-in-law wore his yarmulke; he sat at the table in his suspenders, the sleeves of his expensive shirt pushed up to the elbow; my daughter sat in her high chair and rolled peas onto the floor; my mother-in-law remained on her feet through most of the meal, fetching and clearing. My husband ate with his eyes lowered and a small reluctant smile playing around his lips; how could he help reverting to adolescence with parents like his around?

And for my part, I sat contentedly—"lapping up the marrow"—in the midst of the penumbra of family happiness that my parents-in-law shed around us. Somehow this happiness was compatible with any amount or kind of resentment—at my mother-in-law's apologetic but absolute commandeering of my kitchen, for example, or my husband's emotional retreat, or my father-in-law's conversion-to-Judaism sales pitch, a loop seemingly without beginning or end, delivered to me sotto voce in his heavy German accent. All this was secondary and quite bearable when we were sitting together at the table. And so was the sense, wordlessly but unmistakably conveyed by my in-laws, that in my house we were all camping out, improvising, making do. Many another daughter-in-law would find that insulting, I felt sure. Perhaps the kind of woman who would take offense was exactly the kind of daughter-in-law my parents-in-law would have chosen. But now I had attached myself to them by a bridge of flesh, and in spite of their reservations they had no choice but to accept me. And as for camping out: wasn't that what Jewish history was all about?

My parents-in-law had fled the Nazis. They came to the United States via Palestine, where they met, and Paris, where they married. My father-in-law began as a janitor in a plastics factory in Newark, New Jersey, and in spite of his poor English, which never substantially improved, managed to learn the ropes of the business so quickly and thoroughly that in twenty years he owned his own plastics factory. A true Horatio Alger story, a rare instantiation of the familiar myth, but even people as strong as my father- and mother-in-law could hardly be expected to survive such a history without pain and damage. It amazed me that in spite of their wealth my parents-in-law felt themselves to be such wanderers in the world that they often turned to me for advice. *Mischling* though I was, both sides of my family had been in the States for a few generations and my knowledge of the culture was fluent and idiomatic.

Once I took a walk with them along a bicycle path just above Lake Champlain. They were both looking particularly prosperous and handsome that day, wearing tweed and denim and their newly acquired Rockport walking shoes, and they were vehement in their appreciation of the wide blue lake and the brilliant fall morning. They walked so vigorously that I had to extend my stride to keep up with them, but after a quarter mile they slowed down and our walk took on a more leisurely quality. My parents-in-law both began to speak about their retirement, about the difficulty they faced in relinquishing the habits of compulsive thrift and deferral of gratification that had brought them prosperity and security, but which were nearly useless to them now. They had spent their lives hurtling into the future—and now what? They spoke earnestly, finishing each other's sentences, inviting me to be the auditor of an ongoing conversation.

They were not, as my father-in-law put it, "typical American Jews." While they enjoyed acquiring nice things, they would not make a career of wandering through malls, nor would they fritter away the inheritance they hoped to pass on to their three sons. They would not move to Miami. My mother-in-law would not waste her afternoons gossiping on the phone with female friends.

But how many mornings could my father-in-law spend on the leather couch in his den, listening to Beethoven's late quartets played very loud? How often could they rearrange the furniture in their living room, rehang their collection of paintings? What they were feeling was not despair but a balked, puzzled optimism. All through their lives they had applied themselves to problematic situations with intense concentration and they felt sure that the dilemmas of leisure would yield to this time-proven method—but how?

It's the problem of heaven on earth, I said, and my father-in-law nodded emphatically. Now we had passed the mile-and-a-half mark and they were beginning to puff a little as they walked and talked. But I was just beginning to hit my stride; it seemed to me that this was a rare and rather Olympian occasion. I felt exhilarated, touched by their trustfulness, tender toward them. They seemed for the moment like two promising and conscientious children, and I was the respected teacher in whom they had chosen to confide. Even if the compliment they were paying was a left-handed one—apparently they had identified me as an expert in the management of anomie—I could not help feeling flattered.

And I was glad, for once, to be helpful to them. I knew I was nothing like the *balabusta* daughter-in-law (or "dodd-in-law," as my father-in-law pronounced it), the practical and energetic woman they would have wished for. This daughter-in-law would have given birth to three children by now (but no more; my parents-in-law looked askance at the giant families produced by the Orthodox in Israel). She would have been fierce in her defense of her maternal territory, and my intrusive, overbearing father-in-law would have felt her wrath more than once. But that would have been as it should have been.

My detachment, my penchant for speculation, my literary leanings: these were the traits, along with slovenliness and disorganization, that my parents-in-law had always found alienating in me. They knew I admired and appreciated them, loved them for the dangers they had passed, defended and interpreted them to their son. (And did they know how bitterly I envied him the taken-for-granted security that allowed him to give them the back of his hand without losing their love?) But all I had been able to offer them so far had been my own neediness and one grandchild—nothing like the rich and secure entrenchment in extended family that the feisty *balabusta* would have given them.

But what could I have been thinking? The relevant fact was that I was a half-Jew! And a half-Jew was worse than no Jew at all. I knew this because during the seventh month of my pregnancy, when my father-in-law had finally prevailed on me at least to talk to the local Conservative rabbi and we were parked outside the synagogue in the purring Lincoln, he gave me my final instructions: "Don't tell the rabbi your father was Jewish. Let him think you're one hundred percent gentile." Why, I asked. My father-in-law's hoarsely whispered reply: because you're a *momser,* and *momser*s cannot be converted. Only later did it occur to me that if I were an unconvertible *momser,* so my daughter would be, and her children too—in spite of any conversion performed under false pretenses—and so on into eternity. (A few years ago I learned from an authoritative source that this fine point of Jewish law was as much a product of my father-in-law's imagination as the *balabusta* daughter-in-law was an invention of mine.)

III.

Kafka described himself as "the most typical Western Jew," but in a characteristic reversal he also wrote in his diary: "What do I have in common with the Jews? I have hardly anything in common with myself and should stand very quietly in a corner, content that I can breathe."

I began by reading the letters and journals, acquainting myself with the scenes and circumstances of his life. And oddly enough, I found myself identifying Kafka with my parents-in-law. He began to seem like a long-dead distant relative by marriage, my husband's grandmother's younger cousin perhaps, someone my mother-in-law would have known through family legend. His unmistakable face might almost be spotted among the faces of extended family in sepia-toned group photographs taken before the war at weddings or bar mitzvahs, posed in orderly ranks under the harsh light of a chandelier in a rented ballroom. Granted, he was Czech and not German, but even so, I could readily imagine the adolescent Franz Kafka in the third row back, the *Gymnasium* student with the wolfish grin and an air of shy distinction, self-conscious in his high white collar, but a good enough sport to keep the children amused by pulling handkerchief mice from his cuffs with his long, nervous fingers.

The vividness of Kafka's life, as I was learning it, shortened the perspective with which I viewed twentieth-century history. The early part of the century, which had seemed unimaginably remote, suddenly moved closer, and I found (with the help of a book of photographs) that I could visualize scenes of his Prague boyhood. I could picture the claustrophobic family apartment, full of the intrigues of his sisters and the intolerable shouting and banging of his father. In my mind's eye, the apartment was crammed with bedding—outsized puffy mattresses and ballooning comforters, unmade beds glimpsed through doors left ajar in the early mornings. I think I got this notion half from the details of the father's bedroom in "The Judgment" and half from what I knew of my mother-in-law's father's pre-war bedding manufactory in Cologne.

For most of a year, I simply bathed in reading, but eventually, under gentle pressure from my adviser, I began to work toward a thesis. I focused my attention on the productions of Kafka's early maturity, the break-

through of "The Judgment," followed by "The Metamorphosis," taking account of the circumstances of Kafka's
life, his agonized attachment to his father, and his ambivalence about the prospect of marriage to Fräulein Felice
Bauer.

After several false starts and many days wasted wandering through the local shopping mall and watching
daytime TV, I somehow arrived at an idea—one I happened to believe was true—that would enable me to har-
ness the arguments of the critics I had been reading in the
service of my own. My organizing idea was that very early
in his career as a writer, Kafka "outgrew" his Freudian
beginnings. Here I quote myself:

> While "The Judgment" represented a psychologi-
> cal and literary breakthrough for Kafka, it also
> marked for him the beginning of a transcendence
> of the psychoanalytic mode. Psychological puzzle
> became ontological mystery.

(Not bad, I think, re-reading this, and neither is the rest of
my introduction. But as I read further into my thesis I
note with dismay the variability of my writing style,
sometimes vigorous and punchy, sometimes plodding and
rhythm-sprung.)

I planned to demonstrate that psychoanalytic interpretation becomes redundant when applied to any of Kafka's
work written after "The Judgment." This story *requires* psychoanalytic interpretation, but once its dream metaphors are
properly aligned with the particulars of Kafka's internal

life—when the doddering old father who suddenly and terrifyingly throws off the covers of his bed and capers about radiant with insight is understood to represent Kafka's internalized father, the dream ally of Kafka's artistic side and the enemy of the Kafka who aspired to married life—the Kafka code has been definitively broken. As Anthony Thorlby, another critic on whom I leaned heavily, observes in a discussion of "The Burrow": "The more closely we look at this and other stories by Kafka, the more we discover, of course, that he is forever narrating, in a basically static, symbolic manner, the same situation." To look for this situation is always to find it, but to find it, over and over again, is pointless, or worse than pointless, because viewed in this way, Kafka can only seem what he most certainly is not—a bore.

My adviser liked my idea, but he cautioned me that I would need to devote a section of the paper to an examination of some examples of the psychoanalytic literature on Kafka. My library researches turned up three of this kind of critic. Two of these, Kate Flores and Selma Fraiberg, were eminently respectable. Flores offered the careful and intricately detailed psychoanalytic reading of "The Judgment" on which my argument rested, and Selma Fraiberg provided an ingenious analysis of what she called Kafka's "dream technique," his ability to retrieve "naked specimens of unconscious productions." I was impressed by her analysis and therefore all the more disappointed with Fraiberg's final assessment of Kafka as a "crippled writer":

The disease which produced extraordinary dreams exerted its morbid influence on the creative process as well. The striving for synthesis, for integration and harmony which are the marks of a healthy ego and a healthy art are lacking in Kafka's life and in his writings. The conflict is weak in Kafka's stories because the ego is submissive; the unequal forces within the Kafka psyche create no tension within the reader, only a fraternal sadness.

"A healthy ego and a healthy art": this doctrinaire notion put my back up. And what was so negligible, for that matter, about the "fraternal sadness" that Kafka evokes in the reader?

The last of the three psychoanalytic critics, Ruth Tiefenbrun, was neither respectable nor smart, but she too was useful. To pretend to take her book seriously was an act of conscious intellectual dishonesty, but one I was unable to resist, because *Moment of Torment* was the answer to a graduate student's prayer. It was a one-note rant, brittle and unmodulated, made to order for a novice's target practice. Its thesis is simply expressed: the key to an understanding of Kafka's works is his secret knowledge of his own homosexuality:

We must state that an internal examination of all of Kafka's creative works, as well as his diaries, letters, conversations and dreams, reveal that Kafka considered himself to be a homosexual; and all of his major characters, both human and animal, who are mirror images of Kafka, suffer eternal torment because they are all members of the most despised, the most maligned, and most harassed of all minority groups.

The body of Tiefenbrun's book is given over to the dogged application of her theory; she plows through Kafka's oeuvre, finding it riddled with correspondences and code words. *Moment of Torment* was so baldly simple-minded and repetitive a document that I found it impossible to summarize respectfully, and I spent far too much of my thesis quoting it.

But, as I say, it was useful. Merely by displaying three of the requisite psychoanalytic critics, arranging them along a "pretty good"–to–"very bad" continuum, I inadvertently managed to produce an illusion of analytic progress. A quick reading of my thesis would give the impression that I had succeeded in discrediting the psychoanalytic approach by demonstrating that the sophisticated analyses of Flores and Fraiberg could be reduced to the primitive level of Tiefenbrun.

One of the frustrations of writing this kind of research paper was that the more I fortified myself with critical opinions, the less maneuverable my thinking became. By the time I reached the midpoint of my paper I had encumbered myself with so many critics and biographers that I could only wheel around slowly and lumber off in the general direction of whatever I wanted to say, staggering under the combined weight of Slochower, Sokel, Brod, Pawel, Thorlby, Flores, Fraiberg, Tiefenbrun, et al.

So in my concluding chapters I unceremoniously dumped my critical load and began to speak more or less for myself, using Greenberg and W. H. Auden to amplify and underscore my voice. Kafka, I contended, was a writer for whom the usual distinction between art and life did not apply. My reading of Kafka's letters and journals had convinced me that for him life and art were very nearly fused, and as a result he was uniquely vulnerable, both as a writer and as a man. ("Naked" was the word Milena Jesenská used, and countless critics and biographers followed.) I found support here from Greenberg: Kafka, he says,

> keeps out of his story as stage-managing author just precisely by flinging himself right into the middle of it as K., without retaining a shred of advantage for himself as author.

While much in Kafka is baffling, nothing (after "The Judgment") is hidden. Psychoanalytic criticism, which works by exposing an author's self-betrayals and unconscious contradictions, seems in Kafka's case both unsporting and irrelevant.

To hell with psychology! Now I deployed Greenberg to demolish Fraiberg's claim that Kafka was a "crippled artist." He was surely a sick one, but he was also courageous. Greenberg recognized the bravery of Kafka's struggle to penetrate the depths of his life-fear and his life-failure. Though there is a morbid admixture of self-abasement and self-abnegation in it, his dominant effort is to affirm himself in spite of fear and failure, *through* his fear and failure.

My Greenberg-fortified insight about life and art in Kafka gave me a purchase on another point as well, and here Auden came to my assistance. A knowledge of Kafka's life could serve as a corrective to various wrong readings, the most common of which—as Auden said, and I concurred—was to find in Kafka's work a confirmation of "the gnostic-manichean notion of the physical world as intrinsically evil." At times Kafka comes perilously close, Auden concedes, to accepting this worldview. But a knowledge of Kafka's biography, of what Auden called his "passion for the good life," can correct this misapprehension.

"If ever," Auden wrote, "there was a man who hungered and thirsted after righteousness, it was Kafka." How I marveled at this pronouncement—bold, moving, absolutely unsupported by textual references or critical citations, and absolutely right. Merely to transcribe it gave me a kind of karaoke thrill, and I wondered: would it ever be possible for me to find the authority to speak this way myself?

I'VE RECONSTRUCTED THE PROCESS of writing my thesis, but the truth is that I don't remember it very well. Like labor, it was an ordeal nature helped me to forget. I do recall moments of torment when I could see no way to thread my way around or through the critics I had enlisted without committing plagiarism. And I remember the Kate Turabian phase of the job, the numbering and arrangement of endnotes, the alphabetizing of the bibliography, hassles that ordinarily would have driven me crazy, but which the relief of seeing an end to my labors transformed into satisfying tasks.

My "defense" was held on a hot day late in June, in the nearly deserted humanities building. I was ushered into a seminar room that smelled of burnt coffee and summer emptiness. The members of my thesis committee were all dressed in open-necked short-sleeved shirts, and I felt self-conscious in my dress and heels. They talked shop for a little while, moving on to a discussion of the comparative merits of different brands of cross-country-ski wax. My thesis adviser checked his watch, shot an apologetic smile my way and convened the defense. Each member asked me an easy, encouraging question. I began hesitantly, but after a few minutes I felt a suffusion of adrenaline, an accession of clearheadedness, and I was off. Eventually, my adviser raised his eyebrows and pointed to his watch. I was gestured out of the room, the door was closed behind me. I walked down the hall to the ladies' room, smirked at my reflection in the mirror, and splashed lukewarm water on my hot face. By the time I emerged, my adviser was waiting for me outside the seminar room, his hand extended, offering congratulations.

I walked out of the building and across the campus

quadrangle to my house, where my family waited. My daughter was three now, old enough to throw her arms around my neck and tell me that she was proud of me. My husband did the same, but I took the opportunity to pick a fight with him. Why no dinner out? Was I expected to cook, as usual? Was there no such thing as celebration in his universe? It was only after a long session of shouting and tears and two stiff scotches that I achieved enough detachment to acknowledge the sense of stale letdown I felt. It seemed to me now that I understood the slightly sheepish demeanor of my committee members as they congratulated me, their readiness to return to their talk of the university's recent switch to a new insurance carrier. It was not that my thesis was inadequate—even though it was not very good, it was considerably better than it needed to be. It was simply that this credentialing process was a fairly automatic one, and the men on my committee were a little embarrassed by my intensity and eagerness, by the sense that I was taking the whole thing far too personally.

I woke in the middle of the night with a gasp of dismay, a familiar sensation much like the sudden panic I had once felt just after an ultrasound during pregnancy. On that occasion, as I was walking out of the hospital to the parking lot, car keys jangling in my hand, my heart suddenly lurched and I stopped in my tracks, jolted by the primitive and irrational conviction that I had left my child on the ultrasound monitor, seething restlessly in that inchoate gray world I had strained so hard to understand and the technician had taken such pains to interpret for me. Now I thought: I've lost Kafka.

IV.

Before my pregnancy, my affective palette had been composed of mixed and murky colors, with a few hot bright notes scattered here and there. Pleasure and excitement were familiar to me, but happiness was a new discovery. After the queasiness and anxiety of the first trimester, I began to feel like an egg dipped in rosy dye. This joy sprang paradoxically out of fear of the trial of birth—a great universal. Pregnancy had reassured me that I, who at times felt myself to be painfully odd and anomalous, perhaps internally malformed in some occult way, was actually quite healthy and even normal. I had been stamped with nature's imprimatur, and I had as much claim to self-satisfaction as anyone else. Through the months of my pregnancy I watched myself in the mirror, monitoring my milky, blue-veined burgeoning with curious delight. These days I watch myself age with an oddly similar satisfaction.

At the end of my pregnancy my blood pressure shot up and I was hospitalized. The night before my labor was to be induced I felt no unmanageable fear, but instead a sense of mobilization and focus, almost—like a soldier on the eve of battle—joy at the prospect of being subjected to this test.

I entertained a hallucination during the delivery. What I heard was the nurses urging me on, the doctor imploring me to push and then not to push, but what I saw was a grouping of tables, protected from the sun by fringed umbrellas. This was an outdoor café of some kind, an elevated flagstone patio in a public place like a zoo or a park, looking down on a gently gradated succession of floral terraces. Nobody was in sight, but it was apparent that a group of people had just now gotten up and left one table in particular, because chairs had been pulled away from it at odd angles and crumpled paper napkins had been left to flutter in the breeze.

Such a sober and modest vision, such a pleasant and particular place. It was full of the feeling of late afternoon, a sustaining sense of fulfillment and resignation, a residue of human warmth. It seems odd to me that this vision came to me during childbirth: it had nothing to do with beginnings, everything to do with looking back.

The scene I saw has faded a little, but the feeling that permeated it has stayed with me ever since. I think of it as something akin to a yolk sac, a private supply of highly concentrated psychic nourishment. It returns to me predictably in public places where municipal arrangements have been made for the cultivation of a mild and civilized human happiness—at a botanical garden, for example, where family groups thread their way along graveled pathways through stands of bamboo, pausing dutifully to read the informational signs. It also visits me when I go for morning walks through suburban neighborhoods, past blank-windowed houses recently vacated for the day and still humming with the aura of habitation. Ever since that antivisionary vision in the delivery room, I've been after the spoor of very short-term, very small-scale human history, and the frisson of species recognition that rewards its discovery.

"The only strange thing about me is my nature," says

the dog narrator of "Investigations of a Dog," "yet even that, as I am always careful to remember, has its foundation in universal dog nature." Kafka's late stories, those "affections and acceptances," as the critic Carl Woodring called them, the ones narrated by Talmudic animals who construct complex and subtle but ultimately self-sabotaging arguments and make endlessly qualified distinctions: in the course of writing my thesis on the darker and better known early work, I came to love these tenderly anthropological "thought-stories" best.

The narrators of "Investigations of a Dog" and "Josephine the Singer, or the Mouse Folk" are conscientious creatures, proudly identified with their dog and mouse kin, continually at pains to educate the reader in the ways and rules of their "people," and to describe the process by which dogs and mice who stand apart from society are ultimately accommodated by the commonality. The dog-investigator who boldly inquires into such matters as the "scratching and watering of the ground" and the "calling down of food" is brought to a confrontation with his fear that he stands "outside our people, outside our humanity." Ultimately he is reassured by his own observations about the phenomenon of the "soaring dogs," those canine artists who are "invariably seen alone, self-complacently floating high up in the air." The narrator reminds himself that he is "not in the least queer outwardly." "Now if," he goes on to reason,

> not even the soaring dogs live in isolation, but invariably manage to encounter their fellows some-

where or other in the great dog world, and even to conjure new generations of themselves out of noth-ingness, then I too can live in the confidence that I am not quite forlorn.

NOT QUITE FORLORN: this was how the company of Kafka made me feel at this particularly lonely time in my life, when I was undergoing the first of many separations from my daughter and descending into paranoia at the day care.

I had spent my daughter's first year in a semiconscious daze of absorption; I carried her with me everywhere, staring down into her small oval lake of a face. Then she began to walk and talk and I fell from that state of grace. Having a child had not cured me of my disease of apart-ness, it seemed, only masked its symptoms. My adolescent self-consciousness and fear of inadequacy returned with a vengeance. I had lost my old resistance; the attitude of facile nihilism into which I once gratefully sank was no longer part of my internal repertoire. Motherhood had trapped me in seriousness.

But such was my crazy resourcefulness that after a morning spent reading Kafka, I came out of the immer-sion coated with his worldview, rendered impervious to the smug maternal sanctimony I found so wounding at the day care. Under escort of the Prague genius I walked through glances and whispers with equanimity.

I must admit that sometimes I used my imagined inti-macy with Kafka to buttress the sense of superiority that always lurks behind my fears of inadequacy. I compared

Kafka's loftily gratuitous vision of the good—that there is a truth but it happens not to be available to us—to the limited and instrumental good I could see expressed in the actions of the mothers at the day care, identifying myself with the former and dismissing the latter with a certain scorn. I knew, even as I indulged in it, that this kind of grandiose identification with Kafka put me in the company of those readers Auden was thinking of when he wrote: "Perhaps, when he wished his writings to be destroyed, Kafka foresaw the nature of too many of his admirers."

Kafka was incapable, as Auden says, of "spiritual snobbery." His ability to admire what he envied was exemplary. He marveled at people who were successful in the world, even, or especially, those who like his fiancée Felice Bauer were "good at business." Childless and unmarried, he embraced the goodness of marriage and childrearing with an imaginative passion.

Late in his life he wrote in his diary: "The infinite, deep, warm, saving happiness of sitting beside the cradle of one's child opposite its mother." I've read this entry many times but never fixed its significance. Sometimes I receive it as a confirmation of my own motherhood, a moving reminder of my luck at being able to identify myself with one member of that lamplit triad. At other times my perspective shifts and I find myself standing apart with Kafka, looking on longingly at this domestic scene, filled with a fraternal sadness.

"The only strange thing about me is my nature": Kafka reminded me that my strange nature finds its foundation in universal human nature. One of the "glittering paradoxes" (Greenberg's phrase) at the heart of Kafka's work is the insight that human beings are defined by a sense of anomaly in the self: to be human is to doubt one's own humanity. Being human, the other women at my daughter's day care also stood apart from themselves and from the human community; they also suffered. This is a lesson I learn and forget, learn and forget.

IT WAS KAFKA'S *momser* status that attracted me so powerfully; he was half writer, half holy man. His religious aspirations were passionate, but he fastidiously rejected any religious consummation. He repudiated everything but his own pain-filled subjectivity. He refused, Greenberg says, to "flinch away":

> It took courage to stare into the Gorgon's mouth of universal senselessness and despair without flinching away cynically or idealistically or religiously or in any of the innumerable ways there are of flinching.

One can "flinch away" psychoanalytically too, and Kafka resisted this as well. After "The Judgment" Kafka took up permanent residence in the impasse between insight and resolution, a place many writers visit, but only Kafka could inhabit. It was an inhumanly harsh outpost; he might as well have slept naked in a freezing cave, like an anchorite. And in fact, it's difficult to contemplate Kafka's purity, his asceticism, his self-mortification and early death without thinking of saintliness. He *was* a sort of saint, I think, or half-saint.

And so, I suppose, my tendency to domesticate Kafka, to press him into service as my invisible friend, was correspondingly only a half-heresy. To treat a great writer this way is offensive, a desecration, but saints have always been subject to invocation by their followers.

My friendship with Kafka was an oddly islanded phenomenon. Sadly enough, it was somehow parasitic on the writing of my useless thesis. When that was finished, he died in my imagination. He became a "transitional object" like one of my little daughter's dolls, a specially favored one hugged fiercely and chattered at for a while and then, in the course of following out the trail of some fantasy, gently abandoned and left to lie where it was dropped.

MY LAST THERAPIST

—

When I remember Dr. B's office I envision it from an aerial angle. I see myself slightly hunched at one end of the comfortable leather couch. I see him flung back in his specially designed orthopedic rocker, his corduroy-sheathed legs outstretched, his ankles crossed, his bald pate gleaming. I see the two of us looking out from our lamp-lit island into a parcel of shadowy office space, in the direction of the darkened alcove where Dr. B typed up his bills and displayed the photographs of his wife and children which, squint and peer and crane my neck as I might, I could never quite make out.

Dr. B was a fit and pleasant-looking man in his early forties with a rather long and slightly horsey face, a little like Prince Charles's, or a Semitic version of John Updike's. He emanated sensitivity and goodwill and he had a fine speaking voice, an anchorman's baritone, which tended to lighten as he grew animated. When I first met him—nearly fifteen years ago—I was impressed by his handshake, a firm grasp, two hard pumps, and a quick release. By the time our acquaintance was five minutes old I had formed an opinion of him which I never entirely abandoned, though I did revise and expand it: ordinary!

Dr. B led me to his office, a small utilitarian space on the top floor of the local hospital. On the wall facing the patient's chair, he had displayed his diplomas and a poster-sized photograph of a sailboat in a storm, its deck half-swamped and drastically tilted. He observed me as I took inventory of his office and smiled. "Checking things out?" he asked. "Yes, indeed," I answered. "As well you should!" he said, emphatically. I recognized the language of consumerism, then a fairly new trend in therapy.

Dr. B declared himself available to work with me before the first session was over. His eagerness did not surprise me: I was a literary kind of person, wasn't I, and didn't he have a reputation as a psychiatrist with a special interest in literature and the arts? Surely I was brighter, I found myself thinking, than a lot of his patients, and more interesting. Reasonably stable, free of drug dependency, capable of humorous self-deprecation, even charm. And almost simultaneously I recoiled: was this what I had come to—finding gratification in the imagined prospect of becoming some shrink's prize patient?

I.

Surely I was too much of a veteran for that. By the time I arrived in Dr. B's office I had been through five therapists, three before the age of seventeen. Two of these were almost comically inappropriate: between the ages of eleven and thirteen, I was the patient of two separate classically trained psychoanalysts.

The first was Dr. V, who was Viennese and practiced on the Upper East Side of Manhattan. Dr. V kept a tank of exotic fish in her waiting room. She had mismatched eyes, one small and weepy, the other hypertrophied and glaucous, like an eye behind a jeweler's loupe. Dr. V was followed by Dr. H, another middle-aged woman, but midwestern and more motherly. Like Dr. V, she put me on the couch and maintained a silence throughout the hour.

But she knitted me a sweater. The cables fell out of her needles fully articulated, like great ropes heaved length by length over the side of a ship. I appreciated the symbolism; the developing sweater was meant to suggest that something was being made here, that in spite of my nearly complete silence, progress of some kind was happening. At the end of my therapy with Dr. H—why it stopped, I had no idea: I could only guess it was because the sweater was finished—she presented it to me. It was very handsome and unbecoming and smelled ever after of Dr. H's Pall Malls.

I failed in these early therapies, or attempts at analysis, as I suppose they should properly be called. How could I have succeeded? And what could Drs. V and H have been expecting? Thrown into deep waters without instruction, I floated mute, Dr. V's great eye like an implacable sun above me. My silence was both anxious and voluptuous. I felt a gentle pressure to speak, but I also felt pillowed by the assurance that silence was all right—good, in fact. It established my bona fides as a sensitive person, because only a sensitive person would remain silent when given the opportunity to speak. The more silence, the more certainty that the surface tension of the silence would break; the more prolonged the silence, the more import it would be seen, once broken, to have had. The first would be last and the last would be first: I had internalized this, the fundamental psychoanalytic dialectic, before I turned thirteen. On the couch I felt like a passenger on a night train, lying in a closed compartment on a gently rocking bed, passive and inert, but hurtled forward by the process of travel.

The waiting rooms of Drs. V and H had the feeling, for me, of sanctified space. I understood Dr. V's aquarium as a metaphor for the unconscious mind: those glittering bits of protein flashing through it—how I wished I could pinch the tails of their analogs in my brain, draw them out wriggling, and present them to her. And the framed reproduction of Rouault's little king that dominated Dr. H's waiting room seemed to me the focal point of a shrine.

I brought a free-floating ardor to my first encounters with psychotherapy, a kind of religious hunger which had gone unfed by my parents' agnosticism, their skepticism, their pragmatic liberalism. As I lay on the couch, my thoughts were runnels of dreamy speculation just below the translucent skin of consciousness, monitored, but not entirely registered. I never actually expressed these thoughts, not because I was secretive—nobody could have been more eager to reveal herself than I—but because I had childishly misunderstood the rules of free association. Somehow I had picked up the idea that only unconscious thoughts were to be spoken. An obvious contradiction, but I blurred this impossibility into a kind of Zen koan. Once I had solved it, I felt sure that enlightenment would follow.

MY THERAPEUTIC EDUCATION broke off while I went away to boarding school for two years. After I was thrown out, I returned to Washington, D.C., where my parents now lived, and began therapy with Dr. G, the first male. He was the most genuinely detached of all my therapists. When I remember him I bring to mind a cartoonist's doodle-drawing of a shrink—one quick unbroken line describing a domed, balding head, continuing with a substantial hooked nose and receding chin, and petering out after tracing the swell of a modest professional's paunch. He had a wry decency that was mostly, but not entirely, lost on me at the time. He seemed, emotionally, to be a smooth dry surface; no burrs to snag my creepers or wet spots to which I might adhere.

My therapy with Dr. G was the first in which I sat up and faced the therapist, the first in which I talked freely, and also the first in which I withheld or distorted the truth. I never mentioned how mortified I was, for example, to notice that the patient who walked out of his waiting room as I entered was a fat obnoxious girl from my school with alopecia and a steady rapid blink, and I never confided my fear that perhaps Dr. G had made the treatment of fat adolescent girls—I *was* fat, though not nearly as fat as she was—his specialty.

With Dr. G, I learned to "talk therapy." This was not a matter of using jargon—I'm proud to say I've never done that—but of recognizing which gambits and attitudes cause the therapist to signal his receptiveness. Even the most poker-faced practitioner will always reward an attentive patient with some small sign, a subtle alteration in the set of facial muscles, a dilation of the pupils. So with Dr. G I reached the "clever Hans" stage of my development as a patient.

And like the novice painter who has learned to use the entire canvas, I finally learned how to fill the hour; now I saw that anything I said could be depended on to color the silences that followed, giving them a plausible opacity behind which I could hide until I found another thing to say. Often what I said was about loneliness, or feeling as if I were enclosed in a glass box. These themes seemed to engage Dr. G, and they gave me a pleasant feeling too. I enjoyed the waiflike image I conjured up of myself, and the resultant gentle tide of self-pity that washed over me, raising the hair on my arms and leaving my eyes prickling with tears.

Throughout my three years as Dr. G's patient, I felt a guilty and unshakable conviction that I was completely sane and that I had health to squander. Of course, my notion that patients were expected to be crazy was a naive one, but I had swallowed whole the familiar ideology that connects madness to beauty of spirit. My knowledge of my strength and sanity was a secret I did my best to keep from Dr. G. I wanted him to see me as vulnerable and sensitive rather than robust. I loved the notion of myself as saucer-eyed and frail, and I was ashamed of the blunt and caustic person I knew I was. I hoped that if I applied myself, I might evolve toward becoming the fragile and purely loveable being I so wished to be. I was looking for transformation, not cure. I wasn't interested in being happier, but in growing more poignantly, becomingly, meaningfully unhappy.

Perhaps the reader wonders: why did my parents put me into these psychoanalytically oriented psychotherapies at such an early age? My mother would have explained that my chronic underachievement in school was the reason, and later she would have added my bad and wild behavior (mild by today's standards). And what was wrong with me? A family systems therapist would have identified me as the family scapegoat, the child designated to "act out" the conflicts between my tense, driven father and my incipiently alcoholic mother, the vent through which the collective rage escaped; a Winnicottean would point to the consequences of early maternal inadequacy (my mother was bedridden with phlebitis for most of my first year); a practitioner with a neurological bent could find evidence of a learning disability.

All these hypotheses have explanatory power. I tend to favor the last one, at least on days when I feel inclined to believe that there *is* such a thing as a learning disability. But they were all equally irrelevant to the subjective reality of the adolescent I was. About her I can only say that if she was angry, she was also extremely passive, and mired in a deep helplessness, and that therapy became a means by which she became even more so.

My therapeutic education did me harm. It swallowed up years when I might have been learning, gathering competence and undergoing the toughening by degrees that engagement in the world makes possible. But worse than this was the effect of my therapies on my moral development: seedlings of virtues withered. An impulse that might have flowered, for example, into tact—the desire to gently investigate another's feelings—fell onto the stony ground of the therapist's neutrality and became manipulativeness, a tough perennial better suited to these desert conditions.

I acquired the habit of the analysand, the ruthless stripping away of defenses. But in my case not much self had yet developed, and surely none of it was expendable. I was tearing away not a hardened carapace, but the developing layers of my own epidermis. By reducing myself to a larval, infantile state I was doing what I felt I was expected to do, and what would please the therapist.

II.

By the time I was sixteen, I had given up any serious college ambitions. I spent the days sulking and smoking in the snack bar of a bowling alley with a group of fellow truants. At the age of eighteen, at loose ends and living with a boyfriend's mother in suburban Indianapolis, I scratched my wrists with a pair of nail scissors. The boyfriend's mother put me on a train the next day, and when I arrived in Washington my parents lost no time in taking me to Dr. G, who suggested that I spend some time in a therapeutic community—Austen Riggs, an open psychiatric hospital in the Berkshires, was his recommendation.

For years, life had been retreating and the space it left filling up with therapy; at Riggs, life *was* therapy. Here I was surrounded by young people, most of them no more apparently disturbed than I was. Our physical circumstances were comfortable; we lived in private rooms in a big high-ceilinged residence, ate good food, and were offered the usual diversions—volleyball and tennis, ceramics and woodworking. We were free to come and go.

From the first I felt something anomalous in our interactions with one another. It was as if we had been positioned at oblique angles to one another and had gotten stuck that way, unable to twist ourselves free so as to stand face to face. We had been planted in therapy, like rows of sunflowers. Our gazes were tilted upward, each toward the face of the therapist. Like acolytes at the feet of masters, we were taught to cultivate a contempt for the distractions that surrounded us. So we lived in communal loneliness and restless boredom. I can still "taste" these feelings; the sight of a jewel-green expanse of lawn or a hanging pot of pink and purple fuchsia can set it off in me as surely as an electrode probing brain tissue can evoke a hallucination.

I stayed for three years, years that I would otherwise have spent in college. I was assigned to an incompetent neophyte I'll call Dr. S (number four in the running count), a research psychologist. After the first year I became an outpatient and Dr. S, who was married and soon to become a father, began to show up at my door with bottles of wine and sheepish smiles. I got no help from the Riggs bureaucracy in my effort to extricate myself from this embroilment; firmly gripping my upper arm, the senior psychiatrists steered me out of their offices. One and all, they told me the same story: what I had mistaken to be Dr. S's feelings for me were merely projections of my own transference. Here I felt for the first time the chill of an encounter with psychiatry in its systematic aspect.

Then Leslie Farber arrived at Riggs, coming in to serve as director of therapy for the new administration. He listened to my complaint about Dr. S, believed me, and—eventually—took me on as a patient.

Dr. Farber never found Riggs congenial, and he was suspicious of Stockbridge, which he regarded as a kind of Potemkin village. He left for New York after a little more than a year, taking me and two other patients with him. It is no exaggeration to say that Dr. Farber rescued us.

How difficult it is to abandon the ironic mode and speak enthusiastically! Although I list Dr. Farber as one in the succession of my shrinks, I do so apologetically, recognizing that this is a gross miscategorization—something like including Kafka in a roundup of Czech insurance underwriters. He was something other and larger than the rest of them, so much so that he eludes easy characterization. I write about him troubled by the well-founded fear that I will fail to do him justice.

He was a thinker and writer as well as a psychoanalyst,

the author of two books of remarkable essays. His critique of psychoanalysis began in his understanding of human will, a category that he believed had been smuggled into psychoanalytic explanations of motive without acknowledgment, an element anatomized in literature, philosophy, and theology, but neglected in psychoanalytic theory.

To understand people only in the reductive terms of the medical model was a drastic impoverishment of human possibility. Dr. Farber shared this belief with others associated with the humanistic or existential schools, but he never shared their wooly and inspirational leanings. He was tough-minded, pessimistic by temperament, and a man of deep emotional conservatism. He was a believer in God who protected his belief from any but the most serious inquiry.

Dr. Farber was in his late fifties when I met him. Though less ravaged, his small-chinned, delicate-boned Eastern European face was nearly as seamed and pouched, expressive and revelatory of character, as W. H. Auden's at the same age. He was a small man, plump and sedentary, but his walk had verve and his motions were graceful. I remember the elegant and efficient way he handled his keys as he opened his office door, one eye squeezed shut against the updraft of smoke from the cigarette in the corner of his mouth.

He exuded melancholy and humor. His gravitas, his distinction, were so immediately and overwhelmingly apparent that even in my deteriorated and boredom-numbed condition I recognized them. It was a revelation to me, this full, rich, pungent, complex humanity. It was as if another self continued to live inside the therapeutic self I had become, lying slack but fully jointed, waiting for some salutory yank to spring alive. My sessions with Dr. Farber were entirely unlike my earlier experience of therapy. I had learned to think of my utterances as soap bubbles rotating in midair, to be examined by me with the help of the therapist. They were the matter of the enterprise. But with Dr. Farber, no such "work" was being undertaken. Instead, we talked. He talked—for example—about his childhood in Douglas, Arizona, and how growing up in the desert had affected his inner life. We talked about his marriages, my boyfriends, his children, my parents, his dismay at watching Riggs patients, most of them young and few really sick, loitering in a psychiatric limbo. We talked about movies and TV and the youth culture; we gossiped freely about the Riggs staff and patients. Dr. Farber expected me to hold up my end of these conversations, to keep him interested. Was I up to it? Mostly, but not always.

My reaction to my earliest view of Dr. Farber's world was something like the "wild surmise" of stout Cortez' men at their first sight of the Pacific. I knew quite suddenly not only that this world was *there* but also what that signified. This was my first apprehension of the realm of the moral, about which my parents had taught me very little, and therapy had taught me nothing.

The notion that another person might have a moral claim on me, or that I might have such a claim on another, was a novel one. So was the idea that a moral worldview had an intellectual dimension which required the careful working out of distinctions, the most significant of which was the distinction between the moral and the aesthetic. This is the one I had, and still have, the greatest trouble understanding. Is there such a thing as a moral style? It has always troubled and confused me that Dr. Farber's influence on me had so much to do with traits that were really more aesthetic than moral—his wordly panache, his toughness.

With Dr. Farber I felt free to express the caustic and humorous judgments I had been squelching for years. He enjoyed and encouraged my rude health. The world, which my therapeutic existence at Riggs had bleached of color and emptied of content, began to fill up again with the materials furnished in my sessions with Dr. Farber— with serious and light talk, with movies, books, music, with gossip and stories—with all the stuff of life.

III.

My move from Austen Riggs to New York City was a jarring transition. I wanted life, unfiltered and unprocessed? Here it was, the real thing, lonely, grubby, and full of jolts. I lost jobs, lived in chaos, and kept my money in a bureau drawer. My gums bled and my menstrual cycle went haywire. I cut my hair myself to save money, and the result made me look like the mental patient I had been pretending to be at Riggs. I got robbed, mugged, raped. At one point, the cockroach colony in my apartment grew so large that it produced an albino strain—translucent creatures whose internal workings were visible in certain lights. I was living on my own, away from home or institution for the first time, and I simply did not do very well. I had envisioned an exhilarating life in some vaguely imagined bohemia. But there was no bohemia anymore, none that I could find. Instead there was poverty and disorder and a series of bizarre low-paying jobs which seem funny and picaresque only in retrospect.

Dr. Farber charged me an income-adjusted fee of $7.50 a session. He and his wife went out of their way to help me get established in New York; they paid me handsomely to stay with their children while they went to Paris for a week, and during one of my homeless intervals Dr. Farber arranged for me to sleep on a cot in his brother's empty studio. They fed me, regularly. How warm and inviting the prospect of roast chicken at their table seemed, as I sat on the clanking, hissing subway train, fighting the temptation to get off at the Farbers' Upper West Side stop, how appealing when contrasted to my hot plate, my canned chili and saltines, my cockroaches. And indeed, it was wonderful to spend time in that bustling, musical, intellectually lively household, which eventually came to serve as a sort of salon for a certain group of New York intellectuals.

Other patients also visited the apartment and got to know the family—Dr. Farber never observed the psychiatric taboo against associating with patients, and for him therapy and friendship were inextricable. But I grew dependent on the Farber household, and as my dependency deepened I grew closer to Dr. Farber's wife and more distant from him. I often felt that he was getting sick of me, always there as I was, in his office and in his home, across the room and across the table, asleep on the couch so that he could not feel free to indulge his habit of wandering through the apartment late at night in darkness.

I knew that my contributions to our talks had grown stilted and falsely animated—willed, as Dr. Farber would have put it. I found that I suddenly had very little to say. The struggles of my daily life—getting to work on time under threat of being fired, making it to the laundromat, avoiding crime, and trying to stay clean when the hot water in my building was more often off than on—all this had apparently drained my head of anything interesting. I arrived at Dr. Farber's comfortable Riverside Drive office, with its high views of the streaky Hudson, blinking in the strong light, feeling dirty and uncertain about how I smelled.

I had found it easier to hold up my end of talks with Dr. Farber at Riggs, where we had the shared world of the institution to complain and gossip about. In New York Dr. Farber offered me a sort of substitute by asking me questions about the culture of protest, the rallies and shutdowns then in progress a few blocks away at Columbia. But I was no authority on this subject; my life was far too proletarian to put me in the way of any student revolutionaries.

The fact is, I had very little to offer. My education had been so impoverished, so radically incomplete, that I had grown up to be a creature of hunches and blurts, and soon even these had dried up. My sketchy views had long since been outlined and exhausted, and all I had to give back to Dr. Farber were flimsily disguised recapitulations of his own.

George Eliot, in a reference to phrenology, the psychology of her day, once spoke of her oversized "Organ of Veneration." Apparently I had one too. I became a furtive taxonomist, dividing up the world into the Farberian and the non-Farberian. What was Farberian I would embrace; what was non-Farberian I would reject. But sometimes—frequently—I got it wrong. Once I told Dr. Farber that I wanted to explore Orthodox Judaism. What I knew of his own tightly guarded belief and his interest in Martin Buber gave me confidence that this would please him. Dr. Farber looked at me with amused incredulity: You want to wear a wig? he said. You want to take a ritual bath every month? Seriously?

DANIEL WAS ANOTHER of Dr. Farber's patients in New York, an intellectually promising and sensitive young man with a yeshiva background who, like me, had languished for several years at Riggs, his prognosis growing steadily worse, before Dr. Farber came along to rescue us.

I had found a job, my most respectable yet, as a glorified coffee fetcher and xeroxer in the academic placement office at Columbia, where Daniel had resumed his interrupted education. I often ran into him on Broadway, at Chock Full o'Nuts and in the bookstores. We talked sometimes on the phone, and though we were not intimate, we maintained a concern for one another's fortunes in the city, a kind of sibling connection.

For a year or so Daniel stayed on the dean's list, but then something gave way in his life and he began to skip classes. Eventually he dropped out. During one of our phone conversations, Daniel sheepishly confided to me that he had not yet told Dr. Farber about this. A year passed, and Daniel continued the deception. I mentioned this to Dr. Farber's wife, during one of our cozy late-night gossips after the children had been put to bed. She passed the information to Dr. Farber, who confronted Daniel during his next session. They agreed that their friendship had been ended by the lie, and parted ways.

The explosion, when it came, was directed at me. I noticed, as Dr. Farber ushered me quickly into his office—no leisurely small talk, no smiles—that he looked grim and haggard, as if he had not slept well. I began to feel anxious, and I searched my mind frantically. Had I forgotten to pay? Had my check bounced? I knew that Daniel had been dismissed. In fact, I had come to Dr. Farber's office that morning glowing with schadenfreude and braced by the prospect of a ready-made interesting discussion. I was even prepared to plead Daniel's case a little; I wanted to remind Dr. Farber about Daniel's history, the oppressively high expectations of his parents, the overshadowing intellectual success of his older brother.

So it was disturbing to me that Dr. Farber stared at the floor. His reaction to my introductory stammerings was a long silence. When he finally raised his head and engaged my eyes, his face was full of angry puzzlement. "How could you . . ." he began, then shook his head and fell silent. I was already weeping.

When he spoke again, Dr. Farber's voice was low and hoarse, his speech discontinuous, as if he were vocalizing only random chopped-off segments of a tormented thought process. But I got the idea. I had colluded with a lie, and that had compromised my friendship with Dr. Farber, and my whisperings to his wife had in turn contaminated, if only briefly, even his marriage: "How could you come into my home and . . . solicit . . . my wife?"

I had meanwhile pitched myself out of my chair onto my knees. Panic and grief had transported me, busted up some internal logjam, and for the first time in months I spoke fluently to Dr. Farber as I crouched on the carpet, sobbing, tears springing from my eyes.

Please forgive me, I said. I had forgotten. Or maybe I never learned. Never learned what? asked Dr. Farber. That things matter, I said. For the first time since I had entered his office Dr. Farber looked at me as if I were a fellow-creature. "Yes, they do," he said, and I was so relieved at this turning that I burst into fresh sobs.

Instantly, I understood that I had gotten it wrong, unconsciously slipped back to the precepts of my early therapeutic education. I had reverted to understanding the relationship between Dr. Farber and Daniel, between Dr. Farber and me, as a game played for therapeutic chips, not as a reality in which human connection was at stake.

But of course Dr. Farber had gotten it wrong too—I think now—because my silence on the subject of Daniel's deception had as much to do with simple reluctance to be a snitch as with any larger failure to honor human relatedness. It was quite innocent, really, and perhaps I should have defended myself against Dr. Farber's unexpected and misdirected anger, which shocked me so much that I was unable to properly assimilate its meaning. It was guilt at my own bad faith—my desperate clutching at a friendship that I knew had ended—that found expression in my tearful contrition.

Dr. Farber granted me a kind of amnesty, but never, I think, real forgiveness. He waved me out of his office with an air of preoccupied disgust, but I could sense that in his exasperation his sense of humor had wanly reasserted itself. Before I left, I won from him the assurance that I could return the next week.

I envied the seriousness of Daniel's transgression. I suspected that Dr. Farber cared more about Daniel than about me; his anger was like a father's toward a beloved errant son. And like an errant son Daniel had been cut decisively free; he left New York and moved to Israel, joined the army, and married there, returning to the States years later with his young family. His dismissal from Dr. Farber's office left him bereft, but it also served to jolt him out of a rut. He got to keep, I think, some of his legacy from Farber, while my lesser, weaker, more equivocal offense kept me tied to Dr. Farber for another year, during which I used mine up.

Or so I understood myself to be doing. But meanwhile I had found a boyfriend and moved in with him. This boyfriend, who was later to become my husband, took a satirical view of my attachment to Dr. Farber. He often compared me to a character in one of R. Crumb's underground comic books, the goofy, loose-limbed Flakey Foont, always in pursuit of his guru, Mr. Natural, an irascible little visionary in flowing robes with a white beard and giant flapping bare feet. At the end of that year, my wedding a few months off, I ended things with Dr. Farber myself. I confessed to him that I had had little to say to him for years. I need to leave, I told him, because I'm in danger of becoming the acolyte who gets the master's message wrong. I knew how little Dr. Farber wished to serve as my guru, and I knew how particularly inappropriate my idealizing impulse toward him was. His tendency was deflationary: he nearly always preferred a modest exactitude to a rapturous generality.

I can see myself, I said, twenty years from now as a barfly, the regular who climbs onto her stool every afternoon at two and by four o'clock is mumbling to anyone who will listen the incoherent tale of the wise man she once knew in her youth. Dr. Farber accepted my resignation with warmth. My confession was true, and he liked it because it was true, and because it had a self-immolating boldness calculated to appeal to him. I offered it not because it was true, but because it was the only way I knew to please him.

IV.

When, twelve years after I exiled myself from Dr. Farber, I first walked into Dr. B's office, I was just emerging from the sea of early motherhood onto some indeterminate shore. I felt that my relation to the future had undergone a subtle change, one that signaled, I can see in retrospect, the onset of middle age. I found I lacked, and had been lacking for longer than I wanted to admit, the unshakable confidence in my own sanity and stability that I had once considered such an embarrassing encumbrance. I felt a vague sense of balked urgency. My husband and I were constantly fighting. I brought with me a tangle of confusion and sadness about Dr. Farber, who had recently died.

Dr. B passed one crucial test during the first session. He recognized Dr. Farber's name and knew a little about him. "Irreplaceable," he said, "life-saving," and I loved him for that. He went on to link Dr. Farber with my father, who had also died recently. "A lot of loss," he said, shaking his head deploringly. My reaction was mild disappointment and annoyance. I didn't like the idea of packaging Dr. Farber and my father together but I let it pass.

Then, a few weeks later, Dr. B said something almost unforgivable; he interrupted one of my many anecdotes about Dr. Farber with what he called "a reality consideration." Dr. Farber, he said, had been well known in the profession as a sufferer from depression. Wasn't it possible, he suggested, that during my years as Dr. Farber's patient, I had tried to compensate him for his sadness, just as I had done with my unhappy mother?

How many things could be wrong with this? Could anything be right? First the "reality consideration": was it implied here that the profession had a corner on reality?

And depression: Dr. Farber had his own views about depression. I suggested that Dr. B go to the library and look them up. What the profession took to be Dr. Farber's depression was actually despair.

But I was too angry to argue; instead I picked up the first wad of ad hominem that came to hand and flung it in Dr. B's direction. I looked up at the ship photograph. That put me in mind of an analogy; I compared Dr. Farber to an oceangoing liner with a great deep hull, and Dr. B to a surface-skimming Sailfish. Two spots of bright pink appeared just below Dr. B's cheekbones, and I pointed them out to him, literally pointed with my finger, all the while registering in one corner of my mind the appalling rudeness of the gesture.

I was working myself into a rage, and I could see that he was calculating how best to backtrack and calm me down. He threw up his hands. O.K., he said. You're quite right. I was out of line. I'm not perfect. Do you need me to be perfect?

No, I said. I need you to be smart. Dr. B absorbed that without comment and we sat in silence for several minutes. I was registering my disgust at the hokeyness of the "I'm not perfect" line and the seductive pseudo-intimacy of "Do you need me . . . ?" I was also fuming at the realization that Dr. B had saved his remarks about Dr. Farber until he had me well roped in as a patient. He had waited until it seemed safe to introduce his revisionist agenda. He was getting off, no doubt, on the idea of rescuing me from my thralldom to a distinguished dead practitioner; this was the old supplanter's story so familiar to the profession.

Here I was, seated in the office of my sixth therapist. Hadn't I decided, with Farber's help and long ago—as far back as Austen Riggs—that what I needed was to recover *from* therapy? Why, then, was I even here? One thing I was *not* doing was undertaking a revision of my views of Dr. Farber. This was such a touchy subject that Dr. B, as far as I can remember, never raised it again. My dismay at my own ugly and fluent anger was apparently to be my punishment for my recidivist slide back into psychotherapy, for my bad faith.

It seems that my life has not been so much examined as conducted in therapy. I brought into my therapies not the problems of life but the problems of therapy. Even the glowingly subversive moral lessons of Dr. Farber came to me under the cloak of therapy.

IN THE EARLY MONTHS with Dr. B, I assumed a new persona. I became hostile and prickly. I sneered at the nautical decor in his new office, especially the coffee table, which was a sheet of glass affixed to an old lobster trap. I took out after his ties, particularly a forest-green one printed with a repeating pattern of tiny mud boots and the legend "L. L. Bean." It's not lost on me, by the way, that the sadistic and grandiose tendency of my behavior toward Dr. B was the mirror image of the masochistic self-abnegation I had shown with Dr. Farber.

I behaved unpleasantly because I was paying to behave any way I pleased, and also because this was my emotionally primitive way of staying loyal to Dr. Farber. I would never have felt free to be so nasty if I had not been supremely confident of Dr. B's regard for me. It was, after all, overdetermined; Dr. B told me that his positive feelings for me were highly useful to our work together, as were my negative ones for him. He explained that he could not will affection for a patient, but if he happened to feel it he made sure to cultivate it for the sake of the therapy.

DR. B KEPT HIS FACE in profile, his eyes lowered and shadowed, but he inclined his large listening ear toward me, and somehow he used that appendage expressively; something about its convoluted nakedness reassured and invited me. He also had a particular gift—how he learned to do this I can't imagine—for conveying, simply by sitting there, a warm satisfaction in the fact of my existence. His body's attitude seemed to say, "You're quite something, all right!"

Dr. B's physical expressiveness sometimes betrayed him; his face colored easily, and I could often see a look of eager anxiety spring into his eyes just as he was about to offer an interpretation. I liked him better silent than talking, because when he spoke he sometimes said the wrong thing, jarring me out of my meditations. His unquestioning acceptance of the tenets of his profession often angered me, and so did the way he turned my challenges back on me by engaging their emotive content rather than their substance.

The only topic I was willing to talk about in more or

less conventional therapeutic terms was my marriage. Here Dr. B acted like an advocate, pushing me to articulate my rancors and to assert what he saw as fundamental rights. He threw into question all my efforts to accommodate my husband's needs—What about *yours?* was his refrain. Of course I enjoyed being the innocent one, the hotly defended one, but I knew that if my husband were the patient he would receive the same treatment—at least, he would if Dr. B had determined this to be in his therapeutic interest. I was dismayed by Dr. B's lack of concern for the complex, nuanced picture of my marriage—indeed, of the whole "life-world" that I was struggling to present. Often I felt as if I had spent the better part of the hour constructing an elaborate imaginary house, trying always to balance a wing of self-justification with one of judicious self-criticism, only to watch Dr. B carelessly kick the thing over in his hunt for the hurt.

Dr. B's advocacy was gratifying, but it unnerved me deeply. To feel rancor was to feel self-pity, and I feared being caught up in its familiar dialectic. The more I struggled against it, the more touchingly valiant I appeared to myself, and the further I felt myself sucked back into a destructive self-cherishing. I learned to hate a certain look on Dr. B's face, a steady wide-eyed gaze qualified by a faint enigmatic smile. I'm waiting patiently, his face said, for you to come off it. To him, my resistance to self-pity was simply a form of denial. To me, resistance was necessary; if I yielded to the seductions of self-pity, my efforts to construct a self would collapse and I would find myself falling back into a kind of watery Boschian hell, a bog where I would rot slowly in a solution of my own tears.

Dr. B and I were talking past one another. When I asked whether my marriage was a good one or not, he understood me to be asking "Is it good for me?" I wanted to know the answer to that question, but I was really after something else, something which I can only phrase, awkwardly, as follows: is my marriage part of "the good"? It should hardly have surprised me that from him I got psychological answers to philosophical questions.

V.

I think of Dr. B as a *tinted* man, an updated and affectively colorized version of the psychoanalytic "gray man." In his office I never endured the silences of Drs. V, H, and G. He was quick to move into relation with me, to offer me a kind of friendship. He was frank about the uses of this relationship: it would serve as a kind of mock-up. Our work together would consist not only of shuffling through my past, but also of examining our own relationship for patterns and tendencies applicable to my outside life. What about his own patterns, I asked. Wouldn't they complicate the matter? I could trust him, he assured me, not to let his own needs intrude, or if that was impossible, to inform me of their presence. This he did, sometimes rather oddly. When I was talking, for example, about having been raped when I lived in New York, he interrupted me and confessed that this story was making him very anxious, and that I should probably discount any reaction he offered.

Dr. B operated under an extraordinary constraint, which was to keep his own humanity out of our relationship unless it served a therapeutic purpose. If that was not possible, if some errant tendril worked loose and struggled past the therapeutic boundary, it was subject to examination and extirpation on the spot. But he was also quite free to stir up my feelings deliberately, to flirt, to manipulate, do any and all of these things as long as they were justified by the realistic expectation that they would serve a therapeutic end.

For my part, I was also severely limited. I was free, of course, to express anything, but the rules of the game did not allow me, like Dr. B, to manipulate without disclosure. I was also obliged to live with the knowledge that what transpired in Dr. B's office, however powerful its emotional charge, was not real. Dr. B was fond of saying that what went on between us was *very* real, but of course the use of the intensifying "very" immediately threw up scare quotes around the "real."

Therapeutic gerrymandering had shaped the territory of our relationship strangely. Between us we had it all covered, but the shared portion was nearly nonexistent. Everything was possible between us—everything, that is, but mutuality. It's not exactly accurate to say that I longed for that crucial element, I was too wary of Dr. B to really miss it much.

What I did feel was an intensification of my growing disgust at myself for having returned to therapy like the proverbial dog to his vomit, and for staying in therapy in spite of that disgust. After all, I knew better! I knew that whatever its ends, therapy was a sad, manipulative parody of authentic relation. But I also knew that in the outside world, therapeutic notions had become so omnipresent and pervasive as to be inescapable.

WHY DID I GO BACK into therapy? I was very unhappy when I sought out Dr. B, but I don't believe that unhappiness was the proximate cause of my return. I think it was more a pervasive social loneliness that herded me back, a sense of panicky disconnection from a central social tradition—a feeling to which young mothers have become particularly susceptible.

I believe I returned to therapy not only because it had been my element for so much of my life, but because it was the place I had seen everybody *else* go. By the time I became Dr. B's patient, therapy had overflowed its professional vessels, flooded the culture, and seeped into the groundwater. However I resisted it, every one of my interactions—as wife, daughter, sister, friend, and especially as mother—was subject to mediation by my own therapeutic notions and those of others. I was like an ex-smoker trapped in an unventilated designated smoking area, inhaling so many secondhand fumes that continued abstaining seemed pointless. I returned to therapy because, in a sense, I was already *in* therapy, but I felt myself to be placed uncomfortably on its periphery rather than securely inside it. I went back into therapy because it had become the central institution, the hearth, of my society.

—

ONCE WHEN I HAD been agonizing about my husband and the difficulty of keeping myself from being swamped by the intensity of his ambition, the vehemence of his anxiety, I ended my catalogue of complaint by saying—But he's a good person. Dr. B leaned forward and whispered, in audible italics, *"You've never said anything different!"* At this I burst into tears of gratitude. I was touched that Dr. B had been keeping track and that he handed me back the raw data in such a generous spirit.

In retrospect it seems to me that this incident marked an end to the struggle between Dr. B and me and the beginning of a real, if very minimal, friendship. Human nature is such, after all, that given time and proximity, mutuality will take root even in the least hospitable of environments.

More and more now—as the leaves turned red and yellow outside Dr. B's windows, as fast-food restaurants and discount outlets sprang up on the outskirts of the small New England city where we all lived, as the snow flew and the years passed and my daughter grew and my husband wrote his books and my hair began to turn gray—I did the talking. I did the interpreting too, in my own terms. My hand was on the tiller and I was yawing wildly all over the lake in my maneuverable little Sailfish, and it was fun. It occurs to me now that perhaps one of my many motives to return to therapy was a desire to try my mettle against it, to seize control of therapy for my own purposes.

My talking was mostly narrative and descriptive; I went on at great length about faces, recounted events in intricate detail. When I spoke analytically or speculatively, I did so in general or philosophical, rather than psychological terms. Sometimes Dr. B's eager-to-interpret look flashed momentarily across his face, but I could usually depend on him to quash the impulse. What I had begun to do, of course, in Dr. B's office, was to write aloud.

In the years since I left Dr. B's office I've begun to write in earnest, and writing has allowed me—as nothing else, even the wisdom of Dr. Farber, ever has or could—to escape the coils of therapy. I don't mean that writing has been therapeutic, though sometimes it has been. The kind of writing I do now is associative and self-exploratory—much like the process of therapy, except that the therapist is absent and I've given up all ambition to get well.

Let me give Dr. B his due. He was more than competent; he was really good at what he did, and got better as he went along. Eventually he became a kind of adept. He learned to vaporize at will like the Cheshire cat, leaving nothing behind but a glow of unconditional positive regard, allowing me a spacious arena in which to perform my dance of self. In resisting his impulse to lure me back into the charted territory of psychoanalytic explanation, he granted me my wish to be released into the wilds of narrative.

VI.

Once, five or six years before I became Dr. B's patient, I left my husband and took the bus from our town in

Vermont to New York City. I moved in with an ex-roommate, found another job at Columbia, and made an appointment with Dr. Farber.

He had given up his office now, and was seeing patients at the apartment. When I arrived, late in the afternoon, he shook my hand cordially and led me through the living room, past the familiar row of big dusty windows overlooking West End Avenue and into the kitchen, where he fixed us both Old Fashioneds. I stood at the counter and watched the assembly process, the slicing of the orange and lemon, which he carefully dotted with drops of bitters and sprinkled with sugar, the "muddling" with the back of a spoon and the pouring of a jigger and a half of good bourbon into each sturdy glass.

We retired to Dr. Farber's study with our drinks in hand. When I asked Dr. Farber for permission to smoke—he had suffered a stroke a few years earlier, and had given up his cigarettes—he encouraged me to do so, and to blow the smoke his way. When I told Dr. Farber of my decision to leave my marriage he nodded gravely and with evident approval—he was no fan of marital strife.

I had a sudden impression that in the five years since I'd last seen him, Dr. Farber had moved into old age. He looked wryer, more elfin, a little in need of a haircut. The essential strength and depth of his spirit were still present, but it seemed to me that he had begun to conserve and protect himself. The Sturm und Drang of my life was only one of many clamorings, I felt sure, from which he had now begun, gently but implacably, to turn away.

When I asked Dr. Farber if he would take me on as a

patient once again he said no. We continued to talk for another half hour, reminiscing about Riggs and my New York days, and the tone of our talk was warm and relaxed. I returned to my husband and my life in Vermont a few days later. I believe, though I'm not entirely sure, that this was the last time I saw Dr. Farber. The news of his death reached me five years later, when I was on sabbatical with my husband in North Carolina and happened upon his obituary in *The New York Times*.

THE LAST TWO YEARS of my therapy with Dr. B were marked by a long wrangle about what he called "the termination process." We had not yet entered this phase, he cautioned, and so the end of therapy could not yet be envisioned. How far away in time was the beginning of the termination phase from the end of therapy? That varied, said Dr. B. How would we know that the process had begun? When the work of therapy had been completed.

But it seemed that under the terms of our therapeutic detente, the work of therapy could never begin, and so, of course, it could never end. I could go on writing aloud, basking in the warmth of Dr. B's unconditional positive regard forever, or until my insurance ran out.

Real life intervened in the form of my husband's second sabbatical leave. Dr. B and I both accepted this as a stalemate-breaker, and the termination process was compressed into a few summer months just before my family's year-long removal to Princeton. During these last sessions Dr. B often interrupted my monologues to introduce the theme of attachment and loss, but the stream of my thought continued to ripple along as it always had, picking up no traces of this effluent.

So it was a surprise to me when at the end of our last session, just as I was about to stand up, Dr. B, who since our initial handshake seven years earlier had never once touched me, rose from his orthopedic rocker and stood before me. In what took me a moment to realize was a clumsy, mistimed attempt at a hug, he grasped my head in his hands and pressed it against his stomach, hard enough so that I could hear the gurgle of his digestion and feel his belt buckle bite into my cheek.

Never have I felt such a congestion of sensations; only in retrospect can I separate and order my reactions—first bewilderment, then a panicky vicarious embarrassment, then a flash of sexual arousal quickly extinguished by my realization that Dr. B's embrace was an awkward eruption of affection and not a pass, then a suffusion of amusement and tenderness. I got to my feet and returned Dr. B's hug, planted a kiss on his cheek, and left the office.

FANTASTIC VOYAGE

—

I.

The preparations for my husband's colonoscopy were more unpleasant and elaborate than we would have thought, but he followed his doctor's printed instructions to the letter. He fasted from lunchtime onward the day before and spent the evening swallowing three and a half liters of a nauseating cherry-flavored solution of mineral salts in eight-ounce increments every ten minutes, sucking on quartered lemons to kill the taste. The explosive purgation began on schedule, and before long what came out was nearly as clear as water. But we saw that a few shreds of what the instructions called "solid matter" still floated in the bowl, and in spite of my assurances that he had done as much as could reasonably be expected, my conscientious husband forced himself to swallow the final half liter. He spent the hour that followed struggling not to vomit. Teeth clenched and shoulders hunched, shivering, he paced the floor of our bedroom while I lay watching late-night comedians on TV.

Neither of us got much sleep, so we were both groggy and irritable as we pulled into the hospital parking lot just before dawn. I had slowed down our departure by taking my time drinking my coffee—he wasn't allowed any— and my husband spent most of the half-hour car trip complaining about that. I countered by pointing out that we were ridiculously early, and would have to sit in the waiting room for at least forty minutes before he was called.

But we were not the first to arrive at the hospital that morning. The lot was nearly full, and as we made our way, squabbling quietly, through the hospital grounds and along a walkway that separated its two pavilions, we saw that we had joined a loose procession. In groups of two and three and four, people were approaching. An obese woman, noticeably lame, wearing khaki pedal pushers and a nautical jersey, pushed a wry-necked adolescent boy in a wheelchair. Two other women brought up the rear: perhaps they were sisters of the wheelchair-pusher, aunts to the boy. Two husky, laughing young men with sketchy goatees supported a frail old woman between them. A pair of elegantly dressed WASPs in late middle age walked together, their long strides matched, their facial expressions neutral. They seemed to be united in an intention to dispose of an unpleasant errand with verve and dispatch. Impossible to tell which of them was the patient, unless you guessed from the magazines in the woman's leather carryall that it was the man, but this would not have been a safe inference. She might have brought them to occupy herself during her own hospitalization, or even carried them for him, to read while he waited for her to undergo some procedure. These two had a long-married look, and it was anyone's guess what arrangements had evolved between them.

The lobby was a big, humming, low-ceilinged rotunda, and everyone in it moved as if according to a preestablished harmony. The light was indirect and timeless, but the day was evidently well advanced: a flight of newly discharged patients in wheelchairs, their belongings bagged in plastic and stashed in their laps, were rolled out to waiting cars while a fast, steady traffic of nurses and orderlies and deliverymen pushing loaded dollies crisscrossed the space diagonally. My husband and I found our way to a desk in a shadowy alcove, where a hospital functionary asked him questions about his insurance coverage. He sat down in a chair across the desk from her, but I chose to stay on my feet, hovering over him a little to assert my proprietary status.

I had been thinking that I envied the lives of the hospital workers—the way their time was caught up and regularized by the rhythms of the institution. How cheerful the nurses and doctors and orderlies seemed as they crossed the lobby in pairs—the small Pakistani walking with the big, raw-faced blonde, both wearing pale blue scrubs and surgical moonboots, both taking swigs from water bottles and smiling brilliantly at some shared joke. To a writer who works alone, and struggles to observe a self-imposed schedule, the prospect seemed attractive. But looking at the middle-aged woman with whom my husband was disputing the amount of his deductible, I revised that judgment. Unlike the free-ranging nurses and orderlies, this person was a fixture, rooted to a desk in front of a jointed, fabric-covered panel that concealed the financial heart of the hospital. The light at her desk was most unflattering; it illuminated her face from below, making powdery floodlit caverns of her nostrils. A hand-shaped shadow reached from the crown of her cap of bleached hair down to her cheekbones, obscuring her eyes.

WE RODE THE ELEVATOR to the third floor, arriving at the endoscopy waiting room. I noticed that the handsome WASP couple were already seated at the far end. The man had put on his bifocals and was reading *The New York Times*. The woman was simply waiting, one spare, exemplary knee crossed over the other.

How old were they, those fast walkers? Early sixties, I guessed. Only one actuarial notch past us—my husband is fifty-eight and I'm fifty-three—but they had a dry, settled dignity the two of us will never achieve. The thought actually left me with a moment's relief, a sense that by failing to be severely handsome, my husband and I had cleverly escaped the common fate. But then, of course, I realized I'd gotten caught up in an aesthetic non sequitur. Whether or not our aging becomes us, we are aging, and will continue to do so.

But even so, I also felt sure that we'll continue to experience ourselves as juicy, not yet dry. At least we'll feel ourselves to have juicy centers. For us, the problem is not so much resistance to the inevitability of aging as it is a sense that we're being slow to catch on to its ways.

But then the fast walkers probably feel juicy too; to

feel juicy is to feel alive. People in their seventies say they feel thirty; they find the sight of themselves in mirrors unrecognizable. This is one of the few observations about the subjective experience of aging I can think of that has become a commonplace; apart from complaints about stiffness and dimming vision and the alarming acceleration of perceived time, there really isn't a lot of lore handed down from the old to middle-aged initiates like my husband and me. Aside, I mean, from upbeat magazine articles about the refusal of the elderly to accept the limitations of aging, their insistence on continuing, or beginning, to sky dive and tap dance and go to medical school—articles that miss the point entirely.

Just the other day, my husband and I had been asking ourselves why nobody had ever pointed out to us that for the aging each step along the continuum is always an advance into unknown territory—that growing old is a matter of constantly encountering the new. Which offers a partial explanation, I suppose, for the rarity of dispatches from the old. Each age cohort—and the time periods they encompass grow shorter as age advances—awaits briefings from the one just ahead, until by turns each goes over the cliff, unenlightened and unable to enlighten.

Youth is full of norms; age is anarchic. Youth is a roundup; age is a dispersal, a proliferation of paths by which everyone reaches the same end. How many of these sessions of brooding about age have ended with a sudden rush of mortification at the almost ungraspable banality of

my thoughts? Time is running out. Death approaches.
Well, duh!

THE WAITING ROOM was huge, the size of a stockyard,
and chilly, and rapidly growing crowded. One roped-off
section was reserved for families with children; a few picture books had been flung into a corner, and a partially
assembled plastic playhouse lay on its side. I counted five
children, but only one was doing anything that could be
described as playing. Three sat huddled on the floor,
watching a closed-circuit TV program about the preven-
tion of osteoporosis. The fourth was a tiny wide-eyed
Mexican toddler who sank into her mother's skirts, sucking two fingers.

I turned to my husband. "How are you doing?" I
asked, and patted his knee. He looked up from the professional journal he was reading and smiled, then shrugged.
"Well as can be expected?" I asked. He smiled and
shrugged again. I knew this response; he was acting like
an adolescent boy with an oversolicitous mother. I also
knew that he found it gratifying to behave this way. What
had just transpired between us was an apology from me
for having been less attentive than I should have been and
an acceptance of that apology from him, along with an
implicit bid for further sympathy. He was nervous, of
course. In his place I would have been even more so—so
much more so that in fact I wouldn't have been there at all.

Nothing scary had precipitated my husband's decision
to undergo what he jokingly called a "fantastic voyage."

There had been no pain, no blood in his stool. He was simply following the screening protocol recommended by the A.M.A. He was sensible enough to be willing to lie down and be put into a stupor—I couldn't rid myself of the image of a drooling anesthetized tiger I once saw on a show about the care of zoo animals—so that the walls of his bowels could be explored by a long probe with a camera on one end while his doctor followed its sinuous progress on a TV monitor.

All morning I had been feeling small spasms of primitive resentment toward him. He's so good, I was thinking, as I've thought many times in the course of our nearly thirty-year-old marriage. As a child he kept a log of every book he took out of the library. All his life he's been disciplined, rational, well-organized, prompt, truthful—most of all, prudent. Once again, I found myself toying with a question that my husband, who happens to be a professional philosopher, has never been able to answer to my satisfaction: why should prudence be counted as a virtue?

He comes from a long line of careful people, my husband does. When an airline lost his mother's suitcase, she was able to produce an inventory of everything she had packed, and the original sales slip for each item. A triumph, said a therapist I once told this story to, of compulsiveness.

My resentment was colored by an admixture of superstitious dread. I could not shake the irrational sense that by subjecting himself to a screening test like this, my husband was tempting fate. And added to my faint resentment and fainter dread was a certain envy. He was the one who had made himself pure and ready, while last night's furtively eaten supper of leftovers rotted invisibly in my own unexamined colon. He was the one who would walk into the waters of anesthesia this morning; he was the one who would emerge on the other side while I remained in this anteroom, fully dressed and conscious, a fugitive from medical justice.

Assured of the health of his lower intestinal tract, he would enjoy a brief respite from his chronic anxiety, or at least a respite from this particular anxiety—a part that for a week or so would stand in for the whole. A temporary palliation, but still an enviable one. And besides, for the rest of the day at least, he'd have a legitimate claim on everyone's attention and solicitude, especially mine.

II.

Keeping up an aggressively cheerful line of sports patter, a wiry black attendant in purple scrubs led us across the hall and through a set of swinging double doors into another long chilly room, this one windowless and lined with rows of cubicles hung on three sides with drapery. It was a space so big and white and undifferentiated that it made me think of a tent city on the Siberian steppes. Or it would have, if it hadn't been for the glimpses I caught in passing of the patients and families through gaps in the curtains—the gleams of pink or brown flesh, the flashes of colored cloth, the quick impressions of recumbent and bending bodies.

The attendant ushered us into our own drapery nook,

which contained a chair and a hospital bed, both on wheels, and monitoring equipment bolted to the wall. "You the designated driver?" he asked me, and handed me a hospital gown. "Get him out of his clothes and into this. He needs to take it all off except his socks. The nurse'll be along in a moment."

I sat down on the chair while my husband removed his shirt, belt, pants, undershirt and underpants, and finally his shoes, handing me each item. I tried to help him into the hospital gown, but he put an arm into the head hole at first, and when he got that right, I snapped it up wrong, so that it hung down too low on one side and I had to unsnap it and start over again. My husband had not eaten for more than twenty hours now. He stiffened and sighed as I fussed over him.

This was an old story between us: in all our years together we have yet to learn how to cooperate when puzzling out a thing like a hospital gown. But I felt particularly stung on this occasion because my husband's shivering nudity made him seem so vulnerable, and I had been feeling so tender toward him. I was just about to tell him to do it himself when the nurse flung open the curtains. "Having a little trouble?" she asked, and smoothly remedied the problem.

The nurse was a woman of action; her movements were whippet quick. In what seemed one continuous motion, she pushed my husband gently onto the bed, popped a thermometer into his mouth, and clapped a blood-pressure cuff around his left arm. She ripped open a foil pouch and pulled out an IV needle; after a brief exploration of the back of his hand, she settled on the crook of his elbow as the site for insertion. I looked away, and as I did so I remembered my own stay in the maternity ward twenty years ago when our daughter was born. Every morning, a technician appeared at my bedside to draw blood. "I love coming to this floor," she told me once. "You new moms have such nice big veins."

When I turned back, the nurse had finished, and was securing the needle with a Band-Aid. "I think he's a little chilly," I ventured. "Don't you want to keep his wallet and keys in your purse?" she replied. "We can't be responsible for items like that." Lying on his back, my husband looked up at the nurse with perfect trust. His eyes were wide, his breathing calm. "Are all those teeth yours?" she asked him, and covered him from his beard to his feet in an insulated blanket. The hands and arms of a second nurse introduced themselves into the cubicle, and my husband slid past me on his high rolling bed. "He'll be an hour or so," said the first nurse, turning back to give me something that looked like a high-tech children's toy. By the time I'd identified it as a pager—exactly the kind of device I'd been handed recently while waiting for tables in restaurants—my husband had been wheeled past the nurses' station into the shadows at the far end of the room. "Goodbye," I called out, and then, inappropriately, "Good luck!"

III.

Where to? The cafeteria was the natural place, and I had had no breakfast, but perhaps I would be out of range of the pager there. Still, I had an hour before I could expect it to go off. But what if I was needed? But why on earth *would* I be needed?

Should I find somebody to ask? I stood, irresolute, in front of the double doors until I realized I was blocking traffic. The attendant in purple scrubs swept by me with another party in tow, strutting and swiveling his shoulders, hamming it up for my benefit as well as for the family he was escorting. I knew this because as he passed me, he winked. The way time was reckoned in the endoscopy service, it seemed I was already an old hand.

I was beginning to be uncomfortably hungry, and I remembered that I had a box of raisins in my purse, but I also remembered a sign on the waiting room door: no food or drink. Could I eat my raisins standing casually by the elevator? Too busy there. I'd feel foolish. Instead, I went into the ladies' room and ate them sitting in a stall. Ten years ago I would have smoked a cigarette in the bathroom at a time like this; now I was furtively stuffing raisins into my mouth. With time, it seems, more and more becomes less and less permissible. When I stood up, the toilet flushed itself.

Back in the waiting room it appeared that every seat was taken. They must set aside a single day each week for endoscopy, I was thinking; how otherwise could they fill a space like this? I took a walk around the perimeter. The room contained, I discovered, four distinct areas, each a square carpeted in a different color, each with its own eye-level aquarium and television. I looked for the fast-walking couple, but they were gone. I looked for the

Mexican mother with the wide-eyed daughter, but she was nowhere to be found.

I was tempted to picture the waiting room as a refugee camp, or a ship's steerage compartment, but that would have been a romanticized vision. There was a lot of humanity in this place, but nobody was dirty or obviously wretched or suffering openly. Actually one person was—a tall, emaciated, unshaven character with a startled-horse expression and metal braces on his legs. He was talking loudly, in Greek, I thought, and groaning. A young woman I took to be his daughter was shushing him gently and patting his hand. Something about her manner made me guess that his agitation was chronic and not specific to this place and time.

Apart from him, the crowd was conspicuously docile, and that made sense. Many of these people were here, I assumed, to be tested for prudential reasons, like my husband. At his desk by the door, the attendant in purple scrubs barked out a name every few minutes, enunciating each syllable with militant precision. From the other end of the room came an occasional softer directive— "Rodriguez family, please come to the nurses' station." This was an efficient operation. Patients walked in, got processed, were rolled out in wheelchairs and decanted into waiting cars, went home.

But what if—I could not help but ask myself—what if, in the course of the explorations of bronchial tubes and esophagi and gastrointestinal tracts that were conducted in the off-limits place where my husband was even now lying on his side under "conscious sedation," something bad was discovered? Better it should be known about: that was the conventional wisdom.

Well yes, if it was a little polyp or discoloration or suspicious spot—something just beginning to make itself known. But what if, in some particular case, a stitch in time had failed to save nine? What if what was discovered during one of these routine procedures was a big fat blossoming out-of-control tumor? What if someone's body had been rude enough to ignore the rules of the screening protocol, which seem to offer a nearly automatic negative result to the patient virtuous enough to observe it? What if, like a drunken party guest who responds to a polite query about his wife with a shocking and unwelcome confession of adultery, this body were to embarrass its host by disclosing a gross pathological secret? What then? Would that throw a spanner into the smoothly functioning works of the endoscopy service?

This question had been swimming around latently in my mind all morning, but no sooner had I brought it fully into consciousness than I witnessed a little scene that answered it. Three official-looking people, one of whom was a doctor—or so I took him to be: he was wearing a white coat and a stethoscope—trooped into the room and surrounded a small Asian woman. It was like an annunciation scene: two of them actually knelt at her feet. Sad news, it seemed, was gently imparted. The woman wept. The committee rose and departed. A nurse led the woman away, presumably to the tent city, where the stricken one lay waiting. The whole thing lasted perhaps forty-five seconds. Now I saw that the functioning of the endoscopy service was no more impeded by the breaking of bad news to a family member than the dinner service at Bennigan's is interrupted when the waiters gather to sing "Happy Birthday to You" to a customer.

I FOUND AN EMPTY seat opposite an aquarium. Two big silver carp were doing rounds; each time they took a corner, rows of scales caught the light and flashed sequentially. A beautiful many-fronded creature like an exploding apricot soufflé hung high in the water. At the bottom of the tank a black bewhiskered scavenger lay absolutely still, its belly submerged in pebbles.

The aquarium was the size of a bathtub, the water inside it clear as the air in the room. I had read somewhere recently that the contemplation of fish is a cost-effective way to lower blood pressure, and it was true that as I watched them I could feel my pulse rate slowing. The fish were tranquilizers for the masses. Perhaps they were meant to represent a parallel, idealized existence. Be like them, the hospital was telling us. They worry not; neither do they think.

BUT WHAT IF the team of three made another entrance, and what if this time it was my feet at which they knelt? (Was it possible that I had invented a meaning to explain that scene? And had the small Asian woman actually wept, or had I imagined it?) What if I was the one led by the nurse back to the place where they were keeping my husband?

He would be coming out of anesthesia, still too groggy to be alarmed. His doctor would be in attendance, and as I entered the curtained-off cubicle, he would turn to me and take my hand in his. His head cocked, a rueful wince wrinkling his forehead, the doctor would look into my eyes, squeeze my hand, and tell me the news. I'm afraid we have a problem, he would say, and while he was explaining his findings and the likelihood that the biopsy would prove positive, and that immediate surgery would be necessary, I would absorb only a fraction of what he was saying. My husband would have propped himself up on his elbows by now. Comprehension would be dawning, and early terror.

Soon enough I would be sitting at my husband's bedside in a real hospital room with solid walls, offering him postoperative sips of apple juice from one of those little foil-topped plastic tubs with flexible straws. I'd settle into a hospital routine, reading aloud to him when he woke, dozing when he slept. I'd roam the halls in search of the elusive nurse. I'd step outside to get myself a sandwich in the cafeteria, call his mother and brothers and colleagues at the university, but only when I made trips home to sleep for a few hours, take a shower and change my clothes, would I register how tired and frightened I was.

I could imagine the consolations that caring for my husband at the hospital would offer me. I would feel a shameful joy at the prospect of relinquishing my writing ambitions in the service of his care. Everyone would marvel at my capacity for self-sacrifice. After thirty years of running behind, I would take the lead in the who's-a-better-person competition, or so it would seem to out-siders. Only I, and my husband, would need to know that to me, certain kinds of self-abnegation come all too easily.

And then, before I was ready, he would be discharged. Clutching a semi-deflated balloon bouquet, he would be waiting in the regulation wheelchair at the patient pickup dock when I brought the car around. When we got home, the house would be dusty and cluttered, unfit for an invalid. He would complain, and for the first time since his diagnosis, irritation would flare up in me. I would find that the mobilizing adrenaline that had transformed me into an angel of forbearance and efficiency in the hospital had run low.

My husband would be waking fully to his fear, and I to my loss—not to the unimaginable loss of him to death, but to the more immediate loss of his companionship. Illness would undo and reveal as incompatible two of the intertwined elements of marriage. In caring for him, in dealing with him instrumentally rather than mutually, I would lose him as my friend—my closest, really my *only* friend. He would become, full-time, the querulous recipi-ent of my care he had been since yesterday, a diminished being, incapable of full reciprocity.

Once, when we were younger, my husband confessed that sometimes he thought about what it would be like to have an affair. He concluded that it would be exciting and fun, but then he remembered that he would not be able to tell me about it, and that realization turned the fantasy desolate. If my husband became ill and I became his care-taker, there would be no "telling about" in that case either.

Our sessions of intimate, freewheeling, playful talk would come to an end. Our fast-walking days would be over.

What had promised to shape up as a gratifying reverie about myself as a caretaking martyr had for some reason changed its nature in midflight and become a grimly plausible imaginative probe of the idea of loss. It was all too real, but then so was the endoscopy waiting room. I found myself wishing I'd been allowed to wait in the tent city, which had somehow become a real tent city in my mind's eye, a wintry settlement under a starry sky where families huddled around central fires on earthen floors.

This waiting room was humane enough, in a minimalist kind of way, but it made no provision for imaginative transcendence. The drama of mortality had been reduced here to a matter of risk reduction. There were no grand prospects, no long perspectives—no sight lines, even. I looked around again and saw rows of anxious compliant patients and their designated drivers.

How could all these people remain so calm in the face of what they were awaiting? How could they allow themselves to be "put under" and be seen in that unguarded condition by strangers who would insert camera-eyed snakes into their orifices in order to learn the secrets of their mortality—all in the name of prudence, and without the compensation of fantasy?

IV.

All through our married life, my husband has played the cautious ant, storing up food against the winter, while I've taken the role of the improvident grasshopper, lounging around in the high grass and playing my fiddle.

The analogy breaks down almost immediately, of course. In the fable, the ant and the grasshopper are not married to each other; the grasshopper has no legitimate claim on the ant's food stores, and the ant is under no obligation to feed the grasshopper. And besides, it's a fable, not a novel. It captures the ant and grasshopper as one-dimensional exemplars, not as complex protagonists. It makes no allowance for the ant's nervous admiration of the grasshopper's style, or the grasshopper's stealthy emulation of the ant.

WHAT HAPPENED TO ALL that time? How is it that next summer we will have been married for thirty years? Once again, I'm stunned into banality.

We spent those years together—very much together, more so than most of the couples we know—but it was two different kinds of time we were spending. My husband's life has been lived according to ant time, by which I mean the careful piling up of day plus day plus day plus day plus day, each one marked by steady, devoted effort.

My husband has held a university affiliation for over thirty-five years, but he's no scholar. In the parlance of the profession, he "does" philosophy. He does it by writing, and he's done that nearly every day of the week since I've known him. Though his pace was sometimes agonizingly slow, he has amassed a large and impressive body of work.

The doggedness of his attack has concealed the spirit of adventure he has brought to it, the daily brinksmanship of a thinker who lives by his wits. A modest, curious, unassuming man, enthralled by intellectual inquiry, he has become an important senior figure in his field. As he's grown older, his work has become steadily bolder, more complex, more original.

My life has been lived according to grasshopper time, marked not by the passage of days but by long, irregularly spaced eras. I've made a mess of time, like a person who wastes wrapping paper by cutting too big or too small a square to fit the present. Usually too big, I suppose: I took twenty years to complete two college degrees, and I drew out the care of my daughter far longer than anybody seemed to think was necessary. I spent thirty years getting ready to write, but only the last ten writing. Like my husband, I've had a success at it, but it's been a thinner one than his and I'm afraid it may already be over, a rise and fall that feels steep only because it has been compressed into one late decade.

But to say I made a mess of time is to concede too much to the ant's way of reckoning it, and thus to disguise the radical difference between my husband and me. To me, time has never been something to make one's life out of, but rather something to travel through.

It seems I was operating under a half-realized imperative; the idea was to submit myself passively to time, and to wait until further notice was somehow given to me. My life has been like the changing views of open fields and woods and urban rooftops that flash by a passenger in a train. Time has never seemed like an accumulated or accumulating thing to me—not until recently, that is, when I've looked back to see that I've left what looks like an undifferentiated heap of it behind me.

HARD TO IMAGINE a union of opposites more extreme than ours, or one with more potential for conflict. In our bitterest fights—they're mostly behind us now, but every time I say so we have a relapse—I accused my husband of living a willfully monotonous, blinkered life in the service of his ambition, of selfishly putting his writing ahead of me and our daughter. He, in turn, accused me of laziness and parasitism, of demanding that he compensate me for the failure of my own life project.

There were years when a conflagration would burst out of a single word: heightened. It became a code for the ant/grasshopper conflict. What do you mean, "heightened"? my husband would demand. What do you mean, you need things to be *heightened*? As he grew frantic in his incomprehension I turned stony in my mysterious knowledge. These scenes ended with shouting and door slamming, or worse.

Once I marched into his study and swept an entire shelf of philosophy journals, arranged by date and title, off the shelf and into a heap on the floor. While my husband stood over me, his hands flung up in helpless horror, his face contorted like a Yiddish actor playing Lear, I fell to my knees and scrambled the pile of journals, deliberately destroying any vestiges of order that might have survived the original act of sabotage.

—

INTERESTINGLY, THOUGH a number of therapists have tried to recruit my husband and me individually, none has been willing to take the two of us on together. I like to think our combined intellectual power intimidated them, but it's more likely that they saw how readily we would unite in the face of a therapeutic intrusion. No doubt they judged us to be hopelessly "enmeshed." There'd be no clean way to separate us; we'd each come away with bloody pieces of the other hanging off. But then I really don't believe that therapy can heal and restore a marriage. I believe time can—lots of time, that is.

For most of my life I've liked to think that I'm a nihilist at heart, one of those people who feel that they can only profit from a new roll of the dice. I've been fascinated by cataclysm, eruption, abrupt reversal, the dire glamour of life-changing diagnoses, the "heightened" life that my husband has always insisted he doesn't understand.

But I think now that I haven't given myself adequate credit. My attraction to nihilism has always had an element of false bluster—what nihilist stays married for thirty years? It was a face-saving distraction, behind which I was slowly preparing myself to write. But it was also a byproduct of my frustrated ardor for meaning, of my impatience with waiting. My mistake was to confuse meaning with the sensation of meaning; meaning itself is not something that can be experienced. It's a slow, impalpable drip and the evidence it leaves of its workings can be assessed only in retrospect.

From within the safety of my marriage I've displayed a swaggering, swashbuckling contempt for caution. My husband has enjoyed and applauded this performance; even though it has amounted to an assault on him, he's found it diverting. I think perhaps he has even drawn strength from it. But recently, since my long, secret apprenticeship has come to an end, I've arrived at a late conversion, I've come to appreciate the impulse of the ant—the desire to protect and maintain, to keep a careful vigil over what one values. The therapists were right: it was a collusion all along.

SO NOW WE FIND ourselves in deep middle age, survivors of our own long, loyal, close, angry marriage. How can I convey the regret I feel at the years we wasted in fighting? And how can I also convey the satisfaction I feel at the strength of the friendship that those years have forged between us? We're like two boxers who've fought so many rounds together that we've decided to forgo the late ones in favor of an extended, exhausted clinch.

Or perhaps it's not the depletion of energy I'm talking about, but its diversion. For the past ten years especially, ever since I've become a practicing writer, we've found a new ease and harmony. Under the terms of our writing truce, we've established a number of treaties and reciprocal agreements. Routine, which was oddly lacking in our marriage for the first twenty years, has become important to our writing life. We talk in the mornings over our coffee, and then adjourn to our respective studies. We read and edit each other's work. My husband has tirelessly encouraged my writing and taken real delight in my successes. I've come to understand the strictures that writing imposes on a writer's life, the need to keep it regular and calm.

And during those years, while we were busy writing, our marriage built itself around us like a house, its walls strong enough to withstand the force of any internal explosion—unassailable, even by me. I wish I had known, twenty-five years ago when we were in the worst of it, how the passage of time can turn a marriage into an edifice, a great house almost indistinguishable from all the other great houses of long marriage. Aging is a dispersal, but one of the works of time is the slow conversion of anomaly into universality; the years are a comb tugging ceaselessly at the knot of singularity.

People tend to conflate time and aging, but they are separate influences, with separate spheres. Aging disintegrates the body, but time is a conservator. As it rubs away at the organic, it reveals meaning and pattern.

Even so, I still don't understand why prudence is a virtue. All I understand is that it's prudent to be prudent. Still, I can't deny that the ant's way makes sense for the years immediately ahead of us, because these will be the years in which almost any change will be a change for the worse.

V.

But now the pager was dancing in my hand, flashing red and green. I made my way out of the endoscopy waiting room, back across the hall and past the elevators, through the swinging doors and down the central corridor of the tent city. Once again I caught glimpses of human color and movement through gaps in the white.

Halfway down the room I sighted the fast-walking couple. It was the woman who was the patient, and I received the sudden, strong impression that she was very ill. I saw it in the yellow, waxen soles of her feet, which seemed to jut out of the cubicle into the passageway, and in the stiff disorder of her long white hair, sprung free of the neat chignon she had been wearing in the waiting room. Dressed in her tweeds she had looked enviably lean, but in the hospital gown she showed herself to be painfully thin, just on the edge of emaciation. Her bed had been raised to a sitting position, but her eyes were half-closed and her head lolled to one side. I was shocked by the way she seemed to have come undone; it was as if a large floppy doll loosely stuffed with rags had been propped up in her place. A nurse stood behind her, adjusting a monitor, while her husband sat calmly at her side, reading aloud to her from *Town & Country*.

But it wasn't only the woman's appearance that conveyed the impression of chronic illness. It was also the curtain left carelessly open, an apparent indifference to the reactions of others suggesting that these two were veterans of a long siege.

Even so, I might have been wrong. My husband has often criticized me for my habit of drawing conclusions on the basis of insufficient evidence. The woman might have been very ill or quite well, just coming to from the anesthesia after a routine screening test. I simply didn't know.

At the nurses' station I handed in my pager and asked to be directed to my husband. A pudgy young woman in flowered scrubs led me back down the corridor, past the fast-walkers' cubicle, where the curtain had been pulled shut. We found my husband lying on his back, his eyes wide open. This was a familiar attitude; many times I've turned over in bed to find him looking just like this, instantly alert after waking, already at work in his mind on the problems of his current writing project.

The nurse closed the curtain behind her and stood leafing through what I took to be my husband's chart. Conscious of her expectations, but also suddenly full of feeling, I leaned down to kiss my husband on his forehead. The nurse discreetly smiled her approval and gestured me toward the chair. "He'll be here a little while, while we monitor him," she said, and I saw that he had been hooked up to a gently beeping machine, and that the waves of his heartbeat were calm and regular. I sat down and took his hand.

This nurse had a sweet dimpled face. A few of her molars were missing on the upper left side. I liked her much better than the hyperefficient nurse who had prepared my husband for the procedure. "He did fine," she said, looking up from the chart. "Nothing in here to worry about." I registered a tiny transient thrill of disappointment. The nurse cranked my husband's bed into a sitting position and continued to page through his chart, jotting down notes.

The nurse put down the chart and left the cubicle. She returned with three tubs of juice, offered one to me and two to my husband. He took the two apples, I the remaining grapefruit. She unhooked my husband from the monitor, and the atmosphere in the cubicle turned quietly festive. I was reminded of the happy half hour my husband and I spent in the recovery room after the birth of our daughter, holding her and marveling while medical personnel bustled peacefully around us. There was the same sense then that the unremarkable was being celebrated; things had gone as they should and usually do; all was well.

While we waited for the doctor to arrive, the nurse told stories about patients who made embarrassing disclosures under the anesthetic, patients who screamed during the procedure and boasted afterward that the whole thing had been absolutely painless. "Did I do anything like that?" my husband asked. Oh no, said the nurse. Not you. You did just fine.

Once again, the nurse excused herself. Left alone, my husband and I listened to the limping rhythms of a chorus of monitor beeps in the cubicles around us. My husband turned on his side and confided to me that he was enjoying lying here with me to keep him company, excused from his labors for a little while by medical directive.

I could see by the slow delight dawning on his face that something interesting was occurring to him. He told me that he retained a hazy memory of seeing the probe on the monitor just as it was introduced. But before that, even before the "conscious sedation" drug had begun to do its work, he remembered being advised by the nurse that while he would experience the procedure, he would remember nothing of it. He found himself, he told me, in the odd position of wondering whether or not to dread what was about to happen to him. How, he had asked himself, could he fear something that he would not remember?

THE DOCTOR, A COMEDIAN, made a flying visit to our tent. He told my husband that everything was normal, though there was some early evidence of the diverticulosis that is almost inevitable with age. The only thing really abnormal about my husband's colon, he told us, was its spectacular length. "A few more feet," he said, spreading his arms wide, "and I would've run out of scope."

My husband got up and put on his clothes as methodically as he had taken them off. Purple Scrubs was waiting outside the curtain with a wheelchair. I took my husband's briefcase, and the three of us rode down the elevator together. While I walked to the parking lot to find the car, getting briefly lost in the process, they waited by the hospital entrance. I pulled up to find the two of them wreathed in smiles and high-fiving one another.

But only when he had opened the car door for my husband would the attendant allow him to get out of the wheelchair; even then he took him by the elbow and solicitously helped him into the front seat. As we drove away, my husband explained that he and the man in purple scrubs had discovered that they were exactly the same age, and that this lively, punctilious, theatrical person who had been shepherding him back and forth all morning had undergone quadruple-bypass surgery just six weeks earlier.

We took the local route home, and that got us embroiled in traffic for half an hour, but even so it was only noon by the time we reached our neighborhood. My husband and I both remarked on how much of the day remained, and how remarkably energetic and alert the procedure had left him. We stopped for lunch at his favorite barbecue stand, and after that he asked me to drop him off at his office, where he would make use of the afternoon by catching up on some work.

BOOK OF DAYS

—

I am a passive woman. I am a gormless woman. My life has been characterized by an extreme and pervasive failure of agency. When I look back at my fifty-four years, I'm appalled at the proportion of my time I've passed lying on couches, smoking, dreaming, sometimes reading.

Disinclined to plan, incapable of self-advancement, I've spent much of my life like a child waiting to be given a gift. My deepest wish has never been to achieve, attain to, or possess any particular object or state; instead it has been to receive something. To tell the truth, I find it hard to believe people when they claim to have a goal. Do they really want to become pharmacists, learn languages, play instruments, start small businesses? Privately, I suspect they're being disingenuous, and what they really want is to be surprised.

I don't mean to complain, as so many feminists have, that I've suppressed my own ambitions in the support of those of others. I know what it is to do that, but gender has never been at the root of my condition. What I'm diagnosing in myself is a syndrome that afflicts the self-involved rather than the self-abnegating. There's a miserable sense of impotence associated with it, and an arrogant exceptionalism. It's a disease of writers and would-be writers. Kafka had it, and Walter Benjamin, and countless others too minor to mention.

My mother, herself a failed writer, passed it on to me when I was very small. She identified me as the literary one among her three children and hoped I might redeem her wishes with my own success. But she was rather passive herself, and too subtle to push. She was a great believer in the magic of talent. "Just you wait," she whispered, and as children tend to do, I took her words literally. What she meant as encouragement I heard as an actual prohibition against taking action. Just you wait, she told me, and so I did, year after year.

As I grew older I learned to use the notion of my special destiny as a hedge against school failure and social rejection. I came to take a certain perverse pride in my own passivity. There was more than a little *sprezzatura* in the idea that, unlike all the strivers around me, I needed only to let time pass until the moment came when I would spring full-blown from my mother's forehead. But as it turned out, she was right. I did become a writer, though a minor and late-blooming one.

I. The Calendar

Just as people have tended to misread my passivity as a failure of self-assertion, so they have sympathetically but wrongly taken me to be gentle. I'm not. I don't mean to say that I'm passive-aggressive—I lack the manipulativeness that is a key element of that syndrome—only that I'm passive *and* aggressive. People tend to see me as shy, pleasant, unassuming, but in truth I'm so full of harsh judgments and barely contained high-handedness that only rigorous self-monitoring allows me to pass for a nice person.

I remember, for example, going to a party at the home of a recently married graduate student in my English M.A. program. I was thirty at the time, several years older than most of my peers, married but not yet a mother, still playing the role of class clown. I watched some of the party from a third-floor landing, looking down on the heads of the congregants as they clustered around the barbecue in the scrubby backyard-driveway, drinking beer and struggling to balance paper plates loaded with grilled chicken and salad.

My husband was then an associate professor at the university where I studied. He was with me at the party, as was our friend Alice, a goofy fellow graduate student. The three of us had taken our bottles of Molson and retreated up the exterior wooden stairs for reasons I don't remember, though I know we were bored, and feeling a little wicked. When we grew tired of looking down at the party we made our way into the apartment and conducted our own unguided tour of its rooms.

Nobody had forbidden us entry, and we found the door open, but the place had a distinctly off-limits feeling. It was furnished in the familiar graduate student style that has remained more or less unchanged for more than forty years—everything minimal, functional, low to the ground. But right away we saw, and smelled, that this apartment was cleaner than the norm. The plants were many and thriving. When we peeked into the small, windowless bedroom, we saw that the bed, or rather the queen-sized box spring and mattress that sat athwart the shining floorboards, was not so much made as elaborately dressed, like an antique doll, in afghans, throw pillows, and a dust ruffle. Next to the bed, on a plain wooden box that served as a nightstand, stood a pyramid of four-sided Lucite photo boxes, showing the couple who shared this bed in various happy attitudes—canoeing and backpacking together, posing hand in hand in front of historic buildings, smiling up at the camera from outdoor café tables. And there were also photographs of extended family—parents, brothers and sisters, small children who might have been nephews and nieces.

Next to the Lucite pyramid sat a lopsided ceramic vase, stuffed tightly with white and purple lilacs, just then in bloom. Marcy, the new wife of my graduate student colleague, herself a graduate student in the psychology department, must have placed it there within the last few hours, because beads of water still hung on the blossoms. The three of us standing in the doorway stared for a moment at this bed-shrine, taking it in, and then, inevitably and simultaneously and partly out of shame, we began to giggle. After a moment we withdrew, still giggling, but reluctant to violate the room's sanctity.

We found the kitchen, and each of us took another beer from the refrigerator. Nothing wrong with that, we reasoned: more of the same was available in large quantities in the cooler downstairs. Still in the grip of hilarity, we cruised the room looking for things to notice, and soon we found an article of interest, a large calendar of the Sierra Club variety, showing a shaft of sunlight slanting down through redwoods. Every square of the current month was filled with Marcy's large round printing. Under Tuesday the seventeenth (I'm reconstructing this, of course) she had written, for example: "Mike's mom's B'day!" and illustrated the notation with a little stylized cake and candles. And under Friday the thirtieth, "Last day to register!" accompanied by a sketch of two tasseled mortarboards.

We gently removed this calendar from the wall, sat down at the kitchen table (which was covered with a blue and white batik tablecloth and set with two yellow straw place mats) and continued our investigations. We found that Marcy had filled every square in the calendar year so far, and illustrated most of them in bright Magic Marker colors. Reminders to Mike to make a dentist appointment, to Marcy to take her turn at the local food co-op, to Mike to bring their two tabbies to the vet for their annual vaccinations, to both Mike and Marcy to celebrate the six-month anniversary of their marriage, upcoming in August: all this and much more was recorded. And on the few dates without reminders or appointment notations, Marcy had filled the squares with short diaristic remarks: "lovely sunset," accompanied by a rosy sun sinking over Lake Champlain, or "climbed Camel's Hump," illustrated by a drawing of two stick figures walking up the side of a stylized mountain.

I'm ashamed to admit that Alice and my husband and I did some minor defacement of Marcy's calendar. All three of us threw ourselves into the desecration with glee, but I was the true instigator. We paged ahead until we found a month with some squares left empty, and while one of us took a turn at the window as lookout, the other two collaborated on parodic entries. I wrote (in pencil) something like "Rotate ears," and my husband, who can draw, contributed an appropriate sketch. I forget what the others wrote, but we were all shrieking with laughter until the ringing of the telephone startled us and we hastily rehung the calendar and fled the apartment. Mike and Marcy must have discovered evidence of our tampering very quickly, because Mike ignored my greeting when I walked past his library carrel the next day. We received no more invitations to their parties, and I never saw their apartment again.

NATURALLY WE FOUND Marcy's bed and calendar ridiculous. She had violated every tenet of cool; her aesthetic sense was at jarring odds with the downbeat funkiness of graduate student life. My husband and I speculated that Mike must sometimes feel a little oppressed by Marcy's take-charge cheeriness, but perhaps we were wrongly attributing our own reaction to him. Marcy came from a boisterously churchgoing midwestern family; she was the first of her many brothers and sisters to aspire to a graduate education. She and Mike were part of a new crop of graduate students no longer in thrall to the sixties. Their cohort was more politically complacent than ours, more frankly careerist, less zealous about keeping up bohemian appearances.

All three of us defacers were snobs, but in my case more than snobbery was at work. Though my reaction was colored by envy of Marcy's obvious happiness, its vehemence was attributable to something more obscure. Marcy's proactive grip on her life called into question my own attitude of fatalistic detachment. Looking around her bright kitchen, at the homemade café curtains and the cascading generations of a glossy spider plant, I thought of my own pale, disorderly kitchen, with its scuffed linoleum and crusty surfaces. I was forced to ask myself a painful question: if she cared so much about her life, how was it that I could care so little about mine?

Marcy was then steering a course through the early days of marriage and graduate school; the next projected life stage would replace two bicycles with one secondhand car, install Mike and Marcy in their careers, and see the births of their children. The years of family life and professional growth would follow, then the launching of the children into college, careers, and families of their own. Then retirement, the deaths of their elderly parents, the births of their grandchildren, the increased vigilance that both Mike and Marcy would prudently bring to bear on their own health, the illnesses that no amount of self-discipline and self-monitoring could prevent, the death of one, the adjustment and continued life of the other. Marcy would anticipate each of these passages. Her calendar notations would function as guideposts, daily chartings of her life's progress, and in later years they could serve as a useful chronology, a means of dating photographs, an aid to memory.

My life plan—if I can be said to have had one—was to continue to stay potential for as long as I could, to keep my future undetermined, my calendar unmarked, to resist for as long as possible the moment when my personality would take its fixed form. One of the rules of this mostly unconscious strategy was to avoid acknowledging any ambition or aspiration. Though I knew that my life was promised to writing, and I had in fact been writing for several years, I was somehow certain that it would be ruinous bad form to throw myself into it unreservedly before I got the signal—which I trusted I'd know when I saw it.

Nor would I allow myself to inhabit my life fully. Instead, I'd stand waiting in the doorway, half in, half out. Unlike Marcy, I would leave no paper trail, the better to leave one later.

II. My Success

Some fifteen years after the Marcy incident, I received the signal. When I think about this moment of recognition, I'm reminded of an old army joke my father used to tell: for months, a soldier was observed by his superiors wandering through the encampment grounds picking up and examining gum wrappers and scraps of paper, muttering "Is that it?" to himself. Eventually, he was judged unfit to serve. As he opened his Section Eight discharge papers, he nodded with satisfaction and remarked, "That's it!"

The signal was embedded in Phillip Lopate's newly published anthology, *The Art of the Personal Essay*. The contents of this book were a revelation to me. I read Orwell's "Such, Such Were the Joys," Natalia Ginzburg's "He and I," Hazlitt's "On the Pleasure of Hating," Lopate's own "Against Joie de Vivre" with delight, as well as with a growing conviction that I had found my genre.

I had known there was something wrong with the stories and novels I had been producing in spurts for decades. (How I managed to write so much without acknowledging my ambition to myself is a continuing mystery.) I was never very good at, or interested in, creating fictional worlds whose parts were set in motion by the force of psychological motivation. I never understood plot. Characterization, though it interested me, put me into a state of panicky agnosticism. I'd never had much confidence in my intuitions about how—as Eudora Welty put it—"some folks would do." It seemed to me that folks might do any number of ways.

I never got the knack of parceling out the voices that made up my internal cacophony among the characters of my fiction; instead I made mouthpieces of my protagonists, allowing them to ruminate at length while living eventlessly, wandering through the halls of universities and the food courts of shopping malls. What I really wanted to do was to examine my experience, to think aloud. Reading Lopate's anthology, I saw that the personal essay was the form that would allow me to do just that. For the essay, the equivalent of plot and characterization was thought. This new kind of vehicle ran on a fuel of which I owned ample reserves—I'd spent my life accumulating them—but whose use I had never understood.

To call oneself a born personal essayist seems implicitly ironic, like calling oneself a born dowager or a born éminence grise. But there are people like that—people like me—who seem to stay latent until a suppressed vocation gene is switched on by the attainment of some appropriate life stage. I remember registering the following thought: now that I've successfully waited out the lived part of my life, my real work can finally begin.

Lopate, in his introduction to the anthology, lists and describes the identifying characteristics of the personal essay: contrariety and irony, the recording of internal dialogues and disputes, humor and intimacy. He characterizes not only the personal essay but also the personal essayist, who tends to be middle-aged, ruminative, observant, disengaged, self-questioning: "Unproblematically self-assured, self-contained, self-satisfied types," Lopate writes, "will not make good essayists." Nobody had ever accused me of being any of these things, I thought when I read this, and if their absence qualifies a person, then personal essayist is the job for me.

And it was. For years, my attempts at fiction had been rejected by literary quarterlies, but my essays were snapped up with an alacrity that startled me. Now that I had been initiated in the uses of retrospection, it seemed to me that I had been right to play my long-odds hunch, right to stay passive and disengaged. Now I could look back on my life as an extended training in the habits of thought that would make me a successful personal essayist.

The intimacy of the essay coaxed me out of my timidity. It granted me the paradoxical authority of self-deprecation. It made use of my passivity. My intellectual bonelessness, cultivated through long hours of reverie, had made my mind pliant enough to shape itself to the essay's free-form architecture, to flow through its irregular passages like a liquid. Encouraged, I wrote more. Three years after my essays first began to appear in literary journals, I published my first (and only) book, a memoir called *Mockingbird Years*. The book was subtitled *A Life In and Out of Therapy*.

III. The Story of the Story of My Life

As many memoirs do, *Mockingbird Years* began as a single essay by the same title, the second essay I wrote after my discovery of the form. It was an account of one of the consequences of an adolescence in which I spent more time in the offices of therapists than I did in the classroom: in lieu of college, my parents and therapist packed me off to spend three years in a genteel psychiatric sanitarium in western Massachusetts. There I had the luck to encounter the remarkable antipsychiatric psychoanalyst Leslie Farber, who rescued me (and two other patients) from Austen Riggs and the life of therapy.

"Mockingbird Years" was first published in a literary journal, and after it was subsequently anthologized, an editor from a New York publishing house called me to suggest that I write up a proposal for a book-length development of the piece. He observed that the essay ended in a way that left me suspended in time—just on the verge of leaving Riggs to follow Dr. Farber to New York. He couldn't help wondering, he said, whether I had deliberately left open the possibility of a longer treatment, one that might bring the story of my life up to the present day.

The editor had a voice like sun-softened caramel. He made it clear that the two of us had something very compelling in common: our interest in me. His voice evoked a feeling I hadn't had in many many years—the sense of submitting, with token resistance, to a stranger's seduction. All the while, as I listened to his flattering persuasions, I felt that my inner skeptic was struggling frantically to scale the smooth walls of his voice, only to slide down inexorably into the pit of honey at its base. Not that I was hesitant to accept his proposal—not for a moment! It was just that I wanted to take enough time about it not to seem unbecomingly eager, and also to extend the pleasure for as long as was decently possible.

Like most seductions, this one ended in abandonment. In the flealike way of his profession, the editor soon jumped to another publisher and lost interest in the project, but his notice had turned me briefly magnetic. An agent took me on. After guiding me through several revisions of the proposal I had hastily written up for the editor, she shopped it around, accompanied by "Mockingbird Years" and two other thematically linked essays.

After six months, she had found no takers. I gave up hope without much struggle and with a certain relief;

from the editor's first phone call, the whole business had seemed unreal and improbable. I consoled myself by rehearsing my very real doubts about the project: Did I want to turn an essay I was proud of into a memoir, a genre I was beginning to consider problematical? And how would I stretch ninety pages to three hundred? But I had been made to understand that no mainstream publisher would be interested in a collection of essays by an unknown like me. Who did I think I was, Cynthia Ozick? My story might be salable; my random thoughts and ruminations were not.

Suddenly, just as I had begun to forget the whole thing, four publishers jumped at the project simultaneously. My agent conducted a phone auction and sold the proposal for a figure that amazed me—not because it was so very much, but because it came to more than all my life earnings put together. A contract was drawn up and signed and I was given a year to write the book. This was one of the calmest, happiest periods of my life. Having a job to do and a limited time to do it in reminded me of my pregnancy twelve years earlier; I felt the same sense of being pulled toward the future. And as I did in pregnancy, I suffered from misgivings so deep I can hardly remember them.

I SUSPECTED THAT there was something a little Faustian about the deal I had made with my publisher, but I found it difficult to fix my attention squarely on my qualms. It seemed slightly ridiculous to berate myself for accepting the terms of the marketplace and turning my essays into a memoir—a bit like putting on airs.

To make a pact with the devil, doesn't one need a motive? And hadn't I always been rather pure in my passivity? I couldn't accuse myself of having done it for the money. I had no interest in money, almost no understanding of it. To me, the advance was a delightful joke, a happy superfluity. I was incapable of taking it as anything but a particularly pretty compliment. I couldn't deny that the whole thing was thrilling, but wasn't I due for a thrill? Perhaps this was what Providence had had in mind all along, to gather up all the gratification I was owed and hand it to me in one big wad.

I got no further than this in my thinking at the time, but now I see that in fact I was harboring two motives that reinforced each other and made me doubly subject to temptation. The first was something more primitive than any articulated ambition—a bottomless, voracious, as yet nonspecific longing. That alone would have been enough to make me susceptible. The second was loftier, but equally vague: my desire to realize my destiny. Was this that? Since destiny is what happens, how could it not be?

I SEE NOW how unconsciously shrewd an idea my memoir was; it was almost as if I harbored an internal self-marketer who rose up in mutiny and overrode the will to passivity that governed my personality. No wonder the proposal brought in a big advance: *Mockingbird Years* was exactly the kind of thing a publisher loves. It was old but new, a novel variation on a familiar theme. It fit neatly into a reliably salable subcategory of the "my story" memoir—the therapy saga—but it was distinguished from others of its kind by a contrarian twist. In my memoir, therapy was not the vehicle of deliverance but the villain: the troubles I brought into my therapies were minor, I argued, but the destructive effects of what I called my "therapeutic education" were not.

I had read very few memoirs of self-discovery at the time I wrote my own, but somehow I had managed to absorb all the conventions of the genre. Perhaps it was enough just to have lived in contemporary society and to have watched TV. But since then I've conducted an informal survey of these books—no doubt the reader has done the same—by skimming some while standing in bookstores, and I can report that nearly every one can be reduced to the following formula, as can my own *Mockingbird Years*:

The protagonist (1) suffers and/or is damaged, often at the hands of parents, but sometimes as the result of an illness or affliction or repressive thought system, and (2) seeks out or encounters a person or institution or vocation or influence that offers escape, healing, relief from, and/or transcendence of the original suffering and/or damage. These persons or institutions or vocations or influences turn out to be false, unreliable, or inefficacious (think of drugs, gurus, false religions, sexual obsessions, bad marriages). (2) is repeated. Each time the protagonist's wish for relief is frustrated, the stakes grow higher: the reader's sympathetic identification grows and the narrative tension increases. Just at the point when the reader's pleasure threatens to become pain, the protagonist (3) stumbles across the finish line. Through the agency of yet another vocation or influence or person or institution, the protagonist at last achieves the relief, escape, or transcendence he has been seeking all along. (In my memoir, therapy was the oppressive force, writing the agent of liberation.) The drive toward narrative closure, which seems to be encrypted in human DNA, is realized in an emotionally satisfying conclusion.

WHEN I THINK of *Mockingbird Years,* I picture it as a crude map depicting the three essays from which it originated as aboriginal landmasses. In my mind, they are connected by a series of narrative bridges, long chains of interlocking "and then, and then, and then(s)." Even though I had adapted the original essays for use in the memoir, I view them as uncontestable territories, pieces of the truth. The narrative bridges, on the other hand, seem to me to be flimsy things, instrumentally constructed, spanning a watery chaos.

I realize that this visual analogy is an idiosyncratic one. Readers of my book generally have no idea that some parts of it are adaptations of preexisting essays and others new construction; as far as I know, nobody but me has even identified the narrative bridging, much less found it to be jerry-built. My map metaphor fails to accommodate the many new analytical passages I wrote for the book. And the mere fact that the embedded essays were written before the memoir gives them no intrinsically privileged status; they were as much my own constructions as the narrative parts—more so, perhaps. To confuse matters further, the original essays themselves incorporate many elements of narrative. I find it hard to account for my settled conviction that they were somehow *truer* than the parts I viewed as narrative bridges.

But even so, I had an uneasy conscience while I was putting the book together. The work went very smoothly; too smoothly, perhaps. More than once I had the disconcerting feeling that some internal gear had failed to engage. But it was easy enough to distract myself from these doubts; as the publication date approached, I found myself caught up in a swirl of anticipatory daydreams.

The book sold indifferently but received a number of visible and highly positive reviews. This was more than I had dared to hope for and enough to turn my head. As is often the case with first books, the reviews dribbled in over a period of many months; just when I had begun to settle down, disappointed but relieved that the excitement seemed to be over, another appeared and I was back on the wheel of craving, satiation, and anomic depression.

I lost my bearings, struggled to write and failed, spent my days checking the fluctuations of my book's Amazon.com ranking number and doing Internet searches on my name. And all this time, fantasies were splattering like bugs against my internal windshield. These were poor specimens, sadly limited in scope. I wouldn't allow myself to imagine winning a Pulitzer; instead, I ran slightly augmented recapitulations of the modest excitements accompanying the book's launch over and over in my mind.

My fantasies were small things, but they came so thick and fast that eventually they no longer seemed like discrete episodes but instead like a continuous condition, a fugue state in which I played host to an ongoing sense of myself as an unlikely heroine, coming into her own at last. It was no coincidence, of course, that the self I represented in the final pages of my memoir was exactly the self of my fantasy—poignant, triumphant, and false. More than once, I moved myself to tears.

IV. The Lie of Memoir

As memoirs go, mine is fairly honest. I take a few liberties here and there with details of decor and landscape, but there are no large-scale inventions, no outright untruths— only a thumb on the scale of emphasis, crucial to my purpose of showing how therapy operated in my life.

Everything that I say happened in my memoir happened, and happened more or less when I said it did: no fact checker could catch me out. But in *Mockingbird Years* I distorted the truth of my life almost beyond recognition—my own recognition, that is. I did so by implicating myself in the tripartite lie of the contemporary memoir. First, I presented what was only one of a multitude of possible autobiographical stories as if it were the story of my life. I did this by following out the suspended narrative line that originated in the essay "Mockingbird Years." Next, I allowed this narrative to influence the selections I made from the nearly infinite set of possibilities—and orderings of possibilities—that my life history afforded me. The result was my "life in therapy." Finally, and most seriously, I wrote from an impossibly posthumous point of view, as if I knew the final truth of my life—as if I were confident that nothing that happened in the future might yet revise it. While I was careful to hedge my bet with irony and a certain tentativeness of tone, I knew in my writer's heart that where I left off, my readers would take over—their passion for narrative closure would finish the job for me. And then they would hoist me onto their shoulders and make much of me, or some of them would. The odd consequence of the lie of my memoir was that my mere, and logically necessary, survival was enough to turn my story into a triumph.

It seems I had assimilated all too well the message I got from agent and editor about the salability of story line—though, typically enough, it was eagerness to please rather than careerist self-interest that made me receptive to their cues. I feel a little ashamed that I was so ready to sell my essayistic birthright for a mess of memoiristic pottage, but I can't deny that my book was better, or at least more readable, for having a story line. A narrative arc is necessary to a memoir of the kind I contracted to write, particularly one that encompasses all or most of a life and brings it up to the present day. It's the length that does it: the brain will submit to the temporary bafflements of an amoebically free-form twenty-page essay, but will balk at the prospect of three hundred pages without a through-line.

The experience of writing *Mockingbird Years* gave me a

new appreciation for "Mockingbird Years." I learned that the memoir and the personal essay are crucially different forms. The memoir tempts the memoirist to grandiose self-representation. The essay, with its essential modesty, discourages the impulse. The memoir tends to deindividuate its protagonist, enlisting him to serve as a slightly larger-than-life representative of the sufferings of a group or community, while the essay calls attention to the quirks and fallibilities we take as marks of our essential separateness. The erratic zigzag of essayistic thinking—the process that E. M. Cioran calls "thinking against oneself"—makes the essay proof against the triumphalism of memoir by slowing the gathering of narrative momentum. The essayist *transects* the past, slicing through it first from one angle, then from another, until—though it can never be captured—some fugitive truth has been definitively cornered.

For two years after *Mockingbird Years* was published, I struggled to disentangle the triumphant narrative self of my memoir from my necessarily nontriumphant real self. I lost touch with my real past, and consequently lost access to the future; I was unable to live and consequently unable to write. Like a character under a fairytale curse, I had no choice but to wait until a sense of the actual past returned to me—until the season of my false triumph had passed and the weeds of authenticity had grown high enough to obscure the orderly garden of memoir.*

The past I longed to retrieve was not just the past

---

* Leslie Farber also describes just such a temporary loss of access to his own history in an essay called "Lying on the Couch."

unmediated by the story of a life in therapy, but the past unmediated by any narrative at all. I wanted to rediscover my history under the aspect of nothing but itself; I wanted to revisit the life I lived before I wrote as if I knew how it had turned out. How did this past look as I turned back to face it? Very much the way the future looked to me as a child: like a great undifferentiated ocean of time. Here and there, events and impressions heaved up to break the surface of the unmapped waters of the past, but I had very little sense of the geography of the region. This was the time I wished I had been more like Marcy, who by then had surely generated enough snapshots, calendars, and mementos to fill a warehouse.

V. Baby Pictures

But I wasn't so unlike her as not to have saved my daughter's baby pictures. Characteristically, I left it to friends and relatives to actually take these photographs. I was inhibited by the obscure fear that if I was the one behind the camera, I'd risk sacrificing the internal for the external perspective—that the image of the baby in the pictures would supersede the one that I carried in my heart. But even so, I hung on to several boxes of these photographs, even arranged some of them in albums—though I never dated them, and had to guess at ages when I tried to order them chronologically. Twenty years later, I page through these books of images as hungrily as an archaeologist examining the artifacts of a lost civilization.

In one of these pictures, my daughter, aged about fifteen months, is standing on the stairs, holding out a disposable diaper as if offering it to the viewer. She looks grubby and sticky, ready for a nap, but her smile is sweetly social. She wears a pair of red denim overalls, and the sight of them brings back the feel of the raised nap of that often washed fabric, and its slightly scorched smell, and that in turn evokes a vivid tactile memory of carrying my sleepy daughter up those same stairs to her crib. I can feel her solidly packed weight resting on my hip and pressing into my ribs as I supported her in the crook of my arm, her dangling sneakered feet bouncing against my thigh, her big domed head lolling against my collarbone. I can smell the residue of baby shampoo in her hair.

I have to acknowledge to myself that I need these photographs; without them I could no longer bring to mind the stages of a face that changed every week. How much more of the lost world of my history might I have been able to reclaim if I had taken more pictures, kept other kinds of records of time as it was passing?

It's not only that the photographs of my daughter help me remember her as she appeared at different ages; they also offer me a foothold in time. Having recovered the red denim overalls, I can also retrieve other details and scenes through association, and thus triangulate my way back into an era of which they have come to be an emblem. Those photographs—or at least a few of them—have become the central nodes of a whole system of recollection.

I remember the provenance of the red denim overalls. They were passed along to me by a friend with a child a few years older than my daughter, part of a shipment of hand-me-downs, freshly laundered and folded and packed into a bulging plastic bag. I remember dragging that bag up the stairs and unpacking it, making one pile of items I thought might fit my daughter, another of clothes I judged to be too small, which I repacked and planned to pass on to the Salvation Army. (They sat in the attic until eight years later, when we moved and I threw them out.)

I spent a pleasant hour or so one summer afternoon sorting through footed pajamas and small pilly sweaters while she napped in her crib. What was I thinking about? As it happens, I remember. I was thinking about the delicate, dark little girl whose clothes these had been and how different she was from my own daughter, who was also rather small, but blond and sturdy, with a big Falstaffian laugh. As I examined each item, I wondered how many wearings it would take to effect a complete transfer of its ownership from Rebecca to Sarah. There was one green velour jersey that carried my friend's daughter's essence so indelibly that I hesitated for a moment before laying it on the pile I planned to keep.

That was in our second house in Burlington, Vermont, a white clapboard one on a rather prim cul-de-sac where I was never quite comfortable. My daughter's nursery was a small, irregularly shaped room on the second floor, tucked beneath the attic stairs. I had never gotten around to replacing its gray and maroon striped wallpaper, which made it feel more like a Victorian servant's bedroom than a child's nursery. I hadn't furnished it with anything more than a crib and a changing table and a braided rug, on which I sat that afternoon sorting clothes. On the rug next to the bag of hand-me-downs lay the book I had been reading to my daughter before she fell asleep, a Mother Goose left open to a page illustrated with a picture of a thatched cottage in a far corner of a snowy field. I remember the text of that particular rhyme by heart:

> Cold and raw the north wind doth blow,
> Bleak in the morning early
> All the hills are covered with snow,
> And winter's now come fairly.

My reverie that afternoon was the kind that often accompanies a repetitive task, a drone state made up of several lines of thought entertained simultaneously by a mind that is active but not quite fully conscious. At the same time that I was contemplating the mysteries of transferability, I was thinking about the word *individual* as biologists use it and dwelling on a larger meaning I saw in these hand-me-downs.

Hovering over this braided rumination was a feeling that never quite left me in those years of early mothering—a sense of happy astonishment that my daughter had been plucked out of the possible and made actual. I enjoyed the chore of sorting through those clothes because I took the passing on of hand-me-downs as a metaphor for the privilege of having been included in the chain of generations. This was a piece of luck I've never quite been able to believe. Even now, it doesn't quite seem real to me that she was that baby and I was that mother. I find it chilling to think that without the aid of the photographic documentation I thought to keep, I might have lost my way back to her.

VI. Triumph and Regret

The narrative of my memoir was a lie, and for some time it made my entire history disappear. As for the larger, looser story I've told myself privately, the one about my passivity and my long, patient wait to hear the saving call of vocation: that accounts for many of the facts of my life, and thus seems closer to the truth. But it, too, was a lie, all the graver for being plausible and comprehensive.

Like every story, it was told after the fact. I had no way of knowing until quite late that I would hear any call at all, and when I did, I seized upon it to justify what was failed in my life. My memory subsequently colluded with this narrative scheme by consigning everything unrelated or potentially antagonistic to it—my studies; my motherhood; my marriage; the pleasures, pains, and struggles of my daily life; the ambition that I could hardly contain, much less conceal from myself; even the writing I did before I pronounced myself a writer—to relative obscurity, so as to dramatize my modest writing success by throwing it into bold relief.

I told myself the passive-waiting story before the fact as well as after. I told it like the precocious memoirist I was, projecting myself imaginatively into the position of a future self looking back on the progress of a past self from an already established endpoint. From very early on I held out the idea of a triumph foretold for myself the way the followers of certain cults promise themselves that the messiah will arrive, and like these believers, I showed a tendency to let things go to hell in the meantime.

MARCY TURNS OUT to have been more prescient than I; she gave her future self an advantage by keeping prospective track of time in the way that seemed to me so pointless as I prowled through her kitchen. In her modest, practical, nonliterary way, she put her mark on the immediate future and so made it accessible to the unforeseeable distant future. I put my own future self under a corresponding disadvantage: my attitude toward the future has made my past an ahistorical wilderness. The only way I seem to be able to reclaim my own experience is to remember it "under the aspect"—under the aspect, that is, of narrative interpretation, which initiates distortions of the past as automatically as a rent in a stocking begins a run.

Even if passivity and long years of waiting were necessary to my becoming a writer, it falsifies my life to say that my passivity and waiting were the precursors of that outcome. What comes later in a life draws its significance from what came earlier, but only in the dead letter of a narrative can what comes earlier draw its significance from what comes later. Life can be read backward, but not forward. My long-odds bet paid off, but even so, my reckless dismissal of so much in my life that did not fit my notion of destiny is something to regret.

Regret. What can I make of this anachronistic sentiment? Regret is the obverse of the triumphalism I've been describing here. Its voice is quiet; in a noisily therapeutic age, all but inaudible. What visited me for the first time in Marcy's kitchen twenty-five years ago was regret—perhaps my earliest experience of it.

That moment of regret was something quite separate from the pang of guilt I felt at my bad behavior. It came to me as a signal—not the one I'd been waiting for, but a signal nonetheless—that Marcy's example might teach me something. Perhaps not for the first time, but certainly for one of the first times, it occurred to me that there was something to be said for planning to make a life instead of planning to make a story of my life.

As I remember Marcy's kitchen, my life at thirty returns, all its choices, dilemmas, and uncertainties spread out before me just as they were then. I had no knowledge then of how my difficult marriage would develop. Whether it would last, or should, was one of my preoccupations. Another was a rankling disappointment at my recent loss of star status in the English department, and a concomitant fading of my interest in hedging my bets by becoming an academic. Another was my attitude toward being a slob; my shame about that had recently taken a turn toward dread.

Yet another element of my "life-world" at thirty was the beginning of my longing to have a baby—a longing that was mixed with fear. To say "the beginning" is to get ahead of myself, of course, but even at the time, I recognized this desire as the leading edge of a development that would ultimately engulf my life. We had studied D. H. Lawrence in a seminar that year, and the moment in *Lady Chatterley's Lover* I found most compelling had nothing to do with fevered couplings and Anglo-Saxon obscenities; it was Connie's nude self-assessment in the mirror, when she wondered about having a baby, and whether she was fit to carry one.

Marcy and I were as yet both childless, but she lived her life in expectation: that was clear from her calendar, and from the evidence of busy nesting I saw around me. What was I regretting as I stood in her kitchen? Almost everything: I regretted the way I had exiled myself from the center of my life, regretted my habit of regarding myself as an observer rather than a participant, regretted the exceptionalism I had used to console myself since childhood. I regretted the habit of fatalism that—even as I was regretting it—disposed me to resign myself to the belief that at thirty it was too late for me to change. Just then, as I stood in Marcy's kitchen, I realized what a drag on my marriage my passivity and disengagement from life must have been. And for the first time I was visited by the thought that my destiny as a writer might not be served by this constellation of attitudes. How many times have I comforted myself with the old saw about how the unexamined life is not worth living? In Marcy's kitchen it occurred to me that in my case the reverse might well be truer: that the unlived life might not be worth examining.

—

BY NOW I'VE reached the age when lives are seen, at least provisionally, to have "turned out." In the years since Mike and Marcy's party I've become the writer I was destined to be. The baby was born and successfully raised; the marriage has survived, and while it continues to be contentious, it thrives. Even so, I find it hard to swallow the blandly unpalatable truth that although my life has been better than I had reason to think it would be, it might have turned out better still—far better—even making allowances for the limitations of my nature.

At fifty-four, there is often nothing to do about regrets but to register them. Still, these sterile regrets have their uses, especially for a personal essayist. Once retrieved, they open up the past by carrying me back to moments when possibility was still alive—moments when I did not yet know how things would turn out. Acknowledged, my regrets can alert me to the consequences of my incorrigible habit of telling stories about my life.

I regret having written *Mockingbird Years*—the memoir, that is, not the essay. Perhaps I should say I regret its dishonesty. It isn't quite candid to say I regret having written it, because if I hadn't, I don't think I would have counted my life a success, and if my life had been the failure it long looked likely to be, the regret would have been intolerable. Regret is painful even so, but it's a privileged kind of pain. Perhaps the truest benefit of my late-in-life success was that it afforded me the luxury of acknowledging what Martin Buber called the "irreversibility of lived time."

It was no sin against literature to write as if the story of my life in therapy had been the story of my life. This kind of representation is a convention every reader has come to understand. Nobody will take me to task for it as a writer. But I think it may have amounted to a sin against myself, or a sin against my life, or—more accurately yet—a sin against the true story of my life, the one I can never tell and never know.

THE PRODIGAL RETURNS

—

When my sister's daughter was married a few years ago, I did everything I could to get out of going to the wedding. First I stalled for several months in responding to the invitation. Then, when my sister called, I invented a previous engagement. She reminded me that I'd received a "save the date" notice early in the summer and pointed out that she and her husband had gone to considerable trouble to make it to my own daughter's wedding the year before. In a final, desperate move, I picked a gratuitous fight, demanding to know why my daughter and her husband hadn't been invited. (I never for a moment believed the omission had been malicious.) Because they'd made a decision not to ask *any* of the cousins of that generation, my sister explained: the groom's family was so large that the guest list had had to be cut. At this point I surrendered, apologized, bought an expensive last-minute plane ticket.

I had a very specific reason for trying to dodge this event. Several years earlier, in 2000, I'd published a memoir that depicted my late parents unflatteringly, and I dreaded the encounter with my father's younger brother,

Les, and my first cousin once removed, Lois. I strongly suspected that they were angry at me, or at least that my uncle was; my cousin I was less sure about. These two had been silent since the book's publication, but that was not a clear indication of their reaction. I'd been out of touch with them anyway. The loose affiliations of my childhood have loosened further over the years, and I've moved to Houston, far from the East Coast, where the remaining members of the extended family I knew as a child— Lois and Les, that is—continue to live. In my adult years I've seen them only at weddings and funerals. My mother's funeral in 1997 had been the most recent of these occasions.

Even so, I like Les and Lois, and I worried about what they thought of what I'd done. In fact, this concern had become a bit of an obsession, one of those occasions for three-in-the-morning rumination, like death or the future of my teeth. Conversely, I was grateful that the memoir has had no bad effect on my relationship with my brother and sister. In fact, it brought us closer, especially in the case of my sister, whom I hardly knew when we were children. We've seen very little of each other as adults, but in recent years we've begun to have long talks on the phone. I suppose I could have asked her just how mad Les and Lois were at me; she has always stayed closer to them than I have. I did make a few inquiries about their doings and states of health, half hoping to open the subject obliquely.

I should interject that it's the paternal Jewish half of my family I'm talking about here, not the Scots/English relatives from my mother's side. My sister's son—the bride's brother—told me at the wedding that he had done Internet research on the history of the family and learned that it originated in Lithuania, where a clutch of Jewish Gordons had been established since medieval times. I had always assumed that Gordon was one of those Ellis Island names, and I think I've had a certain investment in the idea that my genealogy is too tangled and obscure to trace, but now the searchlight of Google had illuminated this great Vilna taproot. Contemplating it, I was visited by a drastically oversimplified vision of Gordons begetting Gordons in an unbroken chain, until, in the fullness of time, my father, Kermit Gordon, was generated, and he was the smartest Gordon of them all. I had to remind myself that of course families can't be reduced to this primitive totem-pole conception. They grow by branching, fulfilling their destinies by becoming more and more unlike themselves.

It's not surprising that I took my father to be the endpoint of Gordon evolution. He won every prize in high school and college, including a Rhodes Scholarship. He was recruited to teach at Williams College, went on to become an economic adviser to Kennedy, and was later named budget director by Johnson. When the Nixon administration came in, he took over as director of the Brookings Institution. My uncle Les has been no slouch either. Until his recent retirement he was always dashing off to places like Nairobi and Karachi for the State Department, and he also taught development economics at Harvard. Like my father, he married a decorative, accomplished non-Jewish girl—she was Beth, a member of the Boston Forbes family—and like my father, he took his aesthetic coloration from his wife. The couples shared a taste for Democratic politics, Danish Modern furnishings, ambitious cooking, and good wines bought cheaply by the case.

These two South Philadelphia boys achieved a lot and traveled an enormous social distance in their lives. Perhaps my grandfather carried all that potentiality coiled inside him, but he died before I was born and I know very little about him except that he sold corsets and bras and that my father disapproved of his gambling and stock-market speculation. My grandmother I did know, and I've always found it hard to believe that she produced two such distinguished sons. She was a very simple woman, clingy and querulous through her long widowhood. Here's a story my father used to tell about her, in dialogue form:

> *My grandmother: Who is that colored fellow,*
>   *Hoagy Carmichael?*
> *My father: Stokely Carmichael, Mother.*
> *My grandmother: Well, I don't like him!*
> *My father: He wouldn't like you either, Mother.*

My Jewish relatives were never religiously observant, but they were inescapably adhesive. Unlike my undemonstrative parents, they were a grabby, expressive bunch. I viewed them with dread and secret gratitude; whenever I disembarked from a train in New York or Philadelphia, I could be sure a delegation would be waiting on the platform, bouncing on their heels and clapping their hands, ready to fall on me with cries and kisses.

I remember staying with my grandmother in her Philadelphia high-rise apartment. I was ten or eleven and hated these obligatory visits, only partly because there was nothing but Louis Sherry sugarless preserves to spread on my toast. My grandmother bored me senseless, crocheting afghans in front of the television, her ankles crossed and her elderly knees spread, complaining about her ailments and making bigoted remarks that offended my puritanical young sensibilities. Every day we'd take the elevator down to the courtyard to find my aunt Esther and aunt Rose, who also lived in the apartment complex. There was a bunch of elderly people who took the sun there in the afternoons, knitting or reading newspapers. Apart from Esther and Rose, who were particularly avid cheek-pinchers, I was never really sure which of these were my relatives and which not. All of them acted the part except for a male mope or two who hung on the periphery. As my grandmother and I approached, the entire group would struggle up from their plastic chairs and throw out their arms, crying "Emmy!" as if I were the Messiah come to earth.

I've been thinking lately about those moments of extravagant welcome, and the complicated sensations they brought out in me. At this age I was at my most pitiable—obese, friendless, failing in school. I knew this was the reason they made a mortifying fuss over me. And yet I craved it; it's quite possible to absorb emotional nourishment even as you refuse it.

This nourishment didn't so much do me good as bring me along, push me toward becoming myself. My relatives' demonstrative warmth was a poultice that pulled to the surface of my consciousness all that was most miserable and most evolved in me. Walking across that courtyard I could see the scene, just as the near dead are said to do, from an aerial angle. I saw my fat young self, head hanging and shoulders hunched, being led like a heifer toward a sacrificial altar. I felt acutely ashamed, but also, paradoxically, thrilled at being able to see myself and my situation from a radically distanced perspective. At this age I was beginning to understand that for me the way out was the way up, into detachment. On the train home I celebrated by walking to the dining car by myself and ordering a pot of hot chocolate.

THE MEMOIR I WAS AFRAID had angered my relatives is called *Mockingbird Years: A Life In and Out of Therapy*. In that subtitle I found my first line of defense against any charges they might level against me. For years I'd been explaining to an imaginary Uncle Les and Cousin Lois (whom I pictured as hovering behind him, looking less angry than anxious) that the book is only *incidentally* about my parents. Its real subject is an examination of a life in psychotherapy, and in order to conduct that examination, it was necessary to tell the story of my childhood. Anything negative I revealed about my parents in the process falls under the heading of collateral damage.

Well, was it worth it? This would be the natural countermove, and I could easily picture my uncle making it. He has always been feisty, less frontally aggressive than my father, but a bit of a waggish provocateur. (One summer, visiting us in Williamstown, he dove to the bottom of the pool at the local Carmelite Fathers' monastery and wrote "Martin Luther" in the muck with his finger.) Yes, I'd have to say. I think it *was*. And worth it not only because of the light it sheds on psychotherapy, but also because I believe my memoir is art, and that art has certain prerogatives. (As I sketch this scene in my imagination, I can even now feel a flush of self-assertion rise to my cheeks.)

But how to support this claim? By quoting reviews? I could all too easily imagine the skeptical expression on Les's face. No, I wouldn't let myself get backed into that corner. Instead, I'd put the onus on my uncle to explain why I owed my parents a debt of loyalty. I'd steer clear of any claim that they were abusive, because they weren't (though one of those therapists who were my real target in the memoir insisted that my father was), and simply ask Les to admit that my father himself was never much for filial piety. Growing up, it was perfectly clear to me that he considered his own parents a hindrance, even an embarrassment. They were to be left behind, like a booster rocket designed to fall away once the shuttle is launched. He never had much use for them, except as a trove of dinner party anecdotes. For that matter, he never had much use for his own children! Considering the example of loyalty he'd shown me, how could I be expected . . . ?

But this was exactly the nonsense my daughter used to give me at age thirteen, when she shouted "I learned that from *you*, Mom!" and stormed out of the room. Sitting in the plane on the way to the wedding, I acknowledged to myself that none of the arguments I'd been wargaming would do. It wasn't that they were false, just that they could never be true enough to redeem the self-justifying defensiveness that motivated them. There was no way to prepare myself for the encounter with Les and Lois: I'd just have to play it by ear.

I ALWAYS ENJOY staying in hotel rooms, or at least I always think I'm going to. I maintain a fantasy, a vaporous one that dissolves into shreds of nonsense when examined, about how I'll feel free in them. To do what isn't clear, though it isn't watching porn or drinking myself into a stupor or plucking chickens as the young Fidel Castro was said to do in hotel rooms, or leaving the carpet littered with ground-out cigarette butts and bloody tampons as Robert Lowell's "dolphin," Caroline Blackwood, actually did. What I want to do, if it can be described at all, is to *sprawl*, not only on the bed but some-how all over the room, as if in the privacy of a hotel room I might relax so utterly that as I lay drowsing, my legs and arms would stretch and drape themselves floppily over the TV, the dresser, the armchair, even the small table where the chamber of commerce brochures are displayed.

But when I'd closed the door of this actual hotel room in the Brunswick, Maine, Days Inn, I was seized, as always, with an almost pathological self-consciousness. The smoke alarm might have been fitted with a miniature camera for all the freedom I felt. Instead of sprawling, or whatever it was I'd had in mind, I walked across the room, jerked open the heavy drapes, and looked out on the darkened parking lot, subvocalizing the words "It's still raining!" (It would continue to do so, Noahically, for the next three days.) Then I stiffly unpacked, just as my husband always insists we do right away when we stay in hotels together, discovering that in my haste I'd packed two tops instead of the top and skirt I'd planned to wear to the wedding. When I put away the items in my toilet kit, I found that while I'd remembered to bring my fully charged electric toothbrush and my dental floss and my traveling Proxabrush and the mouthguard I wear at night, I'd forgotten to pack toothpaste.

That evening I cruised around rainy downtown Brunswick in my rental car, looking for a store I might nip into the following morning to buy a replacement skirt, a pharmacy where I could get a tube of toothpaste, and a restaurant. I found only the restaurant, a storefront surf 'n' turf place I felt sure nobody in my family would think of patronizing. Having grown up in a college town, I know how to recognize a townie establishment, and sure enough, this place was full of hearty table-hopping townies, all the more identifiable because so many of them wore Bowdoin sweatshirts.

This restaurant was the culinary equivalent of a hotel room, an anonymous place where I could order whatever I wanted without penalty, or at least without drawing attention. A lobster was the natural choice, but too much trouble to disassemble. What I wanted was a steak—the townies were eating big ones, I'd noticed—but at the last minute I found myself ordering broiled scallops. This automatic prudence overrides nearly all my impulses now. Most of my life I've been self-indulgent and undisciplined, but in middle age I've fallen under the sway of a not quite fully integrated second personality, a manipulative nanny-self who snatches away the cigarette or the rich dessert before I can form an intention to reach for it. (She makes an exception for alcohol: I'm allowed to drink, but only a little too much.) When the scallops arrived resting in a quarter inch of melted butter, I conducted an internal debate about whether to drain it off into my saucer or to leave it, assuming that the scallops had already absorbed most of what I'd end up consuming anyway.

I was up early the next morning, standing over the four-slot toaster in the hotel's noisy, overheated mint-green breakfast room. Three well-scrubbed but obstreperous children were shouting and scampering around the tables while their parents drank coffee and stared glumly at CNN, which flickered mutely on a wide screen mounted on the far wall. I was assessing the feasibility of carrying an English muffin, a tub of yogurt, a banana, and a cup of coffee back to my room—I could just manage it if I balanced the flimsy paper plate on top of the foam coffee cup and tucked the banana under my arm—and at the same time struggling to eavesdrop on a conversation between three bulky, bearded men at a table just behind me. One of them spoke in a heavy Eastern European accent; the others seemed to defer to him. I heard a few references to galleys and reviews and wondered if they were here for a conference at Bowdoin. Was the one with the accent somebody famous? I stole a quick look, but he had turned away.

Then I heard Les's unmistakable voice—like my father's, but lighter and more plangent—and Lois's distinctive soprano laugh. More accurately, I brought it to consciousness that I'd been hearing that voice and that laugh for a while now, if only as faint threads in a fabric of echoing noise. I turned, and sure enough, there they were, at a table by the door. For some reason I'd assumed they'd be staying at my sister's house, or at another hotel. Lois's husband, Harold, was with them. If I'd been looking at these three with new eyes I would have characterized them as young-elderly and pleasantly unassuming, with an air of highly educated prosperity. They looked like what they are: Harold is a professor of physics at NYU; Les is professor emeritus of economics at Harvard. Lois is a flutist, formerly of the New York Symphony. I must have passed them coming in, and I'd have to pass them again going out. My muffin popped up, and I extracted it from the toaster with fumbling fingers.

I looked again and saw there was no way to avoid an encounter; so I simply turned and faced them. Let them acknowledge me, I thought. Let them take pity on me, trapped as I am. For quite a while I stood there, people edging around me to get at the juice dispenser. Not that anyone seemed to mind; many a family drama is played out these days in hotel breakfast rooms, I'm sure. Harold's back was turned toward me and Les was seated in profile. Lois was facing me directly, talking animatedly. Was she deliberately ignoring me? Was it as bad as that? I was staring now, beseeching. Lois looked up; her gaze caught; her eyes widened. She clapped a hand over her mouth and rose slowly from her chair. "Emmy!" she cried, flinging out her arms. Harold stood next, smiling cordially. Les got to his feet deliberately, like a man called up to a dais to make prepared remarks. Oh yes. He had a grievance all right; I could see it. He followed Lois a little haltingly as she crossed the room to embrace me.

BY TEN O'CLOCK IT was decided that the best way to spend a rainy few hours before lunch was to drive around Brunswick and its environs in Les's Volvo, with an eye toward locating the church where the wedding would take place. Harold sat in front, navigating, as Les took curves with a bit too much verve, I thought, for the slick conditions of the road. I sat in back with Lois, glancing at Les from time to time, trying unsuccessfully to read his attitude from what I could see of the back of his head and occasional glances at his profile. He'd taken to wearing a hearing aid, I noticed, but he'd lost nothing of his lively alertness. We hadn't yet spoken, beyond the mumbled pleasantries that accompanied our obligatory hug in the breakfast room, but this proximity itself could be interpreted as progress. At least, it could be viewed as a portent of progress, in the way that photographs of dignitaries seated in twin armchairs are offered as evidence of a thaw in formerly hostile relations.

Lois patted my hand reassuringly, asked me questions about my husband and daughter and my writing, though on this topic I noticed that she seemed to proceed rather gingerly, or perhaps that was me. How young they all seem, I was thinking. Les and Harold both looked wonderfully vigorous, especially Harold, who had turned handsome and distinguished in his seventies. But Lois was really uncanny. She has become chic in recent years, but in every other way she was exactly as I've always remembered her, still ebullient, still full of disarming non sequiturs, still intensely but weightlessly warm, as if she'd learned the knack of detaching concern from the earlier generation's intrusiveness. She was as girlish at seventy-eight as she'd been forty-five years ago as a bride.

I was thirteen when she and Harold were married. My family had moved from Williamstown to New York City some months earlier, and I'd made a habit of spending evenings and weekends in the apartment of Lois's mother, my great-aunt Helen, being overfed and made much of. Lois's wedding was held in that same small apartment, and I can recall the middle-aged seraglio scene in the cramped bedroom just before the ceremony began, where ten or twelve female relatives were dressing Lois and themselves. They were in a frantic, hissing hurry and immodest by my childish standards; the sight of their washboard thighs and broad speckled backs shocked me a little. I watched from a corner as they wrestled Lois into her dress. Just before we all filed out into the L-shaped living room, where the rabbi waited in front of an improvised chuppa, Lois's mother backed her against a wall, clamped an immobilizing hand on her forehead, and applied lipstick to her mouth with a steady, rough hand. Lois took it with sweet forbearance, standing very straight and still and casting her eyes upward, enduring her tribulation by reminding herself of the reward that awaited her.

My memories of Lois's wedding are provisional. Was her dress long or short? Short, I think. Did she wear a veil? I'm not sure, but I seem to remember a hair ornament of some kind—a gesture toward a veil. The only detail I'm absolutely sure of is the focal point of the entire recollection, the small round Band-Aid on Lois's bare upper arm. I can still bring to mind that dot of mannequin beige standing out against her olive skin, and my oddly outraged reaction to it. How, I asked myself, on this of all days, could she have manifested a sore or a pimple or whatever it was that needed to be concealed? Better to cancel the wedding than to let this lesion compromise its perfection! I saw it as a symbolic representation of whatever it was about Lois that licensed the rough handling she'd gotten from her female relatives. That, apparently, was the way my mind worked at age thirteen.

But I should give my younger self more credit. At the bottom of my squeamish fascination with that Band-Aid was a fugitive insight into the anxieties of an earlier generation—their fears of spinsterhood and penury—and into the volcanic family dynamics from which my great-aunts and uncles derived the warmth that sustained and embarrassed me. When I think of Lois's wedding now I read back into it my adult appreciation of the young woman she was then, lively, talented, appealingly plain, hectored by her devoted mother. I see that Band-Aid as an emblem of her vulnerability and charm, not a mark of disgrace. But at thirteen I had no use for Lois; I dismissed her as a musical goody-goody. It was her brother Dick, an incipiently psychotic hipster still living in the apartment, whom I found interesting. He'd given me a book of Oscar Wilde's epigrams for my birthday and allowed me to tag along with him to the Five Spot in the Village, where I drank a Whiskey Sour, which I later threw on the subway. Dick and I shared a bond, I believed. We both stood outside our families, defiant and misunderstood. I had that all wrong, of course; Dick was trapped for life inside his family, and my own newly adopted attitude of rebellious bluster was only a cover for my suspicion that I was being ejected from mine.

As I sat in the back of the Volvo with Lois, I found that I was replying to her questions a little more elaborately than was necessary, and louder too, to make myself audible to the hearing-aid wearer in the front seat. I was going on about my writing habits and the literary quarterlies where my work is published—or buried, I added, hoping that a little self-deprecation would take the grossness out of my boasts. In the company of Les and Lois I felt like a child—a new child who after a span of years that could comprise four or five back-to-back childhoods had finally become somebody my meritocratic family could accept. I'd had a book reviewed in *The New York Times,* hadn't I?

Except it was very late. I was fifty-seven and my parents were dead, and it wasn't a history of the Balkans or a grand historical novel that had been reviewed in *The Times,* but a memoir in which I'd publicly exposed my mother's alcoholic abdication from motherhood and my father's blinkered ambition. And yes, another thing: I somehow kept forgetting that *Mockingbird Years* wasn't the end of it. I'd written a second memoir as well, this one about my childhood. It was even more unkind to the memory of my parents than the first, and it was due to be published in a few months.

At some point in our seemingly pointless loopings around Brunswick we passed the small rural church where the present-day wedding would take place later that afternoon. Somebody—I forget who—brought up the delicate question of the bridegroom's religious affiliation. None of us had met him. We knew only that he is a musician like my niece and that he is Syrian by birth. None of us knew whether his family was Christian or Muslim, and whether, in the latter case, there might be some tension about the bride's partially Jewish origins (or as Harold observed, perhaps even her partially Christian origins). We all sat in silence for a few miles. Suddenly, in a burst of clarity, it came to me that there could be no problem. "Of course not," I said. "They wouldn't be married in a church." Everyone laughed. After a long considering moment Les muttered, "Good observation." How like my father he can sound sometimes!

We returned to the hotel to find that a chamber music group composed of colleagues of the bride and groom was rehearsing in the lobby. Guests and hotel staff stood around listening with that air of enforced reverence people bring to spontaneous performances of serious music. Under cover of a spatter of applause I eased my way past the musicians to the elevator. I wanted to get back to my room—making a stop, first, at the vending machine for a package of peanut butter crackers—to stare at the stucco ceiling for an hour or so, ruminating about the events of the morning, before it was time to get dressed for the wedding.

THE RAIN CONTINUED, and guests dashed from their cars into the packed, humid church, the interior of which was so plain as to seem deconsecrated. Once again, I found myself seated with Les and Lois and Harold. Lois had wrapped her new suede ankle boots in blue plastic *New York Times* wrappers, held up by rubber bands. My brother, Andy, arrived and joined us. We'd been peas in a pod as children and though we see each other rarely, we remain wordlessly close. I was very happy to see him and during the ceremony I felt quite free to prompt him to stand or sit by elbowing him in the ribs, just as I would have when we were children. Even so, I kept glancing at his beard, once red and now yellow-gray, and the progress his balding had made in the last two years.

My sister appeared, on the arm of her husband. She was smiling tremulously, holding her head high and fixing her eyes on the middle distance. The chamber music group played something difficult and contemporary, full of plucked strings. The officiating minister, a Unitarian, took his place at the pulpit. (Les leaned over and whispered "There's the imam, Emmy!") The bride's attendants walked down the aisle, followed by the bride on the arm of her father, my sister's first husband. She wore an oddly beautiful dress, off-white with a crocheted overlay, which I later learned she had found in a thrift shop. I have the impression she carried daisies. What I found striking about the sight of her was not that she looked lovely, though she did, but that by wearing her hair swept back in that unfamiliar way she had declared full genetic allegiance to her father's side of the family: those cheekbones owe nothing to ours. The groom's elderly father, a retired physician, made his way to the front of the church and spoke haltingly and feelingly about fidelity in marriage.

The groom was tall, stooped, shaven-headed; he looked down at his bride with a gently proprietary air. The couple had written their own vows and I'm sorry to report that the groom's sister read a passage from *The Prophet,* by Kahlil Gibran. My sister and her ex-husband used the same verse—the one about filling, but not sharing, one another's cups—when they were married in the sixties. I asked myself: has no progress been made in the last forty years? How I wished that my husband were there, so that we could exchange glances. I suppose, though, that to some extent the choice of text was mitigated and explained by the groom's family's Syrian heritage.

My brother and I were early arrivals at the reception. We equipped ourselves with a beer for Andy and the first of several glasses of white wine for me—I'm a swiller, not a savoring oenophile like my father—and wandered through the empty, expectant rooms of my sister's house, where the newly polished floors shone like a system of waterways, and floral arrangements stood like welcoming sentinels. Once again I felt like a child, but now I had another child for company. We were too timid to disarrange pristine platters of crudités or to speak in anything but whispers, but we giggled and nudged each other as we took our self-guided tour. Coming around a corner, we nearly collided with a pair of elderly relatives of the groom. We all four threw ourselves into mutely frenetic apologies, like Japanese tourists in a sitcom.

Soon the rooms began to fill and the afternoon began to flow. I went back to the bar and got a second glass of wine, losing Andy in the process. I spoke briefly to my nephew, the bride's brother, and his wife, and was introduced to the wife's parents, there from London, but the rest of my own relatives had apparently migrated to another part of the house. For some reason—perhaps the same one that had led me to seek out a townie restaurant the night before—I made no effort to find them. Some reckoning was in the offing, I felt sure, but for reasons I couldn't have articulated even to myself, it seemed crucial that I do nothing to bring it on prematurely.

A cousin of the groom, a young lawyer, approached me in an ambassadorial spirit and launched into a history of the groom's family. They were Coptic Christians, he explained. The parents had lived in New York for many years but retained a house in Damascus. They returned rarely now; jihadists had taken to planting bombs at the bus stop where children waited to be transported to the Christian school. The groom's father had been Assad Junior's professor in medical school and like ours, the family was an accomplished one. The bridegroom's siblings were doctors, lawyers, artists, executive chefs. I tried hard to fix these points of information in my memory for the benefit of Les and Harold and Lois.

As often happens at parties, my experience of time became jerkily intermittent, as if I were moving under a flickering strobe light. My conversation with the groom's cousin having somehow concluded, I found myself at an hors d'oeuvres station, assembling a precarious tower of cheese-smeared rice crackers on a tiny plate and then, having apparently eaten or disposed of them, I was suddenly in the middle of a much smaller room full of young people, packed in on all sides by jabbering strangers but starkly and painfully alone. Then I was standing against a wall in yet another room, talking to three of my sister's friends, all of whom had read my memoir at her suggestion. They were praising the book, asking flattering questions—exactly what I'm always angling for, except that I hated it, and at that moment realized that to one degree or another I'd always hated it. I tried to respond appropriately, but my attempts at grateful murmurs sounded ingratiating and false. I excused myself, found the bathroom, closed the door behind me, stared into my own pouchy, imploring eyes in the mirror. I asked myself: What *do* I enjoy? Not staying in hotels, apparently. Not gluttony, not parties, not flattery, not multiple glasses of white wine. What I seem to want to do—"enjoy" is the wrong word here—is not to have experiences but to think and tell about them. I'm always looking for excuses to avoid sitting down at my desk to write, but I "enjoy" my life only to the extent that even as I'm living it, I'm also writing it in my mind.

THE WEDDING TENT, where dinner was served, was like the interior of a great peach-colored lantern, mottled with trembling leaf-shaped shadows. After my wanderings in the diaspora of the reception, I was seated, once again, with Les and Lois and Harold and my brother. Just as the evening's program was about to begin, the power went out, to a chorus of gasps, and was quickly restored, to raucous applause.

The bride's father, who twenty-five years ago had managed to unite my deracinated, disaffiliated family in angry condemnation by leaving my sister, came to the microphone and gave a long, fluent, entertainingly digressive toast. He looks the part of a villain, with his attractively goatish face and Vandyke beard. His second marriage is apparently successful, as is his professional life. How the wicked prosper! My sister stood up next and was almost too overwhelmed with joy and pride to speak. Her face—the family face, which she and my brother and I all share, the more so as we age—spoke for her, and everyone applauded her warmly. I'd put away two glasses of champagne now, on top of the wine I'd drunk at the reception, and on some perverse impulse I got up and walked over to my ex-brother-in-law's table. I'd hardly spoken to him since the divorce, but now I put a hand on his shoulder, leaned down and murmured, "I'd forgotten what a good raconteur you are." He caught my hand and squeezed it, and for a moment we understood each other.

The lights in the tent flickered repeatedly. Just after coffee and dessert were served, my brother said goodbye and set off on a long wet return journey to western Massachusetts. Then the bridegroom and a group of his male relatives took the stage with oud and tabla and other Middle Eastern instruments I couldn't identify. Two thirds of the wedding party instantly rose and formed a long, snaking dance line. The ceremony and the reception had belonged to the bride's family; now it was the groom's family's turn. They lifted their hands above their heads, clapped, and shouted; the women ululated. Some months later my sister sent me a snapshot of myself, rising from my own chair at just this moment, stirred, but hesitant to join the dancing. (How young I look in this picture, the lines and shadows in my face erased by the flash.) It was startled delight at the joyful strangeness of the music that brought me to my feet, and also an obscure sensation of alarm. For just a moment I understood the world in the novel and anachronistic terms of blood. I had a quickly passing vision of the groom's people as a tide of it, swamping and sweeping away the bits and pieces that were left of my family—the Jewish side, I mean. We've been dissolving rapidly over the last several generations anyway, I know. I myself am an agent and a product of this process. But now, as I watched the dancing at my niece's wedding, it seemed to me I'd had a glimpse of the final dilution.

Les and I had our talk before the evening ended. He made the first move."Your next book!" he shouted in my ear. "Will it upset me like the first one?" (And how did he know about the second book, I asked myself.) "Oh, no!" I shouted back into his hearing aid. This was a flat lie, but for the moment I believed it. An inauspicious start to an unsatisfactory conversation: we were both tired, the acoustics were terrible, and I'd had considerably more to drink than the little bit too much I allow myself. Still I think we might have done better.

What really bothered Les about *Mockingbird Years,* he went on to tell me, was that I failed to give my father's remarkable career enough consideration. *That's all?* I thought. A softball, and a badly aimed one at that. He'd let me off too easy. Confused and sheepishly relieved, I took the conversation on a tangent of my own, yawing off into a comparison of my mother to Les's late wife, Beth, who died in the seventies. In spite of all her problems, I was saying, Beth was a mensch, while my own mother was essentially a cold woman. In my own ears, this sounded like the kind of belligerently sentimental talk I've overheard in bars, and it didn't help that I had to bellow to be heard over the tabla and the oud. To my surprise and faint dismay, Les was nodding and listening intently, as if by talking in this falsely tough and presumptuously intimate way, I'd finally won him over.

Back in Houston, I sent Les a carefully composed

email. I started by apologizing for my failure to get in touch with him several years earlier, when his second wife died of ALS. I mentioned that Lois had told me how he took care of her during her last two years, and that, like Lois, I greatly admired his unselfish devotion. Then I went on to the matter of the memoir. I wrote: "I know I did some damage to the fabric of things, and I can't hope to restore it completely, but even so I'm happy to be back in touch."

"You are right," he replied. "Our contact does not completely allay my feelings toward you, but it goes a long way."

Since then, of course, the second book has been published. I haven't heard from Les, but I know in my bones that he has read it, or at least examined it. He keeps up with reviews. The "fabric of things" that the first memoir damaged has been torn by the second and any progress I made on that rainy day in Maine has been undone.

IT MADE SENSE to me that Les put aside everything to take care of his dying wife. I can think of other examples of his kindness: when my sister's first husband left her, for example, Les hovered solicitously, invited her to dinner, and kept in touch by phone. In spite of his air of wry skepticism, he is a man of attachments—to the older brother he emulated, to his children, to his two dead wives, to the members of his wider family. I've asked myself why he pulled his punches during our talk after the wedding. Certainly his native kindness had something

to do with it, and also—I'll speculate—cognitive dissonance. Family loyalty comes naturally to Les, but this
impulse conflicts with his training as a good liberal and an
enlightened academic. Filial piety is an antique notion,
backward-looking and dangerously vestigial, especially
suspect when it comes into conflict with anyone's claims to
the making of art. Unable to honor his own visceral
expectation of loyalty, he fell back on an appeal to the
value that came first to my father: merit. Never mind that
a judicious appreciation of my father's career would seem
almost comically out of place in a memoir like *Mockingbird
Years*. (And where would I put it? In an appendix? A long
footnote keyed to the first appearance of the words "my
father"?)

NO DOUBT LES'S INTERNAL conflict left him feeling frustrated. I felt that frustration too, having come to our talk
braced for a confrontation. My talking points, which I'd
devised as responses to direct hits, were rendered useless.
Not that I'd ever really wanted them to succeed—how
could I, when my deeper wishes all opposed them? I'd
traveled to Maine dreading the judgment I expected to
receive, but longing for it. I was looking to be judged,
harshly if necessary, to be made to acknowledge my guilt,
and then to be forgiven. But how can I acknowledge guilt
when I'm not sure I'm guilty?

My father's ambition, on which he acted compulsively
and unthinkingly, was the accumulated ambition of generations. He was his family's last best bet, and in realizing

his talents through his achievements he understood himself to be discharging his debt to them. (Could this be what Les was really saying when he faulted me for not making more of my father's career?) Even if he used his parents as material for dinner party anecdotes, I know he also lived to fulfill their expectations—and these were limitless, because his parents knew almost nothing about the expanding worlds into which his talents would propel him. His life was short, like his own father's, and almost brutally determined, like the life of an insect programmed to perform some species-specific task and then drop out of the air. My own impulse to write—I'm talking about the internal writing I've done all my life as well as the writing I began to publish ten years ago—is just as much an expression of the imperatives of my nature as my father's career was of his. But the symmetry breaks down. First: I write for my own purposes, not as the carrier of generations of unrealized aspirations (though my mother was a frustrated writer). Second: my father may have done harm to his intimates *because* of his career, but he never harmed them *through* it. The tendency of his life was emphatically outward, toward objective accomplishment. I've turned inward to examine my own experience, implicating him and others in the process. (Perhaps my father's career really does represent the family's apogee, and mine the decadence that follows such attainments.) I've turned on him, and perhaps that puts me more in the wrong than his parental negligence has put him.

Still, I remind myself, the harm I did was incidental, not a matter of score settling. Another point in my favor:

my parents were not living when I wrote about them. Can the dead be harmed? And why, for that matter, should I allow the disapproval of a relative I hardly ever see to throw me into such dismay? After all; alienating family members is an occupational hazard for a memoirist. Sometimes it seems to me that these are the counsels of common sense. At other times they strike me as evidence of a coarsened sensibility. The kind of writing I do requires that I cannibalize my own history and its dramatis personae, but also that I stay morally alert enough to register what I've done.

However the comparison between my father and me stands, it's unclear that either of us stepped over any absolute line. But even so, for more than a year after the publication of *Mockingbird Years* I found myself jerked into startled panics. This happened in the midst of the most mundane daily activities, as I pushed a cart down a supermarket aisle or sat in my car waiting out a stoplight. It was like discovering that I'd lost my keys—I dig in my pockets, upend and shake my handbag: where are they? But unlike my keys, which I expect to find when they turn up missing, what I'd misplaced was something I know quite well I'd lost for good: my unimplicated, pre-memoir self.

The question that haunts me is not so much *What have I done?* as *What have I become?* I can't help fearing that even if writing and publishing those memoirs was ethically permissible, it was an offense against decency, the value that Les embodies but could not bring himself to invoke. I've violated a norm of civilized life, like a tribe that leaves its dead unburied.

—

ON THE MORNING AFTER the wedding I was awakened by an early call from my husband. He'd been up for hours, watching news reports about the freakish rain in New England, and he insistently urged me to cut my visit a day short, drive back to Manchester, and spend the night at an airport hotel. Otherwise I might be delayed by the weather and miss my plane. I could hear a sleepless night in his voice; he comes from a family of obsessives who see travel as an obstacle course of hazards that can be negotiated only with careful planning and constant consultation.

On my way to the airport I stopped at my sister's house, where a rolling breakfast was in progress, with runners making periodic trips into town to replenish the bagel supply. My sister came to the door, a mug of coffee in her hand, and for the first time since my arrival we greeted each other properly. She wore festive striped knee socks, a sign that the ceremonial frenzy of the wedding had released its grip. As I followed her into the kitchen I saw that her house had become its recognizable self again as well; the floral arrangements had retreated into the shadows of quiet rooms.

Les had already gone, but Lois and Harold were sitting at the kitchen table with the newlyweds and a group of their friends. My niece wore an orange sweater; she and her husband were punchy with happiness, and the feeling was contagious. When a new contingent of guests arrived, Harold and Lois and I relinquished our kitchen table seats and stood talking in the hall. Caffeine and laughter had loosened me up, and I blurted out a confession about how and why I'd tried to avoid coming to the wedding. Lois was instantly reassuring. Yes, Les was upset, she knew, but she wasn't and never had been. I deftly took the opportunity to put her on notice about the imminence of the second memoir.

At some point Harold withdrew and Lois and I took our mugs and plates out to a porch overlooking a stand of dripping evergreens. She'd been pleased, she began, to see that Les and I had had a talk the night before. My response was a shrug, a smile, a wince. Having watched me intently while I produced this sequence of expressions, Lois mirrored them so perfectly that both of us burst out laughing.

She moved on, tactfully, to ask about my husband and daughter, to catch me up on the doings of her two sons and the details of the deaths of her mother and brother. I apologized for having been too self-absorbed to write when I learned of them—I'd certainly *thought* about them both, I said. Lois threw up her hands in a gesture of amnesty and launched into reminiscence. Some of what she said surprised me. I learned, for example, that my uncle Abie the bookie, my grandmother's bachelor brother whom I'd always taken for a colorful and endearing character, was actually a freeloading louse who slept on his mother's couch for most of his adult life. No idealizing there; her tone was frankly scornful. But when she spoke of my father and Les, she glowed. Oh, she said, they were something when they were young! Both of them were so brilliant and so handsome! Here she paused, feeling the inadequacy of these adjectives. What she wanted to convey, I understood, was the air of promise my father and Les carried, the sense of stir in their lives, of things at their beginnings. And they were so *kind* to her, she said, a tagalong younger cousin they might just as easily have ignored. She used to have a wonderful photograph of Les in his Navy uniform; she'd have to look for it.

We talked about my family and the years in Williamstown. Lois had loved my mother, she said, not so much for her charm and talent as for her sadness, the isolation that overtook and trapped her. And my father: Did I know how proud he was of my mind? How he used to delight in repeating the clever things I said? I was utterly surprised, both by this information and by the realization that I already knew it.

I thought: Have I gotten it all wrong?

IN THE YEARS SINCE the wedding, this lesion of doubt has shrunk to a manageable size. What Lois told me about my father threw me into temporary confusion, but I haven't radically revised my view of him. There's too much else that I remember, and it's too late now anyway. When our conversation on the porch had sorted itself out it was something else that stayed in my mind, a slightly riddling remark she made about herself: "The past is strong in me." It's strong in me too, was my first thought. I'm a memoirist, after all. But perhaps it really isn't, or if it is, it's strong *for* me rather than *in* me.

The difference is all in the preposition. In my memoirs

I've told the story of myself, and in the process some of the family's story. But Lois is the keeper of that story, particularly the part about my father's generation, when the family lost itself in an explosion of merit. Her version is not entirely accurate—whose is?—but it's far more comprehensive than mine. The purposes of the memoirist are radically different from the purposes of the family historian. I can claim the authority of detachment, but hers is the authority of love. I think of Lois as the largest of a set of Ukrainian dolls. She contains me; she contains us all.

I'm starting to understand the tropism toward extended family that people my age begin to feel, the unreconstructed clannish longing that expresses itself in amateur genealogy. Perhaps it doesn't seem quite appropriate in my case, but really, why shouldn't I feel it too? Any family member is eligible for the gathering-in—my father, my schizophrenic cousin Dick, my uncle Abie, me.

TO WHOM DO I APPLY to be entered into the rolls? To Lois, of course. I saw her again a few months after the wedding, when I was in New York to talk with my publisher about the new memoir. We'd planned to meet in the city for dinner, but Harold had developed a sore throat so I took the train out to their house in Larchmont. I'd had the usual exciting, bruising time in the city and I was tired. It was raining—once again—and even though I'd bought an umbrella from a florist on Seventh Avenue, I got damp and chilled as I walked from my midtown hotel to Grand Central.

Lois and Harold's house is a cozy Victorian with a view of the sound from its upper windows. After I'd been given a tour, we adjourned to the sitting room, where Harold had built a fire. Would I like a cup of tea, coffee, a beer? A glass of wine or sherry? Mineral water? A real drink? I chose herbal tea—to start with—and ensconced myself in a corduroy armchair. We sat and talked for an hour. The James Frey scandal had just broken and I'd learned enough about it from the frantic talk of the publishing people with whom I'd been sharing restaurant meals to be able to hold forth like an insider. Lois and Harold listened attentively.

We moved into the kitchen. Lois checked on the progress of the chicken, roasting on a bed of herbs in a ceramic pot, while Harold and I sat at the table. The room was warm and fragrant; the small glass of neat bourbon I was nursing was almost medicinally restorative. Harold was talking about one of their sons, who was responsible, I think, for the algorithm that determines the order in which hits are listed on Google. I was feeling too comfortable and dreamy to follow closely what he was saying. At some point I looked up to see that Lois was standing in front of the stove, her arms crossed over her chest, looking at me steadily. It was a very kindly look, meaning simply "You're here," but I found it a challenge to endure. Before she turned away again she said "Emmy," as I knew she would, but so softly that it seemed an afterthought.

HERE AGAIN

—

From the beginning, philosophy conventions are fun to watch. Philosophers arrive; they struggle to negotiate the revolving doors; they neglect to tip the doorman; they fail to recognize one another; they buzz and blunder about in the hotel bars and coffeeshops and hallways and ballrooms that only a few days earlier were the scene of artful and orderly shmoozing by periodontists or actuaries or matrimonial lawyers. In the aggregate, philosophers behave chaotically, unaccountably swerving away from encounters or simply walking off in the middle of conversations. A video camera looking down on the hotel lobby from the ceiling would record something like the motion of wasps whose nest has just been smoke-bombed.

My husband, George, is a moral philosopher, a senior figure in the profession. He's more grounded and worldly than many of his colleagues, but also firmly identified with them. Since his career began he has never missed a meeting of the eastern division of the American Philosophical Association; for him this last one, held in Philadelphia, was the thirty-fifth. My attendance has been spottier, but I think I've been to at least twenty-five. When our daughter was small I stayed home with her, sulking a little at the deprivation because the week between Christmas and New Year's is a dark one and I enjoy the chance to eat, drink, shop, catch up with friends, explore whatever city the meetings are held in. I also like to drop in on papers that interest me, always sitting near the door so I can make an inconspicuous escape. But mostly I tag along to the meetings because I never tire of the amusement they provide. The very idea seems a setup— "Imagine: from all over the country, philosophers converge on Baltimore"—for a joke, an endearingly pointless shaggy-dog story. This is exactly what these convocations turn out to be, at least for a roving nonparticipant like me.

For all the delight I take in them, I pay a certain emotional price when I attend APA conventions. As the days go by, my husband's guild affiliation tends to take over; when I come upon him in a clutch of shop-talking colleagues he sometimes looks at me rather blankly. We're ordinarily very close, and I find these departures disconcerting, though less so than I did when we were younger. It helps that he has learned to warn me. "Going into convention mode," he'll murmur as we step off the elevator. My main complaint now is that so few of George's colleagues seem to realize that in the last fifteen years I've become a writer. They take me to be the faculty wife I once was (still am, I suppose), and that puts my writerly nose out of joint. It also pitches me back into a time when I had no profession, nothing but my marital connection to distinguish me in the eyes of others.

And there's one other item on this list, not so much a complaint as an observation. Our annual return to the philosophy convention opens up a dizzily vertiginous backward view, an unobstructed sight line that reaches back to the early seventies. Every year it's a longitudinal pit stop, an occasion for reminiscence and brooding.

The 2007 convention was in fact held in Baltimore. It was uneventful, but the year before that, in Washington, D.C., a serious fire broke out on the seventh floor of the hotel at three o'clock in the morning, a few hours after what used to be called the Smoker and is now (officially) called the Reception, had concluded. Philosophers descended the stairs calmly and groggily and gathered outside on the icy hotel driveway while red and blue firetruck lights pulsed stroboscopically over their heads. The staff then directed them to the ballroom where the Smoker had been held, to await the all-clear. Almost immediately, they picked up where they'd left off; George and I watched in astonishment as a sort of dream Smoker got underway, with philosophers in their pajamas gathering once again in earnest shop-talking knots, as if no fire had ever happened.

This incident captures something of the uncanny eternal-recurrence feeling that the philosophy convention has come to have for me. Here we are again, I say to myself, year after year, back here again. Here under our feet is the luridly patterned carpet, so woozy-making after a late night; here is the watery light of the hallway sconces; here is the lurching elevator, packed with philosophers bound for the book exhibits, and there, standing in the Starbucks line—don't stare—is the mortal embodiment of someone very old and famous, someone still with us, someone who is more mind than person.

WE ARRIVED IN Philadelphia late in the afternoon on December 27, spent a few minutes at the Marriott's registration desk straightening out a misunderstanding, the APA's fault. The bellhop—my husband did remember to tip him, and without any prompting from me—directed us to the elevator and accompanied us to the twentieth floor. This year we'd been assigned to a suite, not the usual airshaft special. The reason for the upgrade was political and historical: George's department was interviewing for a junior position, and since feminists in the profession problematized the issue some twenty years ago, the APA has allowed no bed to be visible in a room where interviews are conducted. Departmental budgets must thus be stretched to pay for a level of luxury wasted on unworldly philosophers.

But not on me; I'd been looking forward to the chocolate on my pillow, the balcony with a view. So I was disappointed when the bellhop flung open the double doors to what wasn't really a suite at all, only a big room with a conversational grouping of sofas and chairs, a conference table, and a Murphy bed, the fold-up-into-the-wall kind featured in a number of Three Stooges episodes. We tried experimentally to return the bed to its upright, invisible position, but couldn't get it to retract completely. There was something alarming about the way it jutted out an inch or so from the wall, revealing a sliver of blanket and folded sheet. We both imagined it crashing down in the middle of an interview, a jarring Return of the Repressed.

We unpacked. George made a phone call. I checked my email. There was no event or meeting scheduled for the rest of the afternoon, so we decided to return to the lobby to watch the philosophers, a pastime he enjoys almost as much as I do. As we were leaving the room he gave me an odd look and asked if I thought the piece of flounder he'd eaten for lunch had looked all right.

For years we'd been noticing changes at the convention. Twenty-five years ago, conventioneers of George's generation were hairy and vigorous, a disorderly herd of rational animals. But now as we sat well back in the lobby, watching the action around the registration desk, we saw that many we remembered from that era were frankly elderly and a few looked undeniably seedy, so much so that they might have been taken for bums who'd ducked in out of the cold rain. (Conversely, any bums taking refuge in the lobby might have been taken for philosophers.) We glanced at one another, as we have at every convention for at least the past five years: if his peers were old, then what did that make us? Not yet old, we concluded once again—late-middle-aged.

But this year it also seemed there were more young people in attendance than there had been even the year before. The change had been gradual, but now it was approaching some kind of critical mass. These were not, for the most part, the tweedy fumblers I remembered from the early days. Watching from a distance, I could see by the way they arranged themselves in clusters that many were poised and interpersonally adept. I spotted a shaven-headed fox-faced young man in leather pants, slaloming efficiently through the confused throng. Women in the profession have traditionally dressed like scholarly frumps, but many of these young ones were effectively turned out, even chic. I counted two who were actually fashion forward, with elaborately highlighted and willfully disarranged "bed-head" hair. They wore expensive black and lounged about the lobby with an air of disdainful detachment, as though they'd somehow taken a wrong turn on the way to the MLA.

Now it was a little before six, the hour for restaurant-bound philosophers to begin assembling in the lobby. A group of four people in early middle age gathered by the Christmas tree. Two women arrived first, then a man, and then, after several minutes, the last member of the party, also a man. He threw his hands up in apology as he approached, then laid them on the shoulders of the two women, kissing each one's cheek in turn as she offered it. Gracefully done! If this group hadn't been wearing badges, I would never have believed they were philosophers.

AS IT TURNED OUT, the piece of flounder had not been all right, and neither of us got much sleep that night. In the morning, George still felt ill, but he staggered gamely out of bed and did his best to eat a few leftover pretzels and drink some tea. While he stood under the shower—he was determined to carry out his responsibilities as a member of the interviewing panel—I roamed the halls, looking for a housekeeper. Eventually I found one willing to do the room up early, then ran back to warn George to get some clothes on, promised to bring him some chicken soup at lunchtime, gathered up my own things, and darted out to the elevator. I needed to make myself scarce before the interviews began.

I bought a bagel and coffee at the breakfast cart and found a banquette in a shadowy corner where I paged through the *Proceedings and Addresses* of the APA, looking for a talk that might interest me and not make me feel too stupid. George tells me that my mind has a natural philosophical bent, and I do understand some of the issues philosophers address. But my grasp of the specialized vocabulary and the "moves" of philosophical discourse is deficient. I know more than most laypeople, but not enough not to get lost in discussion with philosophers, at least when George isn't around to interpret for me. There are fewer and fewer "amateurs" of philosophy, and the line between someone like me, who is interested but has limited knowledge, and the occasional crank who will corner a philosopher at a party and demand to be persuaded of God's nonexistence (or existence) is disturbingly thin.

Over the years I've attended many papers at the APA, serious ones, packed with philosophers, the air in the airless meeting room charged with attentiveness. I've been able to follow for minutes at a time, sometimes long enough to bear witness to the uncoiling of an argument. I scribble down tentative understandings on the back of my program and pass them to George, who nods distractedly: I've interrupted his own efforts to follow the train of the speaker's thoughts. But my attention always finds a way to wander; maintaining it steadily is like holding my breath under water. The atmosphere of deep focus in the room, which ought to inspire me, instead alienates me. I find myself hovering outside it, speculating about it rather than entering into it. (The philosopher Thomas Nagel famously asked himself what it would be like to be a bat: I ask myself what it would be like to be a philosopher.) And then my thoughts grow restless and errantly superficial. I hypothesize about the relationship between two grungy young people sitting in front of me. I anticipate lunch.

Today, on my own for the morning, I had no desire to attend an important paper. I was looking for a sideshow, an offering that fell in line with my carnivalesque appreciation of the convention. Here was something appropriately marginal but too obscure, a colloquium called "Against Musical Arousalism." What, I asked myself, is Musical Arousalism? "Musical arousal" I could guess at, but the "ism" suggested a schismatic debate the terms of which I'd have to know to understand the talk. The same was true of "Does Four-Dimensionalism Explain Coincidence?" And here was a real baffler: "On Truth, the T-Schema and Definiendum-Sensitive Definitions." I eliminated that from consideration immediately, and also "Of Women, Bogs and Mollusks: Transcending and Transgendering with Simone de Beauvoir"—too early in the morning.

What about the session on Philosophical Counseling? I'd read a little about this innovation—philosophers offering counsel to troubled people, as psychotherapists and clergy do. Philosophical counseling? Hard to imagine anything but disaster or hilarity resulting from that, at least if it were attempted by any philosophers I know. But even so, I was intrigued. I've written about therapy from a critical point of view, and I found myself wondering whether exposure to the eternal verities really might do more for some patients than the usual combination of pharmaceuticals and excavations of the past. I knew that George would consider philosophical counseling intellectually disreputable, but this session looked like what I'd been searching for, more accessible than many of the others and short, only an hour and a half rather than three hours.

It started at eleven, which left me forty minutes to kill. I would have been happy to amuse myself by philosopher-watching and eavesdropping on conversations, but people I knew kept walking by and hailing me. Glad as I was to see (most of) them, I felt self-conscious about being caught doing nothing. I needed writerly cover, and although I usually scorn the practice of taking notes, relying instead on my myth-generating memory, I took out a notebook and began to record my observations. Here are a few. I saw:

A philosopher with a ZZ Top–style forked beard, ambling slowly toward the escalator, reading as he went.

An exasperated "I'm good" dad, a kaffiyeh knotted around his throat, pushing a toddler in a stroller. He was walking rapidly, and as he passed I saw that a red-faced infant, hanging nearly upside down, was wedged into the crook of his elbow.

Many limps, and almost as many canes as limps. Hadn't I read somewhere that gout has become epidemic in affluent societies?

A transgendered person, female-to-male, the first of four I was to notice at the convention, though it's possible I counted one or more of them twice, because they all wore khaki Dockers and button-collared shirts and bow ties, like a cadre of suspiciously lumpy George Wills.

An old bluestocking beauty, a girl overlaid by a crone, stalking by, gray hair bouncing on her shoulders. Did I know her when she was young?

A guy with a canvas Brentano bag, looking dyspeptic and confused, consulting his APA bulletin while blocking traffic at the foot of the escalator, a fast-walking flying wedge of a flight crew in dashing navy blue trenchcoats dividing and flowing around him.

A pear-shaped young philosopher with long limp curls like the ears of a ceramic Staffordshire dog, stopping to speak to another young somebody sitting near me. "Just get out?" he asked,

cocking his head sympathetically. The other
nodded despondently. "How'd it go?" The
other looked up reproachfully. "Don't ask."

NINE OF THE ELEVEN people in the audience for the Philosophical Counseling session seemed to know one another
and the speaker. Only two—I and an elderly man, also
without an APA badge—failed to stay for the meeting
of the American Society for Philosophy, Counseling,
and Psychotherapy (ASPCP) that followed. All this fa-
miliarity gave the talk an oddly ritualistic feeling; it
seemed almost a reenactment, staged so it could be listed
on a vita.

The speaker was a small, lean, balding man, rather
gray-faced, probably in his early fifties. Did I know him?
A few minutes into the program I realized I did; he'd
been George's student more than thirty years ago, and he
and his wife, who was now his collaborator and was sitting in the front row, came to dinner once at our apartment in Leonia, New Jersey. They'd just been married.
He was shy and tense and she was tense and shy.

Or maybe I was misremembering. Maybe I met them
somewhere on campus and the student I had in mind was
the one who brought along his guitar and played an
extended and embellished version of "The Day the Music
Died" until I wanted to scream. But no, they must have
come to dinner, because why otherwise, looking now at
the set of the speaker's wife's shoulders, would I feel this

powerful sense of retrospective shame? Had I made a fool of myself that evening? Did I get into an angry hissing exchange in the kitchen with George, choke on a Brussels sprout, insult somebody, run from the table in tears? In those days I might well have done any or all of these things.

But enough of that. Pay attention. The speaker was talking about the practice of philosophical counseling, also known as rational emotive therapy (RET) or cognitive behavioral therapy (CBT). The philosophical counselor, he explained, challenges the client to think critically, by which he meant examining and altering certain destructive either/or beliefs. (Several times he alluded to a free "Belief-Scan" CD, shrink-wrapped into the cover of his new book, which was on display at the book exhibits.) If, for example, the client believes he must have that promotion, or must have that girl, the philosophical counselor might ask: "Why 'must'? Why not reframe your desire as follows: it's something I want, but can live without."

What a desiccated notion, I was thinking. What cold comfort. Surely the stoical tradition could offer something richer and more consoling than this. What about the really tragic dilemmas? Could a client reframe his way out of those? I found myself envisioning Freud's couch, draped in Oriental carpet and piled with silk cushions. Color and pattern, myth and narrative, love and death: all these unmanageables had been excluded from the tidily cerebral world of RET (or CBT). I would have eased out of the room if that other nonmember of the APA and the ASPCP hadn't been blocking my way to the door.

—

LUNCHTIME. BRINGING CHICKEN soup to George, I stood outside the hotel room groping for the key and heard orderly voices from within: evidently the grilling of the last candidate had gone into overtime. I retreated to the elevators and parked myself on a wide corner windowsill with a long view of a corridor and watched as interviews broke up. Some candidates were escorted out of the room by members of the interviewing team. Others simply emerged and wobbled forlornly down the hall. A number of them were able to keep a poker face; a few wore dejection on their sleeves; none looked happy. Better them than me, I was thinking. What could be more daunting than to summarize one's dissertation before a panel of philosophers? But for some even that was probably not the worst of it. For them the challenge would be: how to manage and move through the space of a hotel room one's gangly postadolescent body, how to respond appropriately to the greetings and small talk offered on your way in (or not offered—these were philosophers, after all), how not to bolt from the room when the interview was concluded.

Watching them, I was visited once again with the eternal-recurrence sensation: was it possible that these young philosophers making their solitary ways down the hall to the elevator were infants when I first accompanied George to a convention? No, they were unborn. Over the years I've watched the job candidates as they pour through the profession, some lodging in the net of employment. They're as perennial as the grass and as readily mown down (but how can it be that philosophers grow in crops?). Every year I feel the same pang of sympathy for them, as distinctive as the tang of chicory in coffee. It's sincere, but edged by Schadenfreude and a certain envy.

I noticed a girl standing a little apart from the gathering around the elevator, one wisdom-of-the-stairs realization after another scrolling across her face. In past years I'd felt motherly toward the job candidates. This year I felt grandmotherly. I could almost imagine beckoning her over and whispering, "You don't know me, my dear, but I wish you well." Perhaps I could offer prophecies, like some itinerant Gypsy elder: "No, you will not make the list at Brown. But what is this I see? It's growing clearer. Ah yes, an on-campus interview at Ball State!"

THE POST-INTERVIEW HUDDLING going on in the hotel room after the last candidate finally left was so intense that I could hardly get George to acknowledge the soup I'd brought him, which was cold by now anyway. Looking at him you'd never guess how sick he'd been the night before. His color was healthy; his eyes were shining; he was talking and laughing animatedly. Phillip Lopate once observed that recruitment is the Eros of academia, and it's true. There's nothing like it to get an academic's blood flowing.

I'd been present at these sessions before. X is strong, somebody would say, but what about the spouse? That would lead to multi-angled speculation about the dean's willingness to arrange a spousal hire. Y looked good on

paper, but was shy in person. Would teaching be a problem? You never know, someone would say, and a competitive volley of anecdotes about how you really never did
know would follow. Hadn't somebody mentioned some
reservation that Z's adviser had expressed off the record?
Oh yes. The word is he's very bright but green. Needs a
few years to ripen.

And so on. I sat at the conference table and ate my
turkey sandwich. The truth was I felt left out, which was
childish of me, but being privy to a conversation one can't
join will make an adult feel like a child. Of course I knew
that being excluded was no injustice—I hadn't, after all,
been present for the interviews. I knew nothing about the
candidates. I was not a philosopher. I had no university
appointment. But they were having such a good time over
there across the room, gossiping in their professionally
sanctioned, beard-tugging way. I would have enjoyed it.

BUT REALLY, I ASKED MYSELF, would I feel any more a
part of things at a convention of my own kind—the
Associated Writers Programs meetings, for example?
Certainly not. Less so, if anything.

Apparently I was tired. The pleasures of solitary
observation were beginning to pall. I was feeling peevish
about being exiled from the room. I wanted a shower and
a nap and my husband's company, but the afternoon session was about to begin. The members of the interviewing
team tidied away the leavings of lunch. I took my purse
and notebook and left the room.

Stepping into the elevator, I found myself in the midst of a stand of five tall young job seekers, all male, all clean-shaven and smelling sweetly of aftershave, all wearing spit-shined shoes and diagonally striped ties. They looked like MBAs, not Ph.Ds. I'd noticed that many young philosophers are no longer the slobs they used to be, but this *Gentlemen's Quarterly* level of self-presentation surprised me. It also confused me; I'm enough a product of the sixties to recoil automatically at the sight of "organization man" types. I have to remind myself that this notion has been utterly displaced. Nobody's an organization man these days, or everyone is.

During the hour and a half before George got free I attended a three-speaker colloquium on the classification of mental disorders. (Yes, I know. It's a preoccupation.) My fatigue after a sleepless night was beginning to hit me now, and my memories of this session are too jumbled to form a coherent narrative. Instead, I'll simply transcribe my notes:

Cut nature at the joints.
Young woman in red, psychiatrist and philosopher
    of science, no "natural kind" requirement for
    DSM classification.
Psychiatric nosology (what?)
Psychiatry objective and evaluative.
Big swaggering articulate Aussie, like a young
    Charles Laughton. Argues distinction betw
    med diagnosis and psych diagnosis.
Keeps saying "carved out."

Visual system is modular. Mind is not.
Central non-modular STUFF WE CARE
    ABOUT
Middle-aged woman, looks depressed. Theory of
    Dysthymia.
fear and sorrow
Burton's Anatomy of Melancholy.
but in modern times fear and sorrow separate.
Traits and states (?)
At border between path and norm
anxiety and depression [in the margin I'd drawn an
    arrow connecting this line to "fear and sorrow"
    above] coupled, but not same concept.
Alastair rm 720 6:30 Sun

(This last entry was a later addition, scribbled diagonally at the bottom of the page. It referred to a genial
Englishman, my husband's former colleague, who brings
his own portable bar to the convention every year and
holds a cocktail party in his room.)

AFTER THE TALK I met George in the lobby and the two
of us set out on a tour of the convention, now in full
swing. With him at my side, it was a more sociable business than my solitary wanderings had been. The escalator
up to the convention level became a mobile receiving line,
with philosophers taking the down escalator waving and
shouting greetings. As they passed I could see their faces
registering "Oh, that's who she is." I smiled and waved

back forgivingly, even though I knew quite well who most of them were. In some cases I'd forgotten their names, but for years I'd been watching them, asking George about them, taking account of the ways they'd aged.

We hovered for a moment in the hall outside what George calls the hot-sheet interview room, where the APA provides tables for departments unable or unwilling to shell out for hotel suites. It was a purgatorial place, windowless and glaringly bright and buzzing with voices trying to keep discreetly low. Job seekers gathered outside the door, each waiting to be ushered in and seated at the appropriate table by an APA functionary with a clipboard in her hands.

George greeted one of the interviewees as he emerged from the room. He was a stranger to me, a stout young man, carefully groomed and spiffily attired. How'd it go? George asked. The young man paused, considered, answered, "Not bad." When I asked what it was like to be interviewed in a room full of other people also being interviewed, he gave a blandly noncommittal answer. Already, he'd put my back up, this very circumspect young person. What business did he have being so stuffy and stiff? He has no irony, I was thinking. He can't see beyond his own ambition. Like one of those tourists who pester the bobbies at Buckingham Palace, I found myself itching to get a rise out of him.

As the conversation moved on to a cautiously general consideration of the tight job market, the name of the interviewee's current adviser came up. This was a famous philosopher, enormously powerful in the profession, a woman of regal and rather imperious bearing. I had been silent, and bored, but now I saw my chance. "Oh," I said, "the queen! What's it like, working with the queen?" George shot me a nervous look. The student's eyes swiveled toward me and then away. It was too threatening a question even to acknowledge, and it broke the rhythm of the exchange.

I excused myself and headed for the restroom, hoping that George would extricate himself from the encounter. As I stood at the sink running warm water over my hands, I could hear the ugliness of my own hostility in the question I'd asked. I'd taken my shot at that young man from a position of safety. He and I were both outsider/insiders here at the APA, and our positions mirrored one another almost perfectly. He was a low-status initiate, full admission to the profession pending, but contingent on various kinds of academic good behavior. I was a protected nonmember, powerless, but in a position to overhear and observe: a eunuch in the philosophical harem. This was a marginal kind of status, but utterly secure. Nothing I did could ever endanger it, though nothing I did—short of acquiring a doctorate and finding an academic position—would ever put me on the inside either. Even though I knew the institution of the APA well from years of observation, I had no stake in anything at this professional gathering. My cheeky question had affinities with the insolent caperings of a court jester. Even so, it was not harmless; I'd put a vulnerable person utterly on the spot.

The interviewee was gone when I returned. We continued our tour, taking a turn through the book exhibits, where our progress was continually interrupted by encounters with philosophers wanting to talk shop while I stood smiling at George's side, waiting to be introduced. This is a bone of contention between us: he says he's often unsure whether or not he's already introduced me to whoever it is he's talking to at some past meeting, and having hesitated, feels he can't work an introduction into the conversation without interrupting its flow. In this situation, I've told him repeatedly, he can always say, "You remember Emily, don't you?" But in truth I can't imagine a formula like that coming from George; it would be too much to expect him to carry on like some pencil-mustached leading man from a thirties movie. It's enough that he has mastered the basics—the smile, the handshake, the polite inquiry. That puts him far ahead of most of his colleagues. And to be fair, he's gotten better. These days he remembers to introduce me about a third of the time (he says half).

The book exhibit was so crowded at this hour that it was hard to do any serious browsing. I could only note from a distance that the book jackets continued to be birds of brilliant plumage: cobalt blue, fuchsia, acid green, sunflower yellow. This is a relatively recent trend. Thirty years ago the books were dun-colored wrens; the only vivid chromatic note in the room was the red of the Marxist-Leninist pamphlets laid out on a card table at the back—*Philosophy Is No Mystery* was one title I remember. There were many fewer publishers represented then, and the books seemed more sober and serious.

The exhibits have expanded over the years; the publishers' booths seem to snake on forever, like concessions at a state fair. There's a profusion of catchy, punning titles, and in the last ten years a fetish for pluralization has developed—"Judeities," "Perplexities," "Hypocrisies," "Contrarieties." I take this to be yet another sign of the MLA-ification(s) of the profession, as are the dishes of M&Ms and Hershey's Kisses that publishers have started putting out to lure browsers to their booths.

We emerged from the exhibits and took the escalator down to the lobby. It was *l'heure bleu* at the convention: time for philosophers to gather in the lobby bar and then to scatter and colonize all the Thai restaurants in the vicinity. My husband and I went out to dinner with a friend who teaches at a British university, a gentle, urbane man who knows how to keep up his end of a general (non-shoptalk) conversation. Then we returned to the hotel to change our clothes for the Smoker.

JUST AS PEOPLE CONTINUE to call Mumbai Bombay, so most philosophers persist in calling the Reception the Smoker. Interestingly, it's the middle generation, the one that came to maturity in the nineties, that has adopted the politically correct appellation. The young and the old—graduate students, and veterans like George—continue to use the original name, with all its clubby, unwholesome connotations.

There are two Smokers, actually, but the Smoker held on the night of the first full day of the convention is the one that matters. It's much better attended than the one on the second night, probably because free watery beer and smashed potato chips are served, while at the other the drinks cost money. The first Smoker is the apotheosis of the convention, a full gathering of the tribe. It's held in the hotel ballroom. Round tables draped in white are corralled in the center of this great space, each serving as headquarters for a registered university and as "home" to job-seeking graduate students from that university. Philosophers eddy around these tables and huddle in the darkened far corners of the room. They make me think of a colony of migratory birds gathered on some Pacific atoll, hopping from rock to rock and onto one another's backs.

The Smoker used to be called a meat market, but no longer. Nobody is hired on the spot anymore. Instead, bits of leftover business are transacted: candidates who were interviewed earlier in the day are sought out to clarify things they said or to explain gaps in their vitas. Job seekers whose interviews went badly are attended to by their professors, who hover over them like cornermen, reproving and advising and encouraging until they feel ready to rejoin the fray. Catching-up goes on as well, and gossiping, mostly professional, but personal too, especially as the hour grows late. Gossip is a rare commodity among philosophers, and I listen for it. Twenty years ago, among our contemporaries, it had to do with marital breakups and suspected affairs. In the last ten it's been news of illness; in the last five, news of deaths.

Every year as we walk into this great dusky chandelier-lit ballroom, jammed with bodies and thrumming with echoes like the Marabar Caves, I think, "Here again!" It's as if I'd just stepped out for a moment to clear my head of the din and then stepped back in again, and in the interim a year had passed. Everything's the same, eternally the same. There, for example, is the famous philosopher surrounded tightly by a clot of acolytes who have temporarily forgotten him and begun to argue among themselves, leaving him trapped and craning his neck to find a means of escape. He's here every year, or his most recent replacement is, and so are the quarrelsome disciples, or theirs.

And then I remember that it's different, always different and growing more different all the time. Or rather, it's the same and different! Why am I surprised? I used to be able to grasp that elementary puzzle easily enough, but now somehow it stuns me. Same and different: I can't seem to get enough of this shopworn paradox, probably because I feel it viscerally now. I need only look at my own hands to be reminded that I myself am both the same and different.

There was a time when people actually smoked at the Smoker. On one ancient occasion a busty young woman in a red sequined sheath strode brazenly through the crowd, a fat lit cigar clenched between her teeth. She wanted attention, but it seems unlikely the stunt got her any job offers. Back then I was a little wild myself. The professional function of the event was lost on me; instead I viewed the Smoker as a big party, one of the few I ever got to go to as the wife of a young associate professor in a dull college town. Of course it was always a disappointment—a few hours spent milling around in a hotel ballroom is hardly a thrill—but then George went to bed and I took up with a rowdy crew of graduate students and made a tour of the afterparties.

At one of those, I remember, we watched as a barbershop quartet of philosophers sang "Bye Bye Blackbird" on the balcony, their arms draped around one another's shoulders. And another time we ran into a former student of George's and his date, a girl who had briefly been famous for running naked around the Empire State Building block during the streaking craze of the early seventies. And once I left a shoe at some party and had to return to the hotel room for it the next morning. They'd used it in a game of Cinderella, the host of the night before told me. Everyone, male or female, who came to the party was required to try it on. It was a chunky low-heeled shoe, size nine, and I was embarrassed.

Are there still afterparties? I'm sure there are, possibly wilder than the admittedly tame ones I used to attend, though I doubt it. I wouldn't know, because I haven't been to one in twenty years. These days George and I both get tired. We can't drink the way we used to (I mean, more candidly, that I can't; he is naturally temperate and has rarely overdone it). We both suffer from that middle-aged deafness-in-crowds syndrome; it's awkward to keep edging one's ear toward the mouth of someone telling an anecdote. And I've lost touch with the motive for staying late at parties, which always has something to do—however faintly or vicariously—with fantasies of sexual conquest.

This year George was holding up better than I was, in

spite of his stomach bug. He'd been unable to eat much dinner, but here he was at 10:45, happily engaged in a shouted conversation across the table with someone whose name I hadn't caught. I was sitting between a glum graduate student and an empty chair, longing for the chocolate bar and airport bookstore novel waiting for me upstairs in the room. But every time I got to my feet to make my excuses, some old friend or acquaintance appeared. Most of them wanted to speak to George, but he was occupied, so I patted the seat of the empty chair next to me and did my best to act the hostess until he got free.

But not everyone was waiting for George; some wanted to speak to me. The wife of a colleague plunked herself down and told me about the day she'd just spent museum-hopping in the cold rain. We exchanged cell phone numbers and made a date for lunch the next day. Then a couple who'd both taught in George's department thirty years ago came along. They were—still are— ambitious, confident, powerful people, and in those early days they formed a natural political bloc. What went on in the department was officially none of my business, of course, but I was young and habitually indignant and I made up my mind to hate this couple with a passion, so much so that I took it as a betrayal when George lingered for an hour at the office to talk to them. This obsession served as a focal point for the miasmic unhappiness I felt back then, when my writing vocation had yet to be realized.

These days nothing remains of that old antipathy, though I do feel a residual awkwardness when I see these people. I feel gratitude as well, because the man of the couple—a polymath with literary interests—has made a point of encouraging and championing my writing for many years. And more generally, at this stage it seems only sane to declare an amnesty. I can't take old resentments and grudges very seriously anymore. When I try to sort out who was right and wrong in all my ancient interpersonal wars I find that the timeline has blurred and left me with very little on which to base an objective judgment.

Seeing people once a year at the convention, I take note of the ways they've grown older. Some have remained much the same, but others—more every year—seem to have tumbled abruptly into a new category of age. I fear I'm one of these, but the odd thing is that none of us can be sure. The mirror tells a very partial story. It's only the eyes and ears of others that can truly register what time has done to our bodies and minds. Aging is like Indian poker; everyone carries the card of his own mortality on his forehead. Charged with knowing about others what they can't know about themselves, and knowing that others, in return, know what we can't know about ourselves, how can we feel anything but tenderness?

So this formerly hated pair sat down with me and we did a little gingerly reminiscing about the university where we all knew each other thirty years ago. They told me about the recent marriage of their younger son. I told them about the birth of our first grandchild. They excused themselves amid a flurry of good wishes, and a former graduate student I'd been close to several years ago came along and we caught up on one another's news and spent a half hour discussing the vicissitudes of her love life. Then she left and a current graduate student took her place and we talked about his wife's recently announced pregnancy.

The next occupant of the chair was a weary member of that day's interviewing panel. We exchanged a few words, but he wasn't particularly inclined to talk. He wanted only to join me in staring out at the crowd, so we did that for a few companionable minutes, and then he caught sight of a candidate he needed to speak to and disappeared back into the crowd, and not long after he left, yet another somebody I knew sat down. Even allowing for the draw of the empty chair, I was beginning to feel rather popular. Could it be, I asked myself, that I've had no place in the profession for so many years that this noplace has finally become a place—my place?

WE BOTH SLEPT BADLY on the lumpy Murphy bed, but George rose full of grim vigor, determined to get through the last day of the convention in good style. Once again I escaped just before the interviewing panel arrived and ate a farinaceous breakfast from the lobby cart. As always on the second full day of the convention, I felt a little blurry and bloated—too much salty food and alcohol and dry hotel-room air. I sat down on my customary banquette near the escalators with my camouflage copy of the APA "Addresses and Proceedings" and watched the passing philosophers for a while. They looked relaxed, if slightly worn. Some who'd taken care with their appearance the first day had let it slide this morning. Fewer were walking singly, many in laughing groups. There was relief in the air, a sense that for most the worst had been gotten through.

I spent the bulk of the morning at yet another symposium, this one on the subject of art and ethics. After the room was darkened and the slide projector turned on, I think I may have fallen asleep. That would account for the largest of several gaps in my memory. My notes are sketchy. Something about "ethical fittingness theory" (EFT) and a scrawled description of a young woman in the audience who spoke up about the imperialist agenda of Turner's naval paintings—it was her arty-chic clothes that interested me. I did manage to write down something lucid at the bottom of the page: "Even the Triumph of the Will could not be criticized if all extra-fictional perspectives are disallowed." Looking over my notes now, I'm relieved to see that at least one of the speaker's points penetrated my sleep-deprived haze.

I ate lunch at a Vietnamese restaurant with the friend I'd encountered at the Smoker. We talked about grandchildren and ailments, our own and those of others. This friend is an ironic realist, an agelessly handsome woman in her middle sixties. Her signature catchphrase is "What can I tell you?" She delivers it hilariously, with raised eyebrows and a tiny convulsive jerk of the shoulders, and it only gets better with repetition. In my memory, the rest of that afternoon and evening accordionates abruptly—nap,

Alastair's annual cocktail party, a bleary interval at a vegan steam-table restaurant where I sat opposite a graduate student who spoke at length about her five-year plan to penetrate the upper echelons of the administration at some northwestern Florida university, sleep.

ON THE MORNING of the last day at the convention, we ate breakfast in the hotel coffee shop and bar. Appetite now restored, George made several trips to the buffet. I ordered oatmeal and fruit from the menu. He read the *Philadelphia Inquirer* while he ate; I stared idly at the booths and tables surrounding us and out at a collection of people standing in line under a green plastic grapevine trellis, waiting to be seated.

Not everyone could be assumed to be a philosopher. Although further talks and symposia had been scheduled for the morning, the convention was breaking up, and many had already departed. The two men at the bar, for example, one drinking a beer and the other hunched over a Bloody Mary at eight o'clock in the morning, were not. They were businessmen, or possibly airline pilots. Neither were the sleek young couple eating egg-white omelettes in the corner, who looked as if they'd spent an hour in the pool or on the treadmill. But the four middle-aged women in the booth over to my right certainly were, and wore badges to prove it. A few tables away from them was the young man who'd made me think of a Staffordshire dog, looking a little melancholy this morning. He'd been omnipresent over the course of the convention, inclining a sympathetic ear to one discouraged peer after another. I'd begun to think of him as a kind of mascot, but now he was eating breakfast alone, duffel bag at his feet, preparing to go home and assume the burden of his everyday life.

The philosophers were leaving and the hotel was taking itself back. I made an effort now to really look at the staff, the cashier with the heavy down on her forearms, the waitress standing in the alcove by the restrooms making what looked like a furtive cellphone call, the bartender with his back to us, washing glasses. I noticed—how could I have missed it?—the flat-screen TV over the bar, where an anchorwoman was mouthing soundless words while a gathering of Afghan warlords convened in a flickering box over her head. Outside in the lobby I could see a crew of maintenance men wheeling coat racks jangling with wire hangers onto the service elevator. The philosophers were leaving and the hotel was preparing itself for the next convention. Whatever the group—endodontists, audiologists, Civil War buffs, paralegals—its members would swarm and dart through these spaces like tadpoles in a puddle and then they'd be gone. To the hotel staff they were all the same, though just now I remembered an anecdote a graduate student had told me at Alastair's cocktail party. He'd been looking for a bottle of Tylenol in the gift shop when the clerk behind the counter asked if he was with the philosophers. Yes, I am, said the graduate student. Well, said the clerk, you guys are just about the rudest bunch of people we've ever had in here.

The hostess was leading an odd-looking woman past

our table. She was very thin, wearing a winter coat buttoned up to the chin. Her face was as delicate as a bird's and her eyes glittered; I could make no sense of her looks. The first thing that occurred to me was that she had somehow stepped out of an Anita Brookner novel—it must have been her anachronistically stiff helmet of hair and the old-fashioned cut of her coat.

She walked so slowly that the hostess stopped several times to allow her to catch up. I waited until she'd shuffled a few yards past us and turned—unobtrusively, I hoped—to get another look. Now I understood: the woman was dying. That explained the buttoned coat, the emaciation, the wig. She was being led toward the table of women philosophers I'd noticed earlier. As she came into view they all got to their feet, their eyes shining with welcome—she was obviously the reason they'd assembled—and when she had completed her journey across the room they stepped forward one by one and took turns encircling her in their arms. Their hands curved above her shoulders; their lips hovered a millimeter from her cheek. Apparently she was so fragile that even the gentlest touch might hurt her. Instead, with great tenderness, her colleagues offered her this airy substitute for human contact: the idea of an embrace.

While this small drama had been going on, George was making a final trip to the buffet. He returned with a sausage, half a Danish, and a tub of strawberry yogurt. "Is this too much?" he asked. "Am I overdoing it?" "No no," I told him. "You've been sick. You need the calories." He finished the food, then folded the *Inquirer* and put it away in his briefcase. I left a generous tip, hoping in some small way to redeem the APA in the eyes of the hotel staff. We made one last trip up to the room to retrieve our luggage. For complicated reasons, we needed to drive to Newark to return our rental car. After that we'd have a long and tiring day ahead of us, much waiting, many hours of travel before we arrived home.

EMILY FOX GORDON is an award-winning essayist and the author of the novel *It Will Come to Me,* and two memoirs, *Mockingbird Years: A Life In and Out of Therapy* and *Are You Happy?: A Childhood Remembered.* Her work has appeared in *The American Scholar, Time, Pushcart Prize Anthology XXIII* and *XXIX, The New York Times Book Review, Boulevard,* and *Salmagundi.* She lives in Houston.

ABOUT THE TYPE

This book was set in Granjon, a modern recutting of a typeface produced under the direction of George W. Jones, who based Granjon's design upon the letter forms of Claude Garamond (1480–1561). The name was given to the typeface as a tribute to the typographic designer Robert Granjon.